LIFEQUAKES

GOD'S RESCUE PLAN IN HARD TIMES

Leah Weber Heling

Victory Won Publications

Milwaukee, Wisconsin

LIFEQUAKES
God's Rescue Plan in Hard Times

Copyright © 2011 by Leah Weber Heling

Victory Won Publications
Milwaukee, Wisconsin
www.leahheling.com

All rights reserved. No part of this book may be reproduced, transmitted in any form or by any means—electronic, mechanical, photocopy, recording, or by any information storage and retrieval system—except for the inclusion of brief quotations in a review, without written permission from the author or publisher.

Unless otherwise indicated, Scripture quotations are taken from the New King James Version. Copyright ©1982 by Thomas Nelson, Inc. Used by permission. All rights reserved.

Scripture quotations are also taken from the New American Standard Bible, © 1975 by the Lockman Foundation Co. Used by permission.

Charts used with permission from Duluth Bible Church.
Photo images by Cynthia Hart.

"I Will Trust When I Cannot See" a hymn by John W. Peterson © Copyright 1970 by John W. Peterson Music Company. All rights reserved. Used with permission.

Cover Design: Cynthia Hart, Graphic Artist
Interior Design and Typeset: Dawn Pekel, Arising Design

ISBN: 978-0-9820982-4-0
Printed in the United States of America

ACKNOWLEDGEMENTS

I am grateful to my Savior, Jesus Christ, for the privilege of writing *LifeQuakes*, for His guidance and direction, and for providing physical and mental endurance to complete this project. Sincere thanks to Ronnie, my husband, for his loving support and help. I offer heartfelt thanks to Pastors Tom Stegall and Rick Gerhartz for their helpful suggestions and to Randy Zempel, Bible Expositor, for writing the Foreword. Much appreciation to the Christian friends who contributed in numerous ways and for the many prayers offered for the completion of *LifeQuakes: God's Rescue Plan in Hard Times*.

CONTENTS

FOREWORD
INTRODUCTION

1	God Allows Lifequakes to Shake Your Footing	1
2	God's Rescue Plan	23
3	What Do You Rely on During Life's Shake-ups?	45
4	Confidence in God's Sovereign Providence	77
5	The Ultimate Lifequake	99
6	Why Do We Have Trials?	121
7	What Kind of Faith Does God Seek?	145
8	God's Trial Clocks Are Precise	175
9	Life Time Replacements	199
10	Smoking Smudge Pot or Blazing Torch?	233
11	What Determines Your Faith?	265
12	The Spiritual First Aid Kit	285
13	Soaring on Prayer Wings	311
14	The Comfort of His Grace	337
15	Are You Living Victoriously?	357

Definition of Terms 376
Appendix A: His Emergency Phone Numbers 378
Appendix B: Supplemental Scripture Directory 379
Resources 382
Recommended Reading 384

FOREWORD

If you find yourself doubting, wandering, and struggling to stay focused on God, *LifeQuakes* is a necessary book to read. Leah Weber Heling will instruct on principles, precepts, and promises from the Word of God that can eliminate your doubts and fears in the trials of life. In your lifequakes and its aftershocks, God hasn't forgotten you. You may forget God, but God never forgets you.

Fears and doubts are a part of living in this sinful world. When the ground under us begins to quake, we may need to brace ourselves spiritually for a major trial. I have seen Christians' lives crumble before the dust even settles because doubt feeds their discouragement. Having more doubt than hope in Christ is the disheartening condition of many believers. Without the grace of God, doubt is a recipe for double disaster.

The Latin word for doubt is *dubitare* and it means "two." God wants us to be of one mind in believing, but when we doubt in unbelief, we have two minds. During times of trials, we are vulnerable to waver between belief and doubt. James warns us about a (*dubitare*) double-minded man, unstable in his ways (James 1:8). I say, oh merciful God please help us with our unbelief in time of need. *"For in You, O LORD, I hope; You will hear, O Lord my God"* (Ps. 38:15). God doesn't want us for even one second to delay hope!

As we read in Numbers 13:33, when twelve spies returned from the Promised Land, ten said in essence, "There are giants in the land ready to consume us." The word "giants" planted seeds of doubt. The Israelites doubted; therefore, they spent the next forty years in misery wandering in the Sinai Desert. Even in their sufferings, God heard their cries just as He hears yours. Believer, He is a merciful and gracious God who sees your tears.

My hope and prayer is that after reading *LifeQuakes: God's Rescue Plan in Hard Times*, you will have the single mindset of the psalmist and be encouraged to *"bless the LORD, O my soul, and forget not all His benefits"* (Ps. 103:2). I suggest reading this book as a devotional by meditating on nearly four hundred passages of given Scripture. In addition, *LifeQuakes* is filled with charts, hymn lyrics and history, and true-to-life stories. You will read of precious promises, instructional guidelines, and spiritual principles from God's Word. We read from one of Heling's pages.

> God won't rescue a prideful, self-sufficient person who thinks he doesn't need God. Self-confidence is one of our greatest spiritual liabilities. However, one of our greatest spiritual assets is Christ-confidence. Remember, God's servants in the Bible had to be broken spiritually to advance their faith.

By the grace of our precious Lord and Savior Jesus Christ, may this book be of rich blessing to you now and in eternal days to come. To God be the glory!

Humbly by His grace,
Randy D. Zempel
Bible Expositor

INTRODUCTION

Just after seven in the morning, an earthquake struck. Jim was in his office preparing to read faxes when he heard a loud blast; the whole house began to shake. He could barely get out of his office because for the next forty-five seconds the whole house felt like it was falling apart. The earthquake, registering nearly seven on the Richter scale, demolished a portion of his home. God powerfully demonstrated His grace by the survival, without any physical harm, of Jim and his family while everything was crashing in around them.

The earthquake Jim experienced in the physical sense corresponds in intensity to the upheaval believers often experience in the spiritual realm. Believers in Jesus Christ experience difficulties, heartbreaks, and calamities just like everyone else. At times doubt and fear may seem to overtake you; however, God has a survival plan for you in your lifequakes.

The Theme of *LifeQuakes: God's Plan in Hard Times*

Like other believers in Jesus Christ, I have had trials, which caused me to long for the peace of God. *LifeQuakes* will explain the biblical principles for finding *"the peace of God, which transcends all understanding"* (Phil. 4:7). These and other principles in this book are a result of many years of hearing sound Bible teaching.

God's involvement through all trials and the believer's response to His grace are the themes of *LifeQuakes: God's Rescue Plan in Hard Times*. Our independence must lessen and Christ's sufficiency must be magnified, as it is written *"He* [Christ] *must increase, but I must decrease"* (John 3:30).

About This Book

LifeQuakes: God's Rescue Plan in Hard Times provides scriptural insights for growing in faith and thriving during difficult times. Written in an informal style, *LifeQuakes* is a reference manual for teens and busy adults. This guidebook calls upon the Word of God, which convicts, guides, directs, instructs, encourages, and comforts us. *LifeQuakes* frequently incorporates Bible verses because the Word of God has life-changing power.

As a guidebook, the Reflection Questions will help you integrate new information. Reflection Questions (based on the text) direct you to support your answers with Scripture verses. Unless the questions ask for your insights, give God's viewpoint and biblical principles.

In addition, you will read true-life stories (for privacy reasons some names were changed). The Scripture-based hymns interspersed throughout the book offer music for reflection. If you wish to sing them with audio, visit *www.hymntime.com* or the site listed after the hymn. Using *LifeQuakes* as a reference book, you may read chapters or chapter portions, sing, or meditate on hymns and verses to find encouragement and comfort. As a resource book, *LifeQuakes* provides additional information at the end of the book. Of special interest is a comprehensive Scripture Directory that lists hundreds of specific verses to read in times of need.

Ways to Use this Book

LifeQuakes reference guide is geared to directing the reader to God's Word and to Christ, the Author and Finisher of our faith (Heb. 12:2). Uses of this faith reference guide are:

- personal individual study
- family study
- classroom or home school use
- teen study led by parents or youth leaders
- college group study
- adult group study
- as a gift (graduate, prisoner, military personnel, co-worker, etc.)
- as a reading ministry—reading it to those with special needs

When using *LifeQuakes* in the classroom, I suggest omitting academic grading. Answers for Reflection Questions reveal spiritual progress in the student's life and since we can't evaluate faith, it is wise to leave the matter in the Lord's hands. Instead, the teacher could recognize class participation and assignment completion. Learning to apply Gods' principles and promises to trials and leading students to Christ and His sufficiency is the goal of *LifeQuakes*.

The Roots of *LifeQuakes*

A pastor's comforting message after terrible shootings at Columbine High School in Littleton, Colorado encouraged me to write *LifeQuakes*.

On an April day in 1999 in a suburban high school, two of its own students mercilessly implemented a shooting spree. In less than fifteen minutes, two student gunmen killed 13 and wounded 21 before turning the guns on themselves—one of the most devastating school shootings in the U.S.

Where did survivors find comfort? Where does a person find peace when faced with trials? *LifeQuakes: God's Rescue Plan in Hard Times* will examine how believers in Christ can experience the peace of God that surpasses human understanding.

CHAPTER 1 PREVIEW

↪ How I Learned to Depend on the Lord
↪ Is It All Right to Ask "Why"?
↪ What God Reveals through Trials

CHAPTER 1

God Allows Lifequakes to Shake Your Footing

A Faith Adventure
God Drew Me Closer

In the first ten years of my marriage my life was shook with major upheavals—*lifequakes* and tremors.[1] The Lord allowed five major trials to occur consecutively thus shaking my life to its roots. My marriage began with the trials of family deaths. In January my uncle passed away and my husband's grandmother died in April.

In the middle of mourning these losses, the Lord blessed us with our first son, *"a time to be born...a time to laugh"* (Eccl. 3). Next my husband's mother died in September at age fifty-two, followed by my mother's death at age fifty-seven, four days after Thanksgiving. The early deaths of both mothers had a devastating effect on us. Since four family members died in the span of eleven months, it was *"a time to die...a time to weep"* (Eccl. 3). Because I didn't know about God's sovereignty over death, I worried about who would die next, my husband or my baby. However, the Lord in His mercy knew that our baby would help ease our sorrow.

Besides these losses, the Lord Jesus tested me with more lifequakes; the '70s and '80s were the most distressing times of my life. During the economic recession of the '70s, my husband was unemployed most of the time—the longest stretch was eighteen months. In addition, my husband was dealing with some personal problems, which were making family life difficult. Our marriage was as weak as a spider web thread and I often felt hopeless.

---

* Lifequakes (trials) are major upheavals such as the death of a loved one, loss of employment, divorce, illness, or natural disasters. Tremors describe difficulties such as insults, disappointments, any minor upset that shakes our comfort level. Tremors can be minor trials.

Despite my discouragement, the Lord continued His grace blessings. When our son was five years old, the Lord gave us the gift of another son—happiness in the middle of difficult times. The joy of two remarkable sons, seeing them develop, playing with them, teaching them was indeed a blessing from the Lord.

As personal suffering increased in magnitude and intensity, the Lord interceded and a friend introduced me to Bible tapes. Through regular Bible study, I began to learn to live by faith, focusing on the Lord and less on my circumstances. The teaching on the tapes gave me a new perspective and more and more I saw the goodness of the Lord. The only thing that kept my entire life from spiraling out of control was maintaining a Christ-centered perspective by learning and applying God's Word to my trials.

God planned another lifequake—severe health problems arose, with over one hundred debilitating symptoms. As I researched for medical answers and sought several doctors for help, I pleaded repeatedly with my Savior for relief. A good prayer would have been, *"Hear me, O LORD, for Your lovingkindness is good; Turn to me according to the multitude of Your tender mercies. And do not hide Your face from Your servant, For I am in trouble; Hear me speedily"* (Ps. 69:16-17). His answer was "wait" and added another trial.

When our oldest son was ten, I substitute taught his fifth grade class. What a shock to see how small my son was compared with his classmates; at age ten, he was the size of a five-year-old. He wore the same size clothes for three seasons; the doctors had told me not to worry and said he was just small for his age.

Teaching school that day was a wake-up call that forced me into action. I hunted for answers with medical specialists. Medical tests ruled out a brain tumor and a bone growth deficiency. With no cause, I had no action plan to help him grow. I turned to the Lord for guidance as I searched for a solution to this problem.

Simultaneous with the four quakes, our younger son was a whirlwind of action and distractibility. One professional diagnosed our son with Attention Deficit Hyperactivity Disorder (ADHD)—the most severe case she had seen in her thirty years of experience. As a teacher, I understood child development; however, this was something new to me. I researched through books, attended seminars and meetings—no Internet in those days. Again, I prayed to the Lord for guidance and stamina.

As I stumbled in the valley of stress and sorrows, I wondered what God's purpose was in all this. Feeling exhausted physically and emotionally I asked how long will the trials last? Often my feelings of helplessness and worry overwhelmed me. I had little social life or relaxation time, only problems surrounding me. Sometimes I resolved that everyone had problems; at other times, I was convinced that others around me had none.

God had plans to give me hope and a better outlook. *"For I know the thoughts that I think toward you, says the LORD, thoughts of peace and not of evil, to give you a future and a hope"* (Jer. 29:11). When I was thinking from God's viewpoint, Jesus Christ was my help. *"God is our refuge and strength, A very present help in trouble"* (Ps. 46:1). God's grace carried me through the trials.

> **AMAZING GRACE**
> Thru many dangers, toils, and snares,
> I have already come;
> 'Tis grace hath brought me safe thus far,
> And grace will lead me home.
>
> ~ John Newton ~

One professional questioned why I was confident and calm as we talked in her office. She said just one major trial like mine was enough to cause a breakdown or a broken marriage, but I had five simultaneously over many years. My answer: Jesus Christ was the "glue" that kept me from a nervous breakdown and preserved my marriage. I am weak but Christ is strong and without Him, I would have caved in to the pressures. Without Christ supplying my needs, I would have given up or fallen apart. The truth of Psalm 55:22 became evident when I trusted during trials. When a believer trusts, the Lord upholds her just as He says, *"Cast your burden on the LORD, And He shall sustain you; He shall never permit the righteous to be moved."* Depending on the Lord became my lifeline to stability; leaning on Christ gave me steadiness and confidence.

God's Answers to My Trials

In His perfect plan and perfect timing, my Lord Jesus answered my prayers with solutions to each trial. My husband's problems continued into our ninth year of marriage. I knew our home situation couldn't continue and I worried about the future. Was a separation unavoidable, I wondered? I didn't want my marriage to end, but my sons and I were struggling in our difficult home life. The thought of working fulltime seemed an impossible option. How could I keep house, help with homework, find loving day care for my youngest son, and still have energy and quality time for my sons? Would I have time to study the Bible? I pleaded with my Shepherd Lord for guidance. I begged Him to reverse our chaotic home life. Through His Word, the Lord was drawing me into closer dependency on Him.

As the years passed, I grew in His grace and the knowledge of Christ—His love, His strength, His power, His sovereignty. A truth I claimed was "out on a limb with God is the safest place in the world." The principle "confidence in God brings courage towards man and circumstances," which I learned from the Bible tapes, became a reality to me. Gradually I started believing my Savior was greater than my problems.

The Lord Jesus was looking for my trust as He was breaking my will. I had come to the end of my solutions; I had failed to overcome the problems. In prayer, I admitted my helplessness. The Lord always knew I was helpless, but it took time for me to realize it.

God encourages us through the apostle Paul in Romans 8:28, *"And we know that all things work together for good to those who love God [believers]."*

God has a perfect plan. He is greater than any problem; therefore, He commands us, *"Be of good cheer, I have overcome the world"* (John 16:33b). I had been gaining confidence in Him to "overcome the world." Since I couldn't resolve my problems, I needed to depend on the Lord. My Savior had positioned me to take a step in faith by confronting my husband.

One summer evening, through my heavenly Father's guidance, direction, and power, I held a one-on-one intervention with my husband. I had decided to trust my Shepherd Savior no matter what the result. His protection overshadowed my anxieties and I could believe *"Because You have been my help, Therefore in the shadow of Your wings I will rejoice"* (Ps. 63:7). In good times and bad, remember His shadow over you—the best and safest place to be.

My Shepherd supplied composure unlike I had ever experienced. As I lovingly confronted my husband, the Lord provided courage, clear thinking, and communication just as He promises. *"For God has not given us a spirit of fear, but of power and of love and of a sound mind"* (2 Tim 1:7). As I prayed silently throughout the intervention, my Savior showered me with His peace. *"Let your requests be made known to God; and the peace of God, which surpasses all understanding, will guard your hearts and minds through Christ Jesus"* (Phil. 4:6b-7). My Shepherd Savior always supplies all my needs.

God delivered my dear husband from his devastating problem and the next day he awoke to a new life. Praise the Lord! My husband had pleaded in prayer and he credited the Lord with delivering him.

Our heavenly Father had indeed arranged everything because He always works for His children. Experiencing God's faithfulness encouraged my faith. Christ had carried our marriage, our family, and me.

God had removed one trial and four remained, which He resolved one at a time. My health problems continued for years until I took a nutritional approach. My Lord revealed Himself as my great Physician.

Concerning my son's growth problems, through prayer and God's guidance, I took my son to one more doctor. Discovering that my son had a hormonal imbalance, the doctor used hormone injections and natural food supplements to help him grow. Praise the Lord, my son started to grow, adding six inches to his height.

Regarding my son with ADHD, the Lord indirectly guided me to professionals and deterred us from using medications, which have adverse long-term side effects. The doctor understood that ADHD is a term for a cluster of symptoms with more than one underlying cause, which we needed to explore. Using several treatment approaches, my son improved and today he is doing well. Praise the Lord for another yes answer to prayer.

Through trials, Christ had sheltered me under His wings. He had become my confidence, my stability, and my security in life. The popular traditional hymn, "Under His Wings," expresses how the Lord carries and shields us when we cast our cares on Him.

> **UNDER HIS WINGS**
> *"Casting all your care upon Him, for He cares for you"*
> (1 Peter 5:7)
>
> Under His wings I am safely abiding,
> Though the night deepens and tempests are wild,
> Still I can trust Him; I know He will keep me,
> He has redeemed me, and I am His child.
>
> REFRAIN: Under His wings, under His wings,
> Who from His love can sever?
> Under His wings my soul shall abide,
> Safely abide forever.
>
> Under His wings, what a refuge in sorrow!
> How the heart yearningly turns to His rest!
> Often when earth has no balm for my healing,
> There I find comfort, and there I am blessed.
>
> Under His wings, oh, what precious enjoyment!
> There will I hide till life's trials are o'er;
> Sheltered, protected, no evil can harm me,
> Resting in Jesus, I'm safe evermore.
>
> ~ William O. Cushing, 1823-1902, & Ira D. Sankey, 1840-1908 ~

Have you ever personally experienced the trial of an earthquake? For most of us, we can only remember terrible images of the devastating earthquakes we saw in a movie or news report.

Jim's Earthquake Experience—Hawaii 2006

Jim describes his experience as it happened,

> It was just after 7:00 am when the earthquake struck. I was in my home office preparing to read some faxes when the earthquake hit my house with what seemed like a loud blast. Immediately following the blast, the house began intensely shaking and vibrating. I could barely get out of my office. The hallway was moving up and down and sideways and I could barely keep my footing. I felt sure the house would start breaking apart at any moment, but I couldn't do anything other than hold on. For a moment the shaking subsided, then more vigorous shaking. The 45 seconds seemed like minutes, but finally the quake subsided.
>
> The earthquake demolished the interior and everything vertical crashed down throwing debris all over the house. Smashed bookcases and shelving lay on the floor. Broken glass, dishes, picture frame glass were all over. My office and much of the house lay in shambles. Doors failed to swing properly or pinched closed, but the damage to the house was minimal. Considering how violently the house was moving and shaking, I am amazed the foundation was still intact.
>
> My town, Waikoloa was near the epicenter of the 6.6 quake. The seismic scale is logarithmic meaning a change from six to seven is a 10-fold increase in intensity. I speculate if this quake was over seven the damage would have been staggering. But, who can say? I am just glad it was not.
>
> I called a friend on Maui—just twenty-five miles of ocean separate the Big Island and Maui. She was outside during the quake and watched the landscape undulate and houses shake. The damage there was not as severe, but all the islands lost electrical power.
>
> I felt fortunate no one nearby was injured and the island wide injury rate was slight; I heard there were no fatalities. Many landslides of huge boulders and debris closed most of the highways. It was incredible! What an experience! Life can change in the blink of an eye!

Quakes Bring Loss and Pain

The aftermath of a major earthquake can be terrible; everywhere you look is devastation and destruction. A severe quake can cause loss of life and millions of dollars in property damages. Earthquake victims agonize in grief over losses—personal property, their homes and loved ones.

Like an earthquake, a lifequake may affect more than one person, an entire nation, or the world as one did a few years ago. One sunny autumn morning I began my daily routine by having breakfast with my grandson and then driving him to school. I walked him to his classroom and I noticed the teacher's aide looking distraught. As I talked with the aide, she told me about the horrific disaster that minutes earlier had hit New York—the destruction of the World Trade Center on September 11, 2001. When I got back home, I watched the film footage on TV and saw some of the suffering by my fellow Americans—the affects of this disaster rippled across our nation and affected the world. This catastrophe not only changed America, it changed the world. My thoughts and feelings overwhelmed me as I thought about the attack on my country.

In the aftermath of a crisis, victims must make a choice—collapse in despair or stand determined to begin again. Many people "get through" crisis clinging to the old cliché, "pull yourself up by your bootstraps." You can survive a crisis by your own determination as most people do, but God wants believers to do more than survive or endure in a crisis. He has a rescue plan to help you spiritually thrive in a trial.

What Is Shaking Your Footing?

Think about your current or a past lifequake. Maybe you awoke one morning, the sunshine glimmering through your window and life seemed wonderful. By evening a grim medical diagnosis shook your life and filled you with fear, worry, and questions about the future. Perhaps you're having relationship problems in your family—the child you trained in the Lord is uninterested in Him and estranged from you. Are you facing a difficult problem at work with a hostile co-worker whom you want to treat with love, but you find it increasingly difficult to show kindness? The following is a list of upheavals that may shake our footing:

- a divorce
- losing a loved one through death
- a spiritual failure or test
- a tragic accident or injury
- imprisonment, just or unjust
- suffering injustice
- falsely accused
- chronic pain or seeing the pain of a loved one
- a violent attack
- an unfaithful spouse
- a serious health issue
- unemployment or underemployment
- a financial hardship
- some form of abuse
- personal substance addiction; addiction of a loved one
- a rebellious child who is destroying his future
- struggles of single parenting
- raising children alone while your spouse is serving on active military duty
- serving in combat duty in a war zone
- a national crisis
- a natural catastrophe such as a flood, hurricane, tornado, or an earthquake

Like the wavering instability of an earthquake, a lifequake may cause you to feel swallowed or buried in its crevices. Any personal loss penetrates deeply and may invade your soul causing powerful emotions such as anger that boils over, perhaps even directed toward God. Blame may erupt; you may blame yourself, another, or the Lord Jesus because a trial changed your life. Perhaps you wish you could suppress your devastating emotions, you wish you could erase the events, go back in time, and start over, but you are powerless to change the circumstances. You must go on, but your mind spins in worry and fear, and you wonder how you can continue; you feel squeezed in a vice.

Used with permission by Duluth Bible Church.

It doesn't matter, really, how great the pressure is, it only matters where the pressure lies. See that it never comes between you and the Lord — then, the greater the pressure, the more it presses you to His breast.

~ J. Hudson Taylor ~

Fair Is Whatever God Wants to Do

Some think suffering shouldn't happen to believers, especially if they are serving God. When suffering does occur we wonder why me, Lord? Why did my friend, the mother of two small children, have to die? Why did I lose my job? Why must I suffer from debilitating pain? We may think it isn't fair. Are we forgetting that God is in control and He does what is best for us. Because God is supreme, we have no right to tell Him what is fair or unfair. He is in control and has the power to do whatever He wills. He has the power to give and to take away; He is just in whatever He does.

No matter what the trial or heartache you suffer, keep in mind the grace of God towards you. His grace blessings exceed whatever we may feel is unfair.

> *God's grace always gives us better than we deserve.*

Is It All Right to Ask "Why?"

Why do bad things happen to believers? The most obvious answer is that we live in a world corrupted by sin, in Satan's world filled with suffering. However, we remember God is in control and allows trials to draw us closer. He allows some Christians to suffer martyrdom, others to survive persecution, and the rest of us to suffer customized lifequakes.

In a lifequake, our minds may fumble for answers and demand why this tragedy happened. Why did God allow this disaster or suffering? Will understanding help you to feel better? Probably not, the pain will remain. Will understanding restore things to the way they were? Even if God reveals "why," we still may not understand because of our human limitations. Since God uses trials to teach us, it is better to ask, what does God want me to learn? Though God rarely discloses the reasons for trials, He yearns to reveal Himself. Believing God knows "why" is more important than knowing the reasons. *"The secret things belong to the* LORD *our God, but those things which are revealed belong to us and to our children forever, that we may do all the words of this law* [His Word]*"* (Deut. 29:29). Must we insist on walking by sight (knowledge) instead of by faith? Knowing why must not override our faith in our all-knowing God.

Instead of asking why me, Lord, a better question to ask is, why not me? What makes me any better than another believer? I'm a sinner and don't deserve special exemption from suffering; furthermore, Scripture tells us to expect to suffer for Christ's sake (Rom. 8:17; Phil. 1:29).

However, we can take comfort in knowing that because Christ suffered, He understands our sorrow, weaknesses, and disappointments (Heb. 2:16-18; 4:14-16). Christ promised never to leave us (Matt. 28:18-20) and He intercedes for us (Heb. 7:24, 25). Therefore, we can confidently rely on

Christ in times of pain, suffering, and persecution.

We may ask why something happened; however, our questioning attitude must be humble and not demanding toward God. In addition, it is unacceptable to question God's character—His goodness or wisdom. For example, if you are a good God, why did you let this happen? As the psalmist recognized, *"As for God, His way is perfect"* (Ps. 18:30). While we may wonder "why," questioning God's wisdom and authority is prideful. Our attitude is important to God.

When Asking "Why" Is Necessary

After the Sabbath while it was still dark, Mary Magdalene went to Jesus' tomb. When she saw His tomb was empty (John 20:11-18), she wondered where the body of her Lord was. Sometimes the question "why" is not only appropriate, it is necessary. The Lord answered her question and encouraged her at the same time. Mary Magdalene was the first to know why the tomb was empty—Christ had risen just as He had said He would. Being the first to know, God also honored her with the privilege of being the first to see the risen Lord Jesus. Our risen Savior had kept His promise to rise again from the dead (Matt. 17:23; 20:19; 27:63; John 20:18). What a wonderful answer to the "why" question of the empty tomb!

God always knows the answer to our "why" questions. Since He alone knows best, God usually keeps information to Himself. Therefore, it is often better not to ask "why." When asking "why" doesn't resolve anything, we should still simply give thanks to God for His promise: *"We know that God causes all things to work together for good to those who love God"* (Rom. 8:28 NASB).

Why Lord?

Since the first grade I dreamed of being a teacher in a Christian school. I wanted to teach children about Jesus, their Savior. My first teaching assignment seemed ideal—first grade, great staff, in a small rural town only one hour from my parents. I thought, this is what the Lord had planned for me, but He had another plan—illness. I saw a doctor in November, but he failed to diagnose strep throat; instead, his diagnosis was a "case of nerves" and told me I needed a social life. By mid-February, the untreated strep throat led to a blood infection, similar to mononucleosis, which spread to my spleen. After a two-week hospital stay, I was still fatigued and unable to teach. As a result, I didn't resume my teaching position until May.

The doctor told me I would need a year to recover. For that reason, I felt guided to resign from my teaching position—the work of my dreams. Though disappointed, I believed the Lord knew best. I moved back to my parent's home, cared for my semi-invalid mother, and kept house while I recuperated.

Why, Lord? I sometimes wondered, but *"It is the glory of God to conceal a matter"* (Prov. 25:2). I can only presume why God permitted those events in my life. I do believe my all-knowing heavenly Father wanted me back in Milwaukee (His geographic will) for His reasons—His purpose for my life. Although my first teaching experience ended abruptly, that wasn't the end of my teaching career.

By November, I was feeling stronger and the desire to teach children had resumed. I joked with Mom and Dad that I missed the "chalk dust." In His perfect time, the Lord moved me back into a classroom with children. Throughout my life, the Lord provided teaching opportunities and currently I am teaching through writing.

> *God's purposes are greater than our imagination.*

One of my favorite hymns is "I Will Trust When I Cannot See" written by John W. Peterson. People around the world love and sing his music. Mr. Peterson had received many sacred music awards. Let Peterson's hymn "I Will Trust When I Cannot See" encourage you.

I WILL TRUST WHEN I CANNOT SEE

When I cannot understand God's leading,
When I do not know the reason why.
He should choose the path that lies before me,
Still to Him in faith I can reply:

REFRAIN: I will trust when I cannot see,
When I'm faced with adversity,
And believe Your will is always best for me
I will trust when I cannot see.

When I feel the sting of disappointment,
And my dreams lie crumbled in the dust,
When my best adds up to loss and failure,
And the things that happen seem unjust:

When I face the furnace of affliction
And the pain seems more than I can bear,
When I think it strange – this fiery trial
Still I'll tell my blessed Lord in prayer:

~ John W. Peterson (1921-2006) ~
© Copyright 1970 by John W. Peterson Music Company.
All rights reserved. Used with permission.

Things Are Not Always What They Seem
Adapted from Unknown Author

Two angels traveling in disguise stopped to spend the night in the home of a wealthy family. The family was rude and refused to let the angels stay in the mansion's guestroom. Instead, the family provided a small space in the cold basement. As they made their bed on the hard floor, the older angel saw a hole in the wall and repaired it.

When the younger angel asked why, the older angel replied, "Things are not always what they seem." The next night the pair came to rest at the house of a poor but hospitable farmer and his wife. After sharing what little food they had, the couple let the angels sleep in their bed where they could have a good night's rest.

When the sun came up the next morning, the angels found the farmer and his wife in tears. Their only cow, whose milk had been their income, lay dead in the field. The enraged younger angel asked the older angel, "How could you have let this happen? The first man had everything, yet you helped him," he accused. The second family had little but was willing to share everything, and you let the cow die."

"Things aren't always what they seem," the older angel replied. "When we stayed in the basement of the mansion, I noticed there was gold stored in that hole in the wall. Since the owner was so obsessed with greed and unwilling to share his good fortune, I sealed the wall so he wouldn't find it. Then last night as we slept in the farmer's bed, the angel of death came for his wife. I gave him the cow instead. Things aren't always what they seem. Sometimes that is exactly what happens when things don't turn out the way you want. God's ways aren't ours."

www.answers.yahoo.com/questionindex?qid=20081009085510AAfuoZh

Although this story isn't an accurate portrayal of angels (they have no power over life and death), you get the point. We don't know what God is doing and His reasons; yet, we believe He works all things together according to His plan and our good.

The theme of the next hymn encourages us to trust Him because He is sovereign and full of grace. After reading the background of the next hymn, enjoy its spiritual richness.

William Cowper, the writer of "God Moves in a Mysterious Way," whose father was chaplain to King George II, went through the motions of becoming an attorney but never practiced law. He lived near Olney, Buckinghamshire, the namesake town of the Olney Hymns, which he co-wrote with John Newton, author of "Amazing Grace."

"God Moves in a Mysterious Way" has a story (though unsubstantiated) behind it and is reportedly the last hymn Cowper ever wrote. Cowper often struggled with depression and doubt. One night he decided to commit suicide by drowning himself. He called a cab and told the driver to take him to the Thames River, but a thick fog came down and prevented them from finding the river. After a time of driving aimlessly, lost in the dense fog, the cabby finally stopped and let Cowper out. To Cowper's surprise, he found himself back on his own doorstep. God had sent the fog to keep him from killing himself. Even in our blackest moments, God watches over us.

www.blueletterbible.org/hymns/bio.cfm?bio=bio_c_o_cowper_w

GOD MOVES IN A MYSTERIOUS WAY

"What I am doing you do not understand now, but you will know after this." (John 13:7)

God moves in a mysterious way
His wonders to perform;
He plants His footsteps in the sea
And rides upon the storm.

Deep in unfathomable mines
Of never failing skill
He treasures up His bright designs
And works His sovereign will.

Judge not the Lord by feeble sense,
But trust Him for His grace;
Behind a frowning providence
He hides a smiling face.

Blind unbelief is sure to err
And scan His work in vain;
God is His own interpreter,
And He will make it plain.

~ William Cowper, 1731-1800, England~

God Reveals Himself, Not His Reasons

God concealed His reasons for Job's lifequakes from him because getting to know God was enough. Our Father wants us to know Him better and to seek His purpose. He desires that we *"grow in the grace and knowledge of our Lord and Savior Jesus Christ"* (2 Peter 3:18). God reveals what He wants us to know and when (Deut. 29:29).

In addition, struggling to understand God's reasons is failing to see what God is seeking. Does God command us to understand His reasons or the crisis itself? No to both, but He does reveal, *"For My thoughts are not your thoughts, Nor are your ways My ways," says the LORD"* (Isa. 55:8). A better question is "who or what am I going to turn to in this trial?" The Lord commands us to, *"trust in the LORD with all your heart, And lean not on your own understanding"* (Prov. 3:5).

> *Ours is not to reason "why" but to seek God and rely!*

Through Quakes We May Grow

Life is a series of changes; children are born, they grow up, leave home, marry, and start a family and this life cycle continues. Also, throughout our life cycle, losses and sorrows enter our lives. Among all the experiences of life, our Lord God refreshes our lives with joys, good times, and blessings. Our all-knowing God allows believers every trial or joy according to His perfect plan and in His perfect time as Scripture tells us.

> *To everything there is a season,*
> *A time for every purpose under heaven:*
> *A time to be born, And a time to die...*
> *A time to heal; ...A time to weep,*
> *And a time to laugh; A time to mourn...*
> *A time to gain, And a time to lose; ...*
> *A time of war, And a time of peace.*
> (Eccl. 3:1-4, 6, 8)

Trials don't guarantee spiritual growth; however, our response to them determines whether we grow closer to our Savior. If we respond in a manner contrary to God's plan, lifequakes may shake our footholds and leave us useless in the plan of God. When we respond in dependency on the Lord, He can use trials to stretch our faith. I have learned to think of a trial as an adventure—a FAITH adventure.

> **FAITH is a**
> **F**antastic
> **A**dventure
> **I**n
> **T**rusting
> **H**im

Dear believers, as you travel on your faith adventures, look for the pleasure of knowing Christ better, discover treasures (spiritual riches), and experience the fulfillment of His promises.

Through Trials God Stretched My Faith

In retrospect, experiencing some difficult lifequakes gave me a deeper appreciation of my Savior's love and faithfulness. *"Therefore know that the Lord your God, He is God, the faithful God"* (Deut. 7:9a). Even when God doesn't say "yes" to prayers or delays answers, He is faithful.

Reflecting on those continuous years of turmoil and distress, I see Christ developed my faith as He shaped my spiritual life. As Paul the apostle encourages, *"And we know that all things work together for good to those who love God* [believers]*"* (Rom. 8:28). In addition, my Father used trials to prepare me for future health problems, heartaches and losses—the tremors and the quakes of life.

I am grateful for the trials, which taught me about the Lord and how to trust Him more consistently. In His loving-kindness, my Savior knew how long to apply the trials to draw me closer. Because Christ Jesus drew me through His Word, He became more real, more personal to me and I learned to occupy my mind with Him. In addition, He put a new song in my heart, *"I will praise the name of God with a song, And will magnify Him with thanksgiving"* (Ps. 69:30). The lifequakes were worth it, now I have a cherished relationship with my Savior. Jesus is my song!

Hudson Taylor, the great missionary to Inland China, reflects my sentiments this way,

> *My faith was not untried; it often, often failed. And I was so sorry and ashamed of the failure to trust such a Father. But oh, I was learning to know Him. I would not even then have missed the trial. He becomes so near, so real, so intimate.*
> (Hudson Taylor's Spiritual Secret, pp.82-83)

What God Ordains Is Always Good

As you meditate on three stanzas of the next hymn, consider the greatness of our heavenly Father who always knows best. Therefore, without hesitation you can yield to His care. In this hymn count the ways your Father is taking care of you, and then consider how you can respond to His grace. For example in the first stanza, God is always good, He directs me and knows how best to protect me; therefore, I can surrender to His care and will for my life. Continue to contemplate on these stanzas remembering to think about your responses to His grace, even expressing them to Him in prayer.

WHAT GOD ORDAINS IS ALWAYS GOOD

"He is the Rock, His work is perfect; For all His ways are justice, A God of truth and without injustice; Righteous and upright is He." (Deut. 32:4)

What God ordains is always good;
His will abideth holy.
As He directs my life for me,
I follow meek and lowly.
God indeed in every need
Doth well know how to shield me;
To Him, then, I will yield me.

What God ordains is always good.
He never will deceive me;
He leads me in His own right way,
And never will He leave me.
I take content What He hath sent;
His hand that sends me sadness
Will turn my tears to gladness.

What God ordains is always good.
His loving thought attends me;
No poison can be in the cup
That my Physician sends me.
My God is true; Each morn anew
I'll trust His grace unending,
My life to Him commending.

~ Samuel Rodigast, 1649-1708 ~

Reflection Questions

Wherever possible support your answers with Scripture verses.

1. What did you learn about asking "why" in trials?

2. What significant principles did you learn from this chapter?

CHAPTER 2 PREVIEW

⇜ The Good News: Truths You Must See and Believe to be Saved
⇜ Wrong Responses to the Gospel of Jesus Christ
⇜ Eternal Security
⇜ Distinctions between Phase One and Two of God's Rescue Plan

CHAPTER 2

God's Rescue Plan

Before we trusted in Christ we were enemies of God and consequently separated from Him with eternity in hell as our final destination. Our separation from God was our greatest problem. We remained alienated from God until we trusted His rescue plan of salvation from sin's penalty. At this moment we were justified—declared not guilty by God which is phase one of salvation. God's rescue plan for the lesser problems we face, such as natural earthquakes, tremors and lifequakes is phase two of His plan. Before we study phase two, we need to start at the beginning with phase one of salvation.

Have you believed the gospel of Christ? If someone were to ask you if you are going to heaven, would you confess Christ as your Savior and then add "I hope so." This response may indicate whether you're saved. You may not have a clear understanding of the gospel or you may just need assurance of your salvation unto eternal life. You need a "know so" salvation assurance, not "hope so."

Do you acknowledge Christ but add you are a good person? Are you afraid of losing your salvation? How do you know if you are a true believer? Answers to these questions may reveal whether you are genuinely saved. This chapter offers biblical answers.

Maybe you are thinking you are saved so you don't need to read about salvation. Besides confirming your own salvation, this chapter provides information that may help you to share the gospel of Christ with others.

Pay particular attention to this chapter because God's rescue plan for salvation is the basis for living by faith. It is also the source of power for believers in Jesus Christ, so settle in and enjoy.

Are You Good Enough to Enter Heaven?

What must I do to obtain heaven? To discover what a small boy believed, a preacher asked him a series of questions.

"If I sold my house, my car and my possessions and gave the money to the church, would God accept me?" "No."

"If I were good to my wife, went to church, gave money or possessions to the poor, would I get into heaven?" "No."

"If you kept your room clean, helped your parents around the house, didn't fight with your brother, would God let you into heaven?" "No."

"Well, how can we get into heaven," the pastor asked?
The boy shouted, "You have to be dead!"

The anecdote may cause a chuckle, but the matter of salvation is serious. How does one gain the gift of eternal life*? How good must you be to enter heaven? People are so busy earning a living, getting married, raising kids, or having fun, they aren't thinking about their eternal destiny.

Many think if they are good God will let them into heaven. They think morality is the basis for salvation—good people go to heaven and bad people go to hell. Surveys show that people think God will permit them into heaven because they are decent. Moral behavior is the typical survey answer whether the person is Christian, Muslim, Hindu, or some other faith.

What if you died in ten minutes and God asked you, "Why should I let you into heaven?" Would any of the following be your answer?

- I have always tried to do the right thing.
- I am a decent person.
- I was baptized when I was an infant.
- I attend church every Sunday.
- I hope God would let me in.
- I believe in Jesus Christ plus one of the above answers.

---

* Eternal life is everlasting life with God and is a believer's present possession the moment he trusts in Christ. Heaven is the believer's ultimate eternal destiny—a place.

Are you certain you will go to heaven when you die? Because you are an honest, moral person, you may assume that God should let you into heaven. By whose standards are you good enough—by yours, the church, or the standards of others? Do you have first-class deeds to counter your sins? Who decides who will have eternal life? God holds the standards, which determine who will have eternal life and live with Him in heaven.

Comparing Man's Plan with God's Plan for Salvation

Man has a plan to get to heaven, which is in opposition to God's grace plan. This section will compare man's salvation plan with God's and reveal whose plan is sufficient to receive eternal life.

If God Is a Good God, Then Good People Go to Heaven

The reasoning behind "good people go to heaven" seems right on two points. It looks fair. Many believe that people are rewarded for doing well. The diligent worker receives a pay raise or a promotion. The athlete who excels because he practices for large amounts of time wins the prize. The student who does well earns a promotion to the next grade. Religious books like the Bible, the Quran (Koran), and the Book of Mormon speak about God's desire to reward superior behavior. However, the Bible distinguishes between rewards earned by the believer (1 Cor. 3:10-15; 9:24-26; 2 Tim. 4:8) and salvation that is a gift (Eph. 2:8-9). The Bible tells us that God rewards good works resulting from a believer's faith following his salvation, but it never speaks of eternal life as a reward, only as a gift.

Another explanation coincides with the belief that God is a good God. The thinking is, if a good God lives in a good place, He lets good people live with Him. If God is a righteous God and permits good people into heaven but never specifies what He means by good, then just how good is God? For example, imagine that you are competing in a race. You wait on the starting line, but you see no indication which direction you should run—no signs, markers, boundaries and no finish line. Without warning, the official fires the gun and the runners dart in haphazard directions. Would you call that race fair?

Again, suppose on the first day of the semester the history professor informs you that your grade will depend entirely on the final exam. He says the class won't meet until the day of the final exam. He provides no course outline, no reading list, and no textbook. He smiles and says, "Good luck!" Is he an exemplary teacher? Is he fair?

Improbable examples, but you see the point. If God didn't tell us how to receive eternal life, He wouldn't be fair. However, God is fair and good; therefore, He provided the details for receiving the gift of eternal life, as we shall see.

Do You See Yourself as Better than Others?

Are you becoming angry about the evils in our culture? Do you yell at the T.V. hoping to feel better? Do you yell at the politicians? Does it make you feel better? Injustice makes us mad. Is it wrong to get angry about injustices? What do we see on the news every night? Delinquents steal cars or spray paint buildings. Men beat their wives or girlfriends. Adultery and fornication are pervasive in our society and TV and Hollywood portray that as normal behavior. Bullies pick on innocent kids. Some police and judges are corrupt as are many politicians. Con artists prey on seniors and swindle them out of their savings. Extortion, greed, oppression, arson, and bribery are prevalent. Even the sports referees and umpires can't make the right calls. Pervasive corruption often fills us with anger; God knows how mad we are. God isn't pleased about this either, and He warns that He will punish the "unjust"—those who behave contrary to what is right and just. Speaking of wrongful behaviors, have you

- lied?
- hated or gossiped?
- lusted?
- stolen?

- been selfish?
- coveted?
- committed adultery (sex with someone other than your spouse)?
- committed fornication (sex as a single person)?
- always honored your parents?
- failed to put God first in your affections?
- blasphemed His name, using it to curse?
- ever worried, complained, or grumbled?
- been guilty of idolatry (made a god in your own image or considered belongings and people above God)?

If you have done even one of those sins, you are in violation of God's standards. *"For whoever shall keep the whole law, and yet stumble in one point, he is guilty of all"* (James 2:10). If you say you have never done any of these sins, you are deceiving yourself (1 John 1:8). Sin (even one) is like ugly, rotten, stinky garbage. Imperfection can't exist alongside perfection in heaven.

How mad is God about sin? Only punishment in hell will satisfy the wrath of holy God. For the unjust, there will be hell to pay in eternity. When we count every sin of thought, word, and deed, we recognize we sin many times per day. As God tells us, *"For all have sinned"* (Rom. 3:23a).

How Good is Good Enough?

Perhaps you think your good outweighs your sin. An individual may admit sin but imply his first-rate behavior would outweigh his sin. Let us do the math. One sin per day for one year is 365 sins per year. Multiply that by 40 years, which equals 14,600 sins in your lifetime. If your moral behavior offsets your sins, how many good deeds would you need to cancel thousands of sins? How would you ever know if you did the sufficient amount of good deeds to compensate for your sins? You couldn't know.

Perhaps you admit you sin daily, but think you are a decent person so God should let you into heaven. God's requirement for entrance into His presence is perfection. Are you perfect? Your sins are countless, and your good works aren't sufficient to offset the scale in your favor. Good people don't go to heaven; only the perfect can live with a perfect God.

Meet Gus, a respectable person who doesn't smoke, drink alcohol, commit adultery, steal, or lie. Gus drives the speed limit, attends church, gives to charities, and loves his wife and kids. Yet when asked if he is going to heaven, he can only respond, "I hope so." If Gus looks good by man's standards, and can't be certain of salvation, who can? Why do good people only "hope so?" People "hope so" because no one can tell them how good they have to be to gain eternal life.

In His Word, God clearly recorded His standards and requirements for obtaining eternal life. Since God is holy and perfect, He can't tolerate or accept sin. We don't have to guess at His standards because they recorded in His Word, the Bible.

You may be blameless in your own eyes or in the eyes of people, but are you perfect in God's eyes? No one lives up to His perfect standard: *"for all have sinned and fall short of the glory of God"* (Rom. 3:23). Therefore, a decent person who outwardly behaves morally yet commits one sin is still unsuitable for heaven. One sin equals failure to keep God's perfect standard. If you are honest, you will admit you are like the rest of us—imperfect. To enter heaven you must be perfect like God. *"As for God, His way is perfect"* (2 Sam. 22:31a). How does God see our good behavior? He tells us through His prophet Isaiah, *"But we are all like an unclean thing, And all our righteousnesses are like filthy rags"* (Isa. 64:6). Who would want to live with that? A perfect God would not! You can never be confident of heaven based on your virtuous deeds.

You will never obtain eternal life based on your finest works alone or on faith in Jesus Christ plus your "goodness" (Rom. 4:5). Keep in mind, Scripture doesn't tell us not to do admirable works, but compared with God's perfection our works are like filthy rags. Doing right or sinning less isn't God's standard; perfection is His measurement. *"The law of the* LORD *is perfect"* (Ps. 19:7a). No one is adequate to enter heaven because his morality doesn't equal perfection. One sin brands you imperfect, condemns you to hell, and a life without God. To live with God, you must be like Him—perfect.

God promises eternal life to everyone who obeys the Law perfectly (all 613 commandments, which include the Ten Commandments, Ex. 20). However, no one can. For example, Jesus told the rich young ruler to keep these (commandments) and live, but the ruler couldn't even keep the first commandment to honor God above wealth (Luke 18:18-24). Keeping the Law perfectly is also the point of Romans 2 and Galatians 3:13. Do keep the Law (work righteousness), and you will live (eternal life) the Law promises, but it also says, Don't keep the Law and you will die! Have you kept the Law perfectly?

Man's plan to live with God is through moral and ethical behavior. With this belief, you can believe in Christ, add your morality, and God will let you into heaven. In other words, man thinks religion—what he can do for God, morality and meritorious works—is the ticket to heaven. However, that is man's plan, not God's plan for eternal life and residency in heaven.

> *If we could be saved by being good, then Christ didn't have to die.*

Since God knows that no one can keep His Law or standards perfectly, He provided a better way than expecting you to save yourself or to help with your salvation. Our merciful Father didn't want to give us what we deserve—hell. Instead, His plan gives us what we don't deserve—eternal life. Salvation according to biblical Christianity is God's work—the cross work of Christ—on man's behalf.

Instead of your work or help, He does the work of salvation, as His Word declares, *"not by works of righteousness which we have done, but according to His mercy He saved us"* (Titus 3:5a). God tells us that people who don't try to be good enough but only believe will be saved (Rom. 4:5).

> *The choice is faith alone in Christ for eternal life or your perfection.*

Read the next pages to be certain you have eternal life. Part one details God's answer to "How is someone saved?" and part two lists the "Wrong Responses"—how someone isn't saved.

The Good News—the Gospel of Jesus Christ

Truths You Must See and Believe to be Saved from Hell

1. I must accept a Holy God's evaluation of me.

When Isaiah saw God, he cried out *"Holy, holy, holy is the LORD of hosts"* (Isa. 6:3). Our tendency is to view others or ourselves from a relative standard; however, God's evaluation of us stems from His holy nature. He declares, *"For there is not a just man on earth who does good And does not sin"* (Eccl. 7:20).

> *"For all have sinned and fall short of the glory of God"* (Rom. 3:23).

> *"They have all turned aside; They have together become unprofitable; There is none who does good, no, not one"* (Rom. 3:12).

Man's pride thinks he has sufficient merit for God to accept him. Again, the Bible says,

> *"But we are all like an unclean thing, And all our righteousnesses are like filthy rags"* (Isa. 64:6).

> *"There is none righteous, no, not one"* (Rom. 3:10).

This, of course, is the bad news.

2. I must see what God has provided for me through Christ's death and resurrection.

The good news of the gospel of grace centers in what Jesus Christ* completed for us on the cross of Calvary. God's justice demanded punishment of death; Jesus Christ died as our substitute and rose again showing God's "stamp of approval" on His finished work.

> *"For the wages of sin is death, but the gift of God is eternal life in Christ Jesus our Lord"* (Rom. 6:23).

> *"For when we were still without strength, in due time Christ died for the ungodly"* (Rom. 5:6).

> *"All we like sheep have gone astray; We have turned, every one, to his own way; And the LORD has laid on Him the iniquity of us all"* (Isa. 53:6).

> *"But we see Jesus, who was made a little lower than the angels, for the suffering of death crowned with glory and honor, that He, by the grace of God, might taste death for everyone"* (Heb. 2:9).

His sacrifice for our sins paid the penalty in full, satisfying God's holy demands unconditionally.

> *"But this Man, after He had offered one sacrifice for sins forever, sat down at the right hand of God"* (Heb. 10:12).

> *"For Christ also suffered once for sins, the just for the unjust, that He might bring us to God, being put to death in the flesh but made alive by the Spirit"* (1 Peter 3:18).

Why did He do this for us? He sacrificed Himself because He loves us and wants to save us from eternal hell—eternal separation from God in the Lake of Fire.

> *"But God demonstrates His own love toward us, in that while we were still sinners, Christ died for us"* (Rom. 5:8).

> *"In this the love of God was manifested toward us, that God has sent His only begotten Son into the world, that we might live through Him. In this is love, not that we loved God, but that He loved us and sent His Son to be the propitiation for our sins"* (1 John 4:9-10).

---

* Jesus Christ is God. He alone was qualified to suffer the wrath of God as payment for sin. (Col. 1:15-20)

3. I must believe eternal salvation is a gift to me apart from religious works.

Because Christ fully paid the penalty for all our sins when He died, what sins must you pay for by your good works? None! Salvation isn't a reward for good people but a gift of God for sinners who trust in Jesus Christ alone.

> *"For by grace you have been saved through faith, and that not of yourselves; it is the gift of God, not of works, lest anyone should boast"* (Eph. 2:8-9).

> *"For the wages of sin is death, but the gift of God is eternal life in Christ Jesus our Lord"* (Rom. 6:23).

> *"For God so loved the world that He gave His only begotten Son, that whoever believes in Him should not perish but have everlasting life"* (John 3:16).

If you could go to heaven by living a moral life, trying to keep the Ten Commandments, being baptized, or attending church, why did Jesus Christ have to die? His sacrifice would have been for nothing! God says,

> *"I do not set aside the grace of God; for if righteousness comes through the law, then Christ died in vain"* (Gal. 2:21).

> *"Therefore we conclude that a man is justified by faith apart from the deeds of the law"* (Rom. 3:28).

> *"But to him who does not work but believes on Him who justifies the ungodly, his faith is accounted for righteousness"* (Rom. 4:5).

Good works should be the result of salvation, never the way to salvation. As His Word tells us,

> *"Not by works of righteousness which we have done, but according to His mercy He saved us, through the washing of regeneration and renewing of the Holy Spirit"* (Titus 3:5).

"This is a faithful saying, and these things I want you to affirm constantly, that those who have believed in God should be careful to maintain good works. These things are good and profitable to men" (Titus 3:8).

4. I must rest by faith in God's promise and assurance to me.

You receive God's free gift of eternal life through an act of childlike faith in Jesus Christ as your personal Savior. *"But as many as received Him, to them He gave the right to become children of God, to those who believe in His name"* (John 1:12). You don't have to wonder any longer about your eternal destiny. Read God's promise to the one who transfers his faith from his works to Christ's finished work.

> *And this is the testimony: that God has given us eternal life, and this life is in His Son. He who has the Son has life; he who does not have the Son of God does not have life. These things I have written to you who believe in the name of the Son of God, that you may know that you have eternal life, and that you may continue to believe in the name of the Son of God** (1 John 5:11-13).

Do you know for certain where you will spend eternity? If you have faith alone in Christ alone, you can be sure that you have eternal life. *"Most assuredly, I say to you, he who hears My word and believes in Him who sent Me has everlasting life, and shall not come into judgment, but has passed from death into life"* (John 5:24).

God is offering the gift (no strings attached) of eternal life because of His remarkable grace (undeserved favor). Jesus Christ, God the Son, has paid for His gift by His supreme sacrifice—He gave His life by shedding His blood to save you.

God's salvation is of no personal value to you until you accept it by trusting in Christ alone. You may have understood faith in Christ is required for salvation, but do you see faith alone in Christ alone is sufficient? Jesus Christ's last words on the cross were, "It is finished!" Christ unconditionally paid the penalty, the debt for sin.

---

* Son of God: " The Bible term *son* signifies that a son has the same nature as the father. In the Old Testament and other later writings, the Hebrew words for *son* were often used to indicate their relationship. God the Father, God the Son and God the Spirit are equal in nature and deity.

Because Christ covered my sin-debt, what remains for me to do?

"It Is Finished"
John 19:30

Religion says...
Jesus Christ did 90% | You must do 10%

This is salvation by works.

"And if by grace, then is it no more of works: otherwise grace is no more grace. But if it be of works, then is it no more grace: otherwise work is no more work" (Rom. 11:6).

"For by grace are ye saved through faith; and that not of yourselves: it is the gift of God: Not of works, lest any man should boast" (Eph. 2:8-9).

God says...
Jesus Christ did 100%

This is salvation by God's grace.

"But this man, after he had offered one sacrifice for sins for ever, sat down on the right hand of God" (Heb. 10:12).

"For Christ also hath once suffered for sins, the just for the unjust, that he might bring us to God, being put to death in the flesh, but quickened by the Spirit" (1 Peter 3:18).

The Great Exchange

God transferred the sin of all humanity to Christ who took the punishment for all sin for all time. In exchange, God transfers Christ's righteousness to us when we believe in Christ's payment. *"For He made Him who knew no sin to be sin for us, that we might become the righteousness of God in Him"* (2 Cor. 5:21). Yes, Christ took our sin debt and paid for it with His blood, so we could go free. He saved us from the sentence of eternal suffering in the Lake of Fire (hell).

Consider the mercy Christ displayed when He paid the supreme ransom for the maximum penalty for undeserving, sin-contaminated human beings. God's love and grace for us caused Him to punish Christ for what He didn't deserve so He could deliverer us from what we do deserve (life without Him in hell). This Great Exchange is God's grace!

English poet and clergyman John Newton (1725–1807) wrote the familiar hymn, "Amazing Grace." As you have just read, the gospel of Jesus Christ offers eternal life to all who believe that Christ suffered the wrath of God for all sins. In addition, our freedom from condemnation can deliver us from despair through the mercy of God. Take time now to meditate on a hymn about God's extraordinary grace.

> **AMAZING GRACE**
>
> Amazing grace! How sweet the sound
> That saved a wretch like me!
> I once was lost, but now am found;
> Was blind, but now I see.
> 'Twas grace that taught my heart to fear,
> And grace my fears relieved.
> How precious did that grace appear
> The hour I first believed!

In summary, the only response to the gospel of Jesus Christ is simply to believe it. God saves people by His grace alone through faith alone in Christ alone based on His finished work alone. The basis for salvation is not our walk (works or behavior) but Christ's finished work. God's method isn't works but simply faith.

> *The good news of salvation isn't doing, but done.*

Wrong Responses to the Gospel of Christ

We distort this gospel or confuse the means with erroneous conditions or wrong responses such as:

- asking Jesus into your heart, since He comes when you believe the gospel, not by asking Him in (John 1:12; 3:16; Rom. 5:1).

- giving your life to Christ. He does not want your "dead-in-trespasses and sins" life; He wants to give you a new life in Christ (John 10:11; 2 Cor. 5:17).

- making a commitment to Christ. Salvation isn't secured by your promise/pledge to Christ, but God's promise/pledge to you (1 John 2:25; 5:13).

- turning over the controls of your life to Christ. The verse Romans 12:1 is an exhortation to believers ("brethren"), not to unbelievers.

- believing plus baptism. A believer's baptism should be a public testimony of one's faith and identification with Christ's death, burial, and resurrection as a result of being saved and not a means to salvation (1 Cor. 1:17; Acts 8:36-38; 18:8). In addition, the Bible says nothing about salvation through infant baptism, a work applied to an infant; salvation is by faith alone. God's salvation plan is through faith in the blood sacrifice of Christ (not water) that washes away sins, and the Holy Spirit works saving faith the moment a person accepts Christ's work (not God's Word spoken at infant baptism). Although the Bible says nothing of infant baptismal regeneration (rebirth), God's grace provides for them. For those with no reasoning capacity (infants and young children) and the cognitively impaired, God by His grace provides salvation. (2 Sam. 12:18-23).

- believing plus keeping the Ten Commandments. God never designed the Ten Commandments to be a way of salvation, but to show us our sin and need of a Savior (Rom. 3:20, 28; Gal. 2:16, 21; 3:10, 24-26).

- submitting to Christ's mastery/lordship in your life. James 4:7-10 is clearly a passage for believers (also: 1:2, 16, 19; 2:1; 3:1, 10, 12; 4:1, 11), not for unbelievers. There is no debate that Christ is Lord. However, the heart of salvation is *"believe on the Lord Jesus Christ and you will be saved"* (Acts 16:31).

- repenting versus confessing/admitting your sins. The verse 1 John 1:9 is a condition for a believer to have "fellowship" with God (1 John 1:3, 6, 7) as a child of God (1 John 2:1), not for the unsaved as a means to be born again (John 1:12-13). One must admit he is a sinner before a holy God to see his need of a Savior, but the solution isn't confessing your sins to God. Otherwise, you would have to know how many sins you must confess to be saved. Confessing sin would become a work to be saved and then repeated to remain saved; thus where is the need for Christ's work. Confession of sin isn't God's plan for receiving eternal life since sin is no longer the issue—all sin had been transferred to Christ and judged. Instead, salvation unto eternal life comes only by believing Christ made full payment for your sins on the cross (1 John 2:2; 4:9-10). One must repent (change his mind) about trusting in his own works and trust in Christ's work alone for salvation (Eph. 2:8-9).

- praying the sinner's prayer (which isn't found in the Bible). Where in Scripture do you find anyone telling someone to pray to be saved?

- coming forward. The concern isn't getting out of your seat, but coming to Christ by placing your faith in Him alone (John 6:35-40) in the quietness of your own mind.

Someone may say, "But isn't this simply a matter of semantics?" Depending on what you mean, the answer to that objection is "yes" and "no." Yes, it is a matter of semantics if you mean that word meanings and definitions are serious. Then again, this isn't a matter of semantics if you mean that "trusting in Jesus Christ alone" and one of these inaccurate, misleading statements is saying the same thing. What God says regarding how to be saved is what matters. When the Holy Spirit directed the writers of Scripture to record in perfect accuracy the inerrant Word of God, He knew the difference between *pisteuō* (believe) and *aiteō* (ask), or *homologeō* (confess), or *hypotassō* (submit), or *didōmi* (give). Over a hundred plus times in the New Testament, the Holy Spirit decided that *pisteuō* (believe) would be the word used to describe the one and only condition of salvation.

If *pisteuō* (believe) was sufficient for the Holy Spirit, isn't it sufficient for you? Don't let your pride ("I've taught that in the past") or your emotions ("I've prayed this with my kids") or your religious traditions ("our church has always said that") stand in the way of truth and biblical accuracy on the crucial subject anyone must address. God's Word states, *"And he brought them out and said, "Sirs, what must I do to be saved?" So they said, "Believe on the Lord Jesus Christ, and you will be saved, you and your household"* (Acts 16:30-31). Please discard spiritual clichés of religious beliefs, practices, and traditions. Instead, look to the authoritative Word of God and accept what the Lord says about eternal life. Beware of those who say we require more than basic faith in Christ to become saved. When people add requirements for salvation, they deny the power and sufficiency of Christ's death on the cross (Gal. 1:6-8; 3:1-5).

In conclusion, salvation is a gift of love from God based on His grace by faith alone in Christ alone. Faith is an open hand receiving, not a working hand doing. Faith isn't a feeling but a decision to believe. Since Christ covered our debt of sin with His sacrificial blood payment, sin no longer condemns anyone to hell. Unbelief in the finished work of Christ condemns people to hell. Besides, to add something (your works, upright behavior, being baptized, or other deeds) to Christ's cross work is advocating another gospel (Gal. 1:6-8; 2:21). In other words, if you add anything to Christ's finished work, you don't believe Christ completed the work of salvation once and forever. Adding to Christ's work causes God to continue to look at you as unsaved, still lost in your sins. Attaching your morality and noble deeds indicates you don't trust in Christ's work alone.

If you don't know whether you will go to heaven, perhaps you haven't believed God transferred your sins to Jesus and judged Him for them. His substitutionary death removed every sin from your sin-debt payment account. Jesus' words, "It is finished," mean there is nothing left for you to do except believe. In addition, *"It is finished,"* in the original language, means "it remains finished." Christ's work isn't a temporary but a permanent payment for sin. Thus, once you accept the finished work of Christ, God saves you forever. If you don't believe in Christ's finished work, you don't have eternal life and you won't go to heaven. In His Word, God clearly tells us unbelief, not sin, is the reason someone isn't saved.

> *For God so loved the world that He gave His only begotten Son, that whoever believes in Him should not perish but have everlasting life. For God did not send His Son into the world to condemn the world, but that the world through Him might be saved. He who believes in Him is not condemned; but he who does not believe is condemned already, because he has not believed in the name of the only begotten Son of God* (John 3:16-18).

> *Sin doesn't sentence anyone to hell but unbelief in Christ's work does.*

Once Saved, Always Saved

When you decide to believe that Christ did the work, God the Holy Spirit will position you in the family of God where He keeps you forever (John 10:28-30). Just as nothing you do merits salvation; nothing you do will cause you to lose salvation. God's grace saves you unto eternal life and likewise, His grace keeps you saved. Remember, God saves you by grace, not by works (Eph. 2:8-9; Rom. 3:28; Titus 3:5), so nothing (lack of works or immoral behavior) you do can separate you from God (Rom. 8:38-39). Once God saves you, you remain saved forever, that is, you have eternal security. God keeps you saved (1 Peter 1:3-5).

If you have further concerns regarding your salvation, see the resource section at the end of the book. Pastors listed there welcome your call, letter, or email. You may check church websites listed there for information on the gospel. For further personal study on the gospel of Christ read the book of Romans and for in-depth audio study visit, *www.duluthbible.org*. Also, read the gospel of John and for in-depth audio study of John, download or use MP3 at *www.wogbc.org*.

> *God's grace keeps you saved forever.*

Take time now to reflect on God's gracious rescue plan from the penalty of sin as expressed in the next hymn of grace. "By Grace I'm Saved" was written over two hundred years ago by Scheidt, a German believer. This hymn based on Ephesians 2: 8-9 summarizes the gospel of Jesus Christ. As you meditate on stanzas one through four of this hymn from the past, may God's magnificent grace rescue plan stir your soul with comfort and joy. (The last three stanzas are in chapter 4.)

To sing this hymn you will find audio music at:
Cyber Hymnal *www.hymntime.com*

BY GRACE I'M SAVED

"For by grace you have been saved through faith, and that not of yourselves; it is the gift of God, not of works, lest anyone should boast" (Eph. 2:8-9).

By grace I'm saved, grace free and boundless;
My soul, believe and doubt it not.
Why stagger at this word of promise?
Has Scripture ever falsehood taught?
No, then this word must true remain;
By grace you too will life obtain.

By grace! None dare lay claim to merit;
Our works and conduct have no worth.
God in His love sent our Redeemer,
Christ Jesus, to this sinful earth;
His death did for our sins atone,
And we are saved by grace alone.

By grace! Oh, mark this word of promise
When you are by your sins oppressed,
When Satan plagues your troubled conscience,
And when your heart is seeking rest.
What reason cannot comprehend
God by His grace to you does send.

By grace God's Son, our only Savior,
Came down to earth to bear our sin.
Was it because of your own merit
That Jesus died your soul to win?
No, it was grace, and grace alone,
That brought Him from His heavenly throne.

~ Christian L. Scheidt, 1709-1761 ~

God's Rescue Plan

Did you know God's salvation plan has three phases? In this chapter, you read about phase one of God's grace plan of salvation through faith alone in Christ alone. Not only did God's rescue plan save you from the penalty of sin (justification*), His grace plan in phase two frees you from the power of sin (sanctification †) in your life. Phase three is deliverance from the presence of sin (glorification ‡) when the believer is in heaven, which won't be discussed in this book.

---

* Justification is when God declared you righteous at the moment of faith in Christ and placed you in His family, thereby moving you from death to life (John 5:24).
† Sanctification is the deliverance from the pollution and power of sin in your daily life. This is present tense deliverance, by faith, from the weakness and the sins of the flesh, faulty thinking, and actions contrary to the will of God (1 Cor. 1:2; 3:1-3; 5:5, also Eph. 4:1; Col 3:1-4).
‡ Glorification is the future deliverance from death including deliverance from the presence of sin. The believer's body will be transformed into a body like the resurrected body of Christ (Phil. 3:21; the possession of eternal life guarantees a future immortal body (1 Cor. 15:44).

Reflection Questions

Support your answers with Scripture verses and/or principles.

1. What does God think about our so-called goodness?

2. What has God provided for you through Christ's completed cross work?

3. Explain why seeking salvation by moral behavior nullifies the results of Christ's finished work on the cross. (Cite verses.)

4. Explain God's gift (no strings attached) of salvation.

5. Salvation comes by _____ alone, in _____ alone, through _____ alone.

6. When you decide to believe Christ did the work, God the Holy Spirit places you into the _____ of God where keeps you forever.

7. Describe phases one and two of God's rescue plan.

Phase two is God's rescue plan for living and the main emphasis of this book. Freedom from the power of sin means the sin nature no longer has control. You can be free from the power of sin to dominate your life; thus, the sins of worry, fear, or any other sin need not steal your peace. In the remaining chapters, *LifeQuakes: God's Rescue Plan in Hard Times* will reveal God's grace provisions for living by faith and overruling the power of sin in your life. Consequently, when you live by faith, He will give you His peace, the peace that exceeds human understanding.

CHAPTER 3 PREVIEW

◦ Your Thinking Determines Your Direction and Behavior

◦ Where Do You Turn, to Whom, on What Do You Rely?

◦ Depending on Our Lord and His Character during Life's Shake-ups

◦ Trust Scriptural Facts Not Feelings

CHAPTER 3

What Do You Rely On During Life's Shake-Ups?

Darla had a history of abuse and blamed her family for her food obsession and obesity. Because she felt alone and rejected by her family, she used food to cover up her emotional pain and emptiness. Only the Lord Jesus could fill the void in her soul.

Where Do You Turn When the Going Gets Tough?

What determines your direction and behavior? Although we aren't merely products of our background, it can influence us. However, our thinking has a greater affect on our decisions and behaviors than our past upbringing. What we think shapes our responses to tremors and lifequakes and either breaks us or carries us through crisis. Focusing on a biblical perspective will carry us through trials with His peace. Unfortunately, believers often choose to depend on something other than faith to help them cope through troubled times. Where do you turn? Do you:

- depend on alcohol, drug use, or food to numb the pain?
- watch excessive TV, gamble, use pleasure to avoid thinking or feeling?
- behave inappropriately or engage in reckless behavior?
- rely too heavily on other people?
- depend on your self-sufficiency?
- wallow in self pity?

Reflection Questions

1. What causes your failure to trust the Lord in a crisis?

2. Currently, what do you turn to in troubled times?

3. Explain how your thinking either breaks or carries you in a crisis.

We may look to possessions, people, or pleasures to cover the hurts or the emptiness we feel. If we are honest and humble, we will admit that food, alcohol, pleasure, material possessions, or heavy reliance on people fail to satisfy the needs of our souls. Only Christ can fill the God-shaped void in our souls. In your next trial, what will you turn to?

> *Walking close to the Lord Jesus in dependency leaves no room for anything to come between.*

What a believer thinks and what he trusts during a crisis is important to the Lord. Christ Jesus desires your trust in Him alone so He can provide His peace. The psalmist affirms, *"Truly my soul silently waits for God; From Him comes my salvation. He only is my rock and my salvation; He is my defense; I shall not be greatly moved"* (Ps. 62:1-2). Since your responses follow your thinking, what you do will reveal your view of God.

Who holds the highest position among your relationships? Who is your "rock" of strength and stability? *"My soul finds rest in God alone;*

my salvation comes from him. He alone is my rock and my salvation; he is my fortress, I will never be shaken" (Ps. 62:1-2 NIV). Can you "hide" in Christ when you have troubles in life?

The hymn, "Hiding in Thee," written by William Cushing reflects Psalm 61:2 and parallel verses of Psalm 62:1-2. This uplifting hymn describes an overwhelmed psalmist who prayed, "lead me to the Rock" which reminds us to trust God, the Rock or stability of life. "Hiding in Thee" pictures the comfort of the believer who "hides" (finds safety and shelter) in Jesus Christ, the Rock of rescue during lifequakes.

"Hiding in Thee" was written in Moravia, New York, in 1876, says Mr. Cushing. It must be said of this hymn that it was the outgrowth of many tears, many heart-conflicts and soul-yearnings, of which the world can know nothing. However, the occasion that gave it being was the call of Mr. Sankey. He said, "Send me something new to help me in my gospel work." A call from such a source, and for such a purpose, seemed a call from God. I so regarded it, and prayed, "Lord, give me something that may glorify Thee." It was while waiting that "Hiding in Thee" pressed to make itself known. Mr. Sankey called forth the tune, and by his genius gave the hymn wings, making it useful in the Master's work.

www.hymntime.com

We find comfort when we cling to Jesus the Rock (the object) of our faith as the words of the next hymn, "Hiding in Thee" remind us.

> **HIDING IN THEE**
>
> *"Lead me to the rock that is higher than I"* (Ps. 61:2b).
>
> O safe to the Rock that is higher than I,
> My soul in its conflicts and sorrows would fly;
> So sinful, so weary, Thine, Thine, would I be;
> Thou blest "Rock of Ages," I'm hiding in Thee.
>
> REFRAIN: Hiding in Thee, hiding in Thee,
> Thou blest "Rock of Ages," I'm hiding in Thee.
>
> In the calm of the noontide, in sorrow's lone hour,
> In times when temptation casts o'er me its power;
> In the tempests of life, on its wide, heaving sea,
> Thou blest "Rock of Ages," I'm hiding in Thee.
>
> How oft in the conflict, when pressed by the foe,
> I have fled to my refuge and breathed out my woe;
> How often, when trials like sea billows roll,
> Have I hidden in Thee, O Thou Rock of my soul.
>
> ~ William O. Cushing, 1823-1902 ~
> ~ Music: Ira D. Sankey, 1840-1908 ~

Unless You Know Him, You Can't Trust Him

The better we know someone the more we can trust him. Therefore, the better we know the Lord the greater our trust will be in Him. The Lord Jesus wants us to know Him and have an intimate, dependent relationship with Him. The Lord wants a treasured relationship with us that surpasses all others.

Because the Lord wants a cherished relationship with us, He reveals Himself in His Word and in our trials so we can see Him in greater ways. For example, maybe your faith needs encouragement like the faith of the disciples at sea when a storm arose. They saw Jesus in a greater way during the storm when He rebuked the sea and the winds

(Matt. 8:23-27). When we believe He is capable, our faith is strengthened.

Trusting the Lord doesn't automatically happen; instead, our loving Father uses trials to gain our trust in Him. Because my reliance in Christ Jesus was inconsistent and weak, I had a closer relationship with my mother than I did with the Lord. Truthfully, I depended on her more than I did the Lord. When she died, I felt shattered, alone and lost. (Never assume God removes people from our lives because of our dependency on them or our lack of dependency Him, although He can. God's ways belong to Him!) Now I see that Christ gradually revealed my misplaced dependency. I learned that the strong bond of love between my mom and me didn't compare to the love of Christ. The Lord Jesus used losses to stretch my faith by revealing Himself to me so I would know Him better and see Him in a greater way.

In your next trial, look for God to reveal Himself in a greater way. Remember, *"God is our refuge and strength, A very present help in trouble"* (Ps. 46:1) and then look for His power and presence in your next trial. Trials offer the chance to know Christ better.

> God designs lifequakes to advance our relationship with Christ.

Expanding Our Attachment to Him

The better we know the Lord Jesus, the deeper our attachment will be to Him. Since the Lord wants us to know Him personally, He reveals everything we need to know about Him in His Word. His character traits are truths about Him. Some traits belong to God alone (e.g., infinite) and some are found in a limited or qualified sense in man (e.g., love). God's attributes are His character, His essence, and His Holy being and not one is independent of the others. Here are some brief descriptions of the countless qualities of God.

Our Lord God is:
- Eternal—no beginning and no end, always was and always will be (Gen. 21:33; Ps. 90:2)
- Faithful—always reliable, loyal, trustworthy (Deut. 7:9)
- Forgiving—washes us clean from sin (Ps. 32:1; 1 John 1:9)
- Gracious—gives us what we don't deserve, or withholds what we do deserve (Prov. 3:34; 1 Cor. 15:10)
- Holy—separate and pure (1 John 1:5)
- Immutable—unchangeable (Mal. 3:6; Heb. 6:17-18)
- Just—always just and fair (Deut. 32:4; Ps. 89:14)
- Love—perfect affection and devotion that is constant and consistent; self-giving for the good of the one loved (John 3:16; 1 John 4:7-8); God seeks the highest good by displaying His love (Eph. 2:4-5).
- Merciful—loyal love; faithfulness to keep His promise to take care of His people, compassionate, understanding and gentle (Eph. 2:4)
- Omnipresent—everywhere, but not in everything (Ps. 139:7-12; Prov. 15:3)
- Omnipotent—all-powerful (Isa. 40:28b; Rev. 19:6)
- Omniscient—knows everything and all possible things (Isa. 40:28b; Matt. 11:21; Acts. 15:18)
- Patient—His calming endurance (Gen. 6:3; Neh. 9:16-21)
- Righteous—perfect goodness, without sin, defect or fault; always does the right thing at the right time (Ps. 11:7; Ps. 97:6; Rom. 1:17)
- Sovereign—King of kings, supreme ruler, in control of every circumstance (Ps. 47:2; 103:19; 145:13)
- Truthful—honest, unable to lie (Ps. 33:4; John 14:6)

We trust the Lord to the extent to which we know Him.

By trusting the Lord moment by moment our attachment with Him develops. The hymn, "Trusting Jesus" by Edgar Stites highlights a lifestyle of faith.

TRUSTING JESUS

"The righteous...His heart is steadfast, trusting in the LORD"
(Ps. 112:6-7 NASB).

Simply trusting every day,
Trusting through a stormy way;
Even when my faith is small,
Trusting Jesus, that is all.

REFRAIN: Trusting as the moments fly,
Trusting as the days go by;
Trusting Him whate'er befall,
Trusting Jesus, that is all.

Brightly does His Spirit shine
Into this poor heart of mine;
While He leads I cannot fall;
Trusting Jesus, that is all.

Singing if my way is clear,
Praying if the path be drear;
If in danger for Him call;
Trusting Jesus, that is all.

Trusting Him while life shall last,
Trusting Him till earth be past;
Till within the jasper wall,
Trusting Jesus, that is all.

~ Edgar Page Stites, 1836-1921 ~
~ Ira D. Sankey, 1840-1908 ~

God's reveals His character to strengthen our relationship with Him. Learning about God's qualities prepares us to lean on His character during lifequakes or tremors.

The following descriptions of God's character are merely a glimpse of Him. We begin with the spectacular love that God displayed at Calvary.

Grace and Love Dependent

Relying on the generous love of God is always a source of spiritual support. Our heavenly Father's consistent love renews us, especially when we reflect on God's indescribable gift—the person of Jesus Christ (2 Cor. 9:15). After salvation, our Father expresses His generous love by providing the means of overcoming sin and gaining His peace in every lifequake or tremor. God's lavish love flows with His grace—His undeserved favor which gives us what we don't deserve.

Appreciate Calvary's Love

Remembering the indescribable love of Jesus Christ for me when I was His enemy is a constant comfort to me. Dear believer, ponder His saving love—a holy God, Jesus Christ took the penalty of your sin. *"But God demonstrates His own love toward us, in that while we were still sinners, Christ died for us"* (Rom. 5:8). Just think, while you were His enemy, God the Father displayed His immeasurable love for you by giving His greatest gift, Jesus Christ.

In addition, nothing and no one can separate you from the supreme love of God that is in Christ (Rom. 8:38-39). Jesus loves you dearly and as He prayed for Peter, He prays for you. *"I have prayed for you that your faith should not fail"* (Luke 22:32a; Rom. 8:34). What stops you from believing that God has matchless love for you, His beloved child? When you think God has forgotten you, you disregard His magnificent love, which He proved at the cross. Can you even fathom Christ's great love and mercy that saved you from an eternity without Him?

Because you are His child, God showers you with many spiritual blessings, excessive grace, and infinite love. The Lord reveals His outstanding love through His promises, through shared access to Christ's inheritance, and by sharing in His victories.

> *The vast love of God is like the ocean,*
> *you see its beginnings but not its end.*

Our love for Christ can't compare to God's love for us as many believers eventually realize. One such believer was Philip Bliss who wrote, "Jesus Loves Even Me." He said this song was suggested to him by hearing the chorus of the hymn "Oh, How I Love Jesus," repeated frequently in a meeting he attended. After joining in the chorus several times, the thought came to him: "have I not been singing enough about my poor love for Jesus and shall I not rather sing of His great love for me?" Under the impulse of this thought, he went home and composed this hymn.

In writing the hymn, Bliss desired to expose the truth that the peace and comfort of a Christian aren't founded so much on his love for Christ as on Christ's love for him. Additionally, that to occupy the mind with Christ's love would produce love and devotion. How much God has used this little song to lead sinners and doubting Christians to look away [from problems] to Jesus, eternity alone can tell. —Major Whittle.

www.hymntime.org

JESUS LOVES EVEN ME

I am so glad that our Father in Heav'n
Tells of His love in the Book He has giv'n;
Wonderful things in the Bible I see,
This is the dearest, that Jesus loves me.

REFRAIN: I am so glad that Jesus loves me,
Jesus loves me, Jesus loves me.
I am so glad that Jesus loves me,
Jesus loves even me.

Though I forget Him, and wander away,
Still He doth love me wherever I stray;
Back to His dear loving arms I do flee,
When I remember that Jesus loves me.

Oh, if there's only one song I can sing,
When in His beauty I see the great King.
This shall my song through eternity be,
"Oh, what a wonder that Jesus loves me!"

Jesus loves me, and I know I love Him;
Love brought Him down my poor soul to redeem;
Yes, it was love made Him die on the tree;
Oh, I am certain that Jesus loves me!

If one should ask of me, how can I tell?
Glory to Jesus, I know very well!
God's Holy Spirit with mine doth agree,
Constantly witnessing Jesus loves me.

In this assurance I find sweetest rest,
Trusting in Jesus, I know I am blessed;
Satan, dismayed, from my soul now doth flee,
When I just tell him that Jesus loves me.

~ Philip P. Bliss, 1870 ~

Signs of His Love

Considering the vastness of God's love, try to understand His desire for a cherished relationship with you. As a believer in Christ's finished work, you are a member of His family; therefore, He takes care of you and doesn't leave you to fend for yourself. In His lavish love and grace He has provided for all your needs (Ps. 23:1) because you belong to Him. However, the Lord wants more than merely having you in His family—He desires a unique intimacy with you. Just think, the eternal God, the Lord and King of the universe, the Savior of the world desires a special friendship with you!

The Lord never stops reaching out to you in love. Because of His extraordinary love, He wrote you a love letter. We know this as His Word, the Bible, which explains how to have this exceptional relationship. God's love letter reveals Himself and thousands of expressions of His love so you can get to know Him. One special expression of His love is "loving-kindness." God revealed the meaning of loving-kindness in the Old Testament book of Hosea.

Treasure God's love letter—the Bible!

Background of Hosea

The book of Hosea is a love story—tragic, and true. Hosea's love and faithfulness to his unfaithful wife Gomer picture the loyal love of God and the spiritual adultery of Israel. Hosea describes the sins of Israel and contrasts them to God's righteousness. As God's messenger, Hosea warned the nation of Israel about God's judgment for their sins of idolatry and empty ritual, but he combined his message with comfort and future hope for Israel. Because of God's love and faithfulness, He will restore Israel in the future. The book of Hosea dramatically portrays constant and persistent love.

The book of Hosea comforts us as it reveals God's love and faithfulness despite Israel's adulterous behavior towards Him. In his relationship to Gomer, Hosea portrayed God's faithfulness, justice, love, and forgiveness toward His people. Hosea's actions of love confirmed that he forgave his wife. Remember love is a choice, a decision, or an action, not a feeling. Beyond the account of a man and his adulterous wife, the book of Hosea depicts God's loyal love for His unfaithful people. Although Hosea's wife and Israel, the wife of the Lord, were unfaithful, God remained faithful.

Despite our unfaithfulness to Him, He remains faithful to us (2 Tim. 2:13). His loyal love is unconditional and continuous; therefore, you can depend on it.

What Does "Wife of the Lord" Mean?

Scripture uses marriage to illustrate the relationship of God to His people. God uses marriage to depict love, intimacy, privilege, and responsibility between the two parties.

Since marriage is the commitment and union of a man and a woman, there is perhaps no greater heartbreak than the violation of marriage vows. In the Old Testament, the Scriptures picture Israel as the "wife" of the Lord. Whenever Israel would desert the Lord through unfaithfulness, God would discipline her for disobedience; Israel would eventually repent (change her mind) and ask God for forgiveness. The Lord would always forgive and restore Israel, she would return to faith and obedience only to repeat the cycle of unfaithfulness. Israel is the forgiven and restored "wife of the Lord."

Wife of the Lord and the Bride of Christ

This "wife of the Lord" association must not be confused with the relationship of Christ to the church (John 3:29). In the New Testament, Paul used the engagement concept to explain the ideal relationship that exists between the church as an innocent virgin being presented to Christ (2 Cor. 11:1-2). Observe that the chaste virgin signifies its purification by the blood of the Lamb. Scripture describes the church as a virgin loyal to one husband, which couldn't be said of an adulterous wife forgiven in grace. While, Israel is the Lord's earthly wife, the church is Christ's spiritual or heavenly wife (John 3:29). The Bible identifies the church as the Lamb's heavenly bride (Rev. 19:7).

Loving-kindness—God's Covenant Love

Notice the faithful love of our heavenly Father as stated in Hosea. *"I will betroth you to Me forever; Yes, I will betroth you to Me in righteousness and in justice, In lovingkindness and in compassion, And I will betroth you to Me in faithfulness. Then you will know the* LORD*"* (Hosea 2:19-20 NASB). To understand the depth of God's loving-kindness we must examine the verse in context, but first some definitions of words in the verse. Betroth means to promise by one's word, to swear, to take an oath. Betrothal (a mutual consent to marry) or espousal was the act of engagement for marriage in Bible times and was as binding as marriage.

Betrothal and marriage consist of a moral and spiritual principle for the home and society. The betrothal regarded the woman as the lawful wife of the man to whom she was betrothed (Deut. 28:30; Judg. 14:2; Matt. 1:18-21). The term betrothal is symbolically used of the spiritual relationship between God and His people (Hosea 2:19, 20). The betrothal was a contract. In the Bible God's promise, agreement, or contract was called a unilateral covenant—one side does the keeping. The Lord binds Himself to His people, Israel, forever and He unites Himself to us, His bride, forever. Our heavenly Father "betrothing" Himself to us forever is our assurance or the guarantee of His unconditional love and His faithfulness to us. Christ's union with us forever reassures us of His betrothal love—His extraordinary expression of love for His bride.

Another term, loving-kindness is the Old Testament's highest expression for love and has a wide-range of meaning. Loving-kindness, an expressive word for our Father's love for us, is the Hebrew word *hesed*, which God uses two hundred fifty times in the Old Testament. In general, there are three basic meanings—strength, steadfastness, and love, which always act together. Any understanding of the word that fails to suggest all three meanings forfeits some of its richness. "Love" by itself easily becomes sentimental apart from the contract. "Strength" or "steadfastness" when used without love suggests only the completion of a legal responsibility. Besides loyalty, loving-kindness also depicts generosity and mercy.

The biblical use of *loving-kindness* often describes someone performing, showing, or keeping this quality. The genuine content of the word is especially obvious when used in the plural; God's mercies, kindnesses, or faithfulness are His specific acts (not feelings) of redemption* in fulfillment of His promise. Our Savior's decision to act in redeeming the world was evidence of His mercy. Loving-kindness encompasses loyalty and faithfulness and emphasizes togetherness in a love relationship. Since God is faithful and He never changes, He will keep His contract of loving-kindness.

How was God's loving-kindness with Israel, His unfaithful wife portrayed in Hosea? Israel was spiritually adulterous and unfaithful, spurning God's love by turning instead to false gods. Israel was thanking false gods for food, shelter, and clothing instead of thanking the true God for those blessings. Specifically, they worshiped and thanked Baal, the god whom they believed controlled weather and farming. They simultaneously brought offerings to Jehovah God.

Israel wasn't merely unfaithful and sinful but also idolatrous. God warned Israel of coming judgment; in His justice He would discipline them. The Lord God gave them many chances to repent, that is, to change their minds about Him and return to Him. Because Jehovah God wanted to restore Israel, He chose to complicate their lives with trials. He placed obstacles of wars, bondage, and persecution in their wayward path thus making the rewards of idol worship deplorable in order to persuade them to return to Him. If He didn't possess loving-kindness, He would have abandoned them.

---

* Redemption—[1]to buy, purchase, or pay a price for something. [2]to purchase "out of." [3]to loose or set free in the fullest sense/ Christ's death not only paid the price our sin demanded but removed us from (out of) the marketplace of sin. Christ's redemptive work secured our freedom from the penalties and bondage of sin.

His acts of loving-kindness and mercy overflowed to them. Repeatedly, God reaffirmed His betrothal promise of faithful love by offering them the opportunity to reconcile. Although Israel was unfaithful, God's commitment continued unchanged; He remained faithful and merciful. Our loving, faithful God is always ready to forgive and restore His people.

God's loving-kindness through deliverance is a theme of the Scriptures. The book of Hosea records an obvious demonstration of God's redemptive love. God commanded Hosea to buy his wife back from an adulterous lifestyle (Hosea 3:2). He saved her from the penalty for adultery* indicating that forgiveness took precedence over stoning or divorce (James 2:13). Hosea's redemption of his harlot wife and restoration to the protection of his home is a parallel illustration of the forgiving love and grace of God for His spiritually adulterous people. What a picture of God's redeeming love and grace!

This same gracious loving-kindness culminated in offering Christ's blood as the purchase price to redeem us—to buy us back from the slave market of sin. The moment we accepted the gift of salvation God attached the price tag that reads, "JESUS."

> We do not deserve the redemption price paid for us—that is God's grace.

God's grace hadn't abandoned Israel despite her unfaithfulness. Likewise, our spiritual Bridegroom, Jesus Christ, daily demonstrates His loyal love to us, His spiritual Bride, despite our frequent failure to trust Him. The loving-kindness of God is always pursuing and always seeking to restore.

---

*Capital punishment was the penalty for adultery (Lev. 20:1; Deut. 22:22-24).

Our Faith Response toward His Loving-kindness

The Father loves us as much as He loves Jesus. God's Word says,

> *"That the world may know that You have sent Me, and have loved them as You have loved Me"* (John 17:23b).

> *"As the Father loved Me, I also have loved you; abide [depend] in My love"* (John 15:9).

Dear believer, always remember that this loving-kindness is an enduring, loyal, generous, merciful, faithful love directed specifically toward you. Therefore, you can rejoice in the greatness of the everlasting loving-kindness your heavenly Father has for you. He affirms, *"Yes, I have loved you with an everlasting love; Therefore with lovingkindness I have drawn you"* (Jer. 31:3b).

When we feel rejected by others, when life seems overwhelming, when the temptation to give up is fiercest, we can find comfort in the depths of our Savior's loyal, loving-kindness. In grief or despair, cling to His loving-kindness and believe in His complete acceptance of you. Leaning on the Lord's love will cause us to thrive, not just survive, the difficult times.

> *God Submerges You in Oceans of His Love.*

Another version of "Jesus Loves Me" speaks of Christ's faithful love to adults. No matter what your age, you can have confidence that Jesus always loves and cares for you since He is the lover of your soul.

> **JESUS LOVES ME**
> Adapted from unknown author
>
> Jesus loves me, this I know,
> When my hair is white as snow
> When my sight is growing dim,
> Still He bids me trust in Him.
>
> REFRAIN: Yes, Jesus loves me.
> Yes, Jesus loves me.
> Yes, Jesus loves me,
> The Bible tells me so.
>
> When my steps are oh, so slow,
> With my hand in His I'll go
> On through life, let come what may,
> He'll be there to lead the way.
>
> When the nights are dark and long,
> In my heart He puts a song.
> Telling me in words so clear,
> "Have no fear, for I am near."
>
> When I trust Him and obey
> For there is no other way,
> To be joyful every day,
> Jesus is the only way.
>
> When my work on earth is done
> And faith's vict'ries have been won.
> He will take me home above;
> Hold me in His arms of love.

Relying on God's Sovereignty

Knowing the Lord is in control of everything gives us a sense of security and frees us from the compulsion to run things. Let's consider some descriptions of His sovereignty.

God has perfect authority over everything and He alone is ruler over everything in the world. *"The LORD has established His throne in heaven, And His kingdom rules over all"* (Ps. 103:19).

Our Lord God is supreme above all nations, powers, and rulers. *"The Lord God Omnipotent reigns!"* (Rev. 19:6b). He is the supreme sovereign and manager over all. No one is like God or equal to Him. *"Now when all things are made subject to Him, then the Son Himself will also be subject to Him who put all things under Him, that God may be all in all"* (1 Cor. 15:28).

Our Lord Christ has authority and power to do whatever He desires, whenever He wants, anyway He wants to, and for whatever purpose He chooses according to His character. Everything He does is perfect according to His righteousness.

Spending time observing the majesty and details of God's creation reminds us of His power and authority in every detail of our lives. *"Ah, Lord GOD! Behold, You have made the heavens and the earth by Your great power and outstretched arm. There is nothing too hard for You'"* (Jer. 32:17). Since nothing is too difficult for the Lord, what do you honestly believe about Him?

Take time now to complete this inventory by truthfully answering questions and skipping those that don't apply.

1. Is the Lord the supreme manager of my finances?
2. Have I given my difficulties with people to Him who knows everything?
3. Has finding a mate become a priority, instead of trusting the Lord to provide?
4. Have I entrusted my health concerns to the Lord who perfectly manages health care?
5. Do I believe nothing is too difficult for the Lord?
6. Am I *"casting all [my] care upon Him, for He cares for [me]"* (1 Peter 5:7).
7. Do I believe the Lord is able to do whatever He chooses? If so, will I surrender my needs, problems, circumstances, even my life to His supreme management?

8. Do I believe the Lord knows what is best for everyone involved in this difficult situation whether He changes something or not?

Believing our sovereign Lord is in control and will do what is best for us, according to His plan, is the belief that boosts confidence in Him.

When I believe that God is in control, I can relax!

God's Justice Triumphs over Injustices

Everyone has suffered injustices. Maybe you were a victim of a crime. Perhaps you experienced the unjust loss of a loved one. How you respond to them concerns the Lord. Will a tragic unlawful loss of a loved one cause you to trust in man or in laws and justice to make things right? Can laws deliver you through the crisis? Neither man's laws nor any human "solutions" can offer genuine peace or remove fear. We read from Isaiah, *"Behold, God is my salvation, I will trust and not be afraid; 'For YAH, the LORD, is my strength and song; He also has become my salvation.' Therefore with joy you will draw water From the wells of salvation"* (Isa. 12:2-3). Only our Lord Jesus can offer true peace; no other solutions will suffice.

Many victims spend time obsessing about injustices and harboring negative feelings about their mistreatment. Others become paranoid fearing the offender will pursue them when the prison term ends. Anger towards the offender or the lack of justice in a court case must not block your confidence in God's ability to defeat evil. Will you believe the Lord is your Deliverer and trust Him to defeat evil in His time?

We can learn from King David, who prayed to God about troubles with his enemies and focused on the mercy of God.

> *"Why do you boast in evil, O mighty man? The goodness of God endures continually"* (Ps. 52:1b).
>
> *"I trust in the mercy of God forever and ever"* (Ps.52:8b).

> *"Have mercy [be gracious] upon me, O God,*
> *according to Your loving-kindness"* (Ps. 51: 1a).

When something bad happens to us, when someone commits a crime against a loved one or us, we may demand justice. We assume we deserve better. We forget *"all have sinned and fall short of the glory of God"* (Rom. 3:23); therefore, we are just as guilty. When thoughts of revenge or punishment toward someone who wronged us consume us, we are forgetting that God is in control. His justice prevails in His time (Rom. 12:19).

When a lifequake of injustice happens, we may not know what to pray. We may ask, how do I trust God, or for what do I trust Him. When we suffer injustice, we may want to get even and ask God to punish the offender. We may trust God to resolve the problem in the manner we want, disregarding God's way for resolving it. Will trusting to have the injustice resolved our way deliver genuine peace and hope again? No, since true peace doesn't come from having our way, or from a change in circumstances. The natural trust of man sees his own solutions. However, God desires that the believer cast his concerns on Him and trust Him with the matter.

When someone gets the promotion, recognition, or a pay raise, we may think that is unfair and yield to man's viewpoint assuming we deserve better. However, we don't deserve better. How often do we sin each day? How often are we ungrateful to God for His daily supplies? Do we trust Him every moment of the day? We must remember the new mercies God gives us every day are better than we deserve.

God's Sovereignty and Love

Most often God's character traits are demonstrated in His actions. The next example pictures at least two qualities of the Lord. Note God's sovereignty and loving care during Joseph's trials. Also notice that Joseph, a victim of injustice, responded in faith believing God would work everything together for good.

Teen Betrayed by Family

Joseph was the second youngest of twelve brothers. These brothers were jealous of him and hated him because their father favored him. Their father, Jacob, displayed his favoritism by making a beautiful multi-colored coat for Joseph. In addition, God had given Joseph multiple dreams with the same implications—Joseph's brothers bowing down to him, which caused his brothers to hate him more.

Sometime later while in the fields, the brothers saw Joseph in his colorful coat approaching them. In jealous anger, they plotted to kill him. Rueben, though afraid of his brothers, felt compassion for Joseph and wished to spare his life so he suggested they throw Joseph into a pit. The brothers seized Joseph, ripped off his beautiful coat, and threw him in a pit to die. While the brothers were eating lunch, Rueben went to another part of the field. In his absence, a company of traveling merchants with their camels became visible and the brothers saw an opportunity to deal with Joseph without killing him. They drew their seventeen-year-old brother Joseph out of the pit and sold him to the merchants for twenty pieces of silver.

After a long journey, Joseph arrived in Egypt surrounded by strangers who spoke a different language from his. His new home amid large cities, beautiful temples for idol worship, mighty pyramids and the great Nile River was a strange site for a boy who previously lived in a tent. In Egypt the traders sold Joseph to Potiphar, an officer in Pharaoh's army and captain of the guard.

Scripture doesn't record Joseph having questions or concerns although he probably did. Joseph had cause for fear and worry because of several unknowns. He didn't know what would happen next, how long he would be in a foreign land, whether he would see his father again, or what would become of him. God didn't provide a road map. Instead, over many years God guided Joseph one-step at a time.

Although the consequences of his brothers' injustice to him continued for years, God didn't forget Joseph. We see here how the Lord blessed Joseph.

> *The LORD was with Joseph, and he was a successful man; and he was in the house of his master the Egyptian. And his master saw that the LORD was with him and that the LORD made all he did to prosper in his hand. So Joseph found favor in his sight, and served him. Then he made him overseer of his house, and all that he had he put under his authority. So it was, from the time that he had made him overseer of his house and all that he had, that the LORD blessed the Egyptian's house for Joseph's sake; and the blessing of the LORD was on all that he had in the house and in the field. Thus he left all that he had in Joseph's hand, and he did not know what he had except for the bread which he ate. Now Joseph was handsome in form and appearance* (Gen. 39:2-6).

Along with the hurt of rejection from his brothers, the grief of separation from his father, and living in a foreign land, Joseph had trials over the course of these years. For example, Potiphar's wife tried to seduce him, but Joseph refused her advances and fled. Because Joseph rejected her advances, she turned against him and wrongly accused him. Potiphar believed her lies and sent Joseph to prison. The keeper of the prison didn't investigate the allegations; therefore, innocent Joseph spent a few years wrongfully imprisoned. After serving his term in prison, the Lord restored Joseph to a position of power and caused him to prosper in whatever he did (Gen. 39:7-20*).

Joseph trusted in God's management of his life and lived by faith and not by sight. Although Joseph couldn't understand God's plan at the time, he trusted God to provide for him and guide him.

God placed Joseph in the right place at the right time for future events regarding his father and brothers. As part of God's greater plan, many years later Joseph helped his family avoid the famine in their homeland by relocating in Egypt. We rarely discover what greater plan God achieves through our trials.

Joseph's faith may seem too difficult to believe and you might even think you can't possibly have faith like his. Dear reader, understand it's

---

*Learn more about Joseph in Genesis 37-50.

not your faith but in whom you place your trust that matters. Trusting the Lord gives us courage to do what is right despite our past or what others think. Since our faith is in the same almighty God that Joseph trusted, we can trust Him in our trials and temptations.

> *God doesn't give us a road map for life;*
> *He gives us something better—Himself.*

Place your confidence in the strength of God's just and sovereign character instead of trusting in the thinking of the world. As the Lord tells us: *"Cursed* [suffering more pain, hurt, and lack of peace] *is the man who trusts in man And makes flesh his strength, Whose heart departs from the LORD. Blessed is the man who trusts in the LORD, And whose hope is the LORD"* (Jer. 17:5, 7; for further comfort read Ps. 94).

> *God handles every injustice in His way and perfect timing;*
> *He works every detail together for our good and His glory.*

Relax in His Perfection

God always does what is right as His Word states, *"The LORD is righteous in all His ways, Gracious in all His works"* (Ps. 145:17). Therefore, He doesn't make any mistakes when He allows lifequakes or the slightest tremor to shake you. He always considers what's best for you although your trial may not seem helpful to you. We can't trust our feelings, but we can trust the truths of Scripture. Since the Lord is perfect goodness, He can never be wrong.

God Never Makes Mistakes

After my mom died, I felt anger towards her incompetent doctor. I believed that if he would have been more thorough and offered treatments to help her, my mom would not have died. After learning more from God's Word, I changed my perspective. Whether the doctor did his job properly is inconsequential since God controls all matters. Since the Lord Jesus has power over death, His management of all events could have delayed her death. However, the Lord had the perfect time and manner for my mom to die. In His perfect wisdom, God determines each person's death day.

My adjusted perspective prepared me for my father's death nineteen years later. Although grieved, by this time I believed God was in charge of my circumstances and I found contentment in the Lord. When lifequakes shake me up, I concentrate on the Lord who knows and controls every detail from beginning to end. Besides, He always allows precisely the best lifequakes and tremors into my life to help me learn to know Him in greater ways. Is anything better than that?

"He Makes No Mistakes" was written by A. M. Overton (1932), a retired pastor, who lost his beloved wife and wrote this poem for her funeral service. Adrian Vermeulen-Miller slightly modernized the words. This poem reminds us to walk with God in faith, not by sight since He alone can see us through the fog of our distress.

> **HE MAKES NO MISTAKES!**
>
> My Father's way may twist and turn,
> My heart may throb and ache.
> But in my soul I'm glad I know,
> That He makes no mistake.
>
> My cherished plans may go astray,
> My hopes may fade away,
> But still I'll trust my Lord to lead,
> For He does know the way.
> Though night be dark and it may seem
> That day will never break;
> I'll pin my faith, my all on Him,
> For He makes no mistake.
>
> There is so much I cannot see,
> My eyesight's far too dim
> But come what may, I'll simply
> Trust and leave it all to Him.
>
> For by and by the fog will lift
> And all things plain He'll make.
> Through all the way, though dark to me,
> He made not one mistake.

Security in God's Constant Presence

A father was shopping with his young sons, Tim and Tom, in the men's clothing section of a large department store. The boys were having fun drifting in and out among the clothes racks and were unmindful of their father. Some minutes passed and the boys noticed their dad was "missing." Tim and Tom wandered around looking for dad but couldn't find him, so they frantically shouted out, "Daddy, where are you?" "Here I am, right behind you. I was here all the time and I was watching over you."

During difficult times, we may feel God has moved away from

us, but He never moves away from His children. God is omnipresent; "omni" means all. He is always present, always beside us. The next time you feel alone and wonder where God is, imagine your heavenly Father sitting on a stationary throne facing you as you sit on a swivel chair. Whenever you swivel (turn your back on God), He remains in the same place watching you.

Often when we need to feel God's presence the most, we choose to rotate away from Him, turning our backs to Him. We spin away because we assume we can manage our problems, only to look back when we see our inadequacies. When we "give up" on the Lord, we do the same. Despite our rotation away from Him, our faithful Father always faces us because He never abandons His own.

> *When God feels far away from you,*
> *remember who swiveled the chair.*

How often we behave like little children when lifequakes or tremors strike. We wander from Christ, think He left us, and accuse Him of moving.

Trust Scriptural Facts Not Feelings

Do you question God's presence? Our feelings deceive us and we may confuse faith with feeling. When feelings or troubles overwhelm us, we may not sense God's presence. Just because we can't see God, doesn't mean He isn't there.

Reliance on our changing feelings conflicts with God's way of living by faith. When we plant our faith in the facts of His Word, our feelings will follow. Anchor your faith on His truth and He will give you the security and confidence of His presence. Our Father wants our trust through dark times and alleged separation.

Whether the following story is true or not, it's a good word picture of the bond between an Indian father and his son, which we can apply to our spiritual life.

The Legend of the Cherokee Indian Youth's Rite of Passage

An American Indian father took his son into the forest to spend the night alone. The father blindfolded his son, told him to sit on a stump the whole night, and keep the blindfold on until the rays of the morning shone through it. Furthermore, the father told him he shouldn't cry out for help because once he survives the night, he would be a man. He was not to tell the other boys of this experience because each lad must come into manhood on his own.

Naturally, the boy was terrified in the dark woods. He could hear forest noises, wild beasts must surely be all around him, or maybe even some human might do him harm. The wind blew the grass, the earth shook his stump, but he sat stoically; he never removed the blindfold — the only way he could be considered a man!

Finally, after a horrible night, the sun appeared and the boy removed his blindfold. To his surprise, he discovered his father sitting on the stump next to him. The father had been watching the entire night, protecting his son from harm.

My Church at *www.mychurch.org*

The Lord desires that you trust when you can't see. He says in His Word, *"For we walk by faith, not by sight"* (2 Cor. 5:7). In the blackest of times, your Father is hovering all around you. His truth reveals He is always with you as the psalmist testified.

> *Where can I go from Your Spirit? Or where can I flee from Your presence? If I ascend into heaven, You are there; If I make my bed in hell, behold, You are there. If I take the wings of the morning, And dwell in the uttermost parts of the sea, Even there Your hand shall lead me, And Your right hand shall hold me. If I say, "Surely the darkness shall fall on me," Even the night shall be light about me; Indeed, the darkness shall not hide from You, But the night shines as the day; The darkness and the light are both alike to You* (Ps. 139:7-12).

Our Father promises, *"I will never leave you nor forsake you"* (Heb. 13:5c). Confidence that the Lord is with you is essential to living by faith.

> *We find the security of His presence when we believe His Word.*

God Knows and Cares

Unlike our all-knowing Lord, sometimes we don't know or understand. The next lighthearted story shows the misunderstanding of children.

Pothole Misconceptions

> After a hardy rainstorm filled the potholes in the streets and alleys, a young mother watched, through her kitchen window, her two little boys playing in the puddle. The older of the two, a five-year-old boy, grabbed his sibling by the back of his head and shoved his face into the water hole. As the boy recovered and stood laughing and dripping, the mother ran to the yard in a panic. "Why on earth did you do that to your little brother?" she angrily asked the older boy. "We were just playing 'church,' Mommy," he said. "And I was just baptizing him...in the name of the Father, in the Son, and in the hole-he-goes."
>
> *www.answers.yahoo.com/questionindex?qid=20090112142302AAQOqZy*

Like children, sometimes we simply misunderstand or don't understand something or someone. However, the Lord Jesus knows everything about you, even the many details we don't know about ourselves. Consider, *"But the very hairs of your head are all numbered* (Luke 12:7a).

Christ Jesus understands what you think and how you feel. Jesus sympathizes with your weaknesses and encourages you with the following verse. *"Seeing then that we have a great High Priest who has passed through the heavens, Jesus the Son of God, let us hold fast our confession. For we do not have a High Priest who cannot sympathize with our weaknesses, but was in all points tempted as we are, yet without sin"* (Heb. 4:14-15). He understands your pain and your tears because He is your compassionate Savior. As your Savior, He knows and plans His best for you.

How often we fail to understand God's plan and purpose for our lives. Most believers don't understand His plan to reproduce the likeness of Christ in us. His plan includes the use of trials to change us to be more like Christ (Rom. 8:29). We may not understand reasons for our trials, but our all-knowing Father understands everything about them. Will you trust the Lord who knows your fears and your failings yet never stops caring for you? The Lord knows the details of every difficulty and the purposes for them. Christ understood your greatest need, and He cared about your greatest problem—how to avoid the penalty of sin. Therefore, He took care of it at Calvary. What more must He do to prove that He understands and cares?

Is Christ Enough for You?

Are you ready to abandon your futile solutions to fill the emptiness in your soul or suppress your painful feelings? Will you stop turning to food, alcohol, drugs, excessive pleasures, other people, or yourself? Have you become more convinced that Christ is the answer to life's problems?

As we learn to know the Lord, we realize He can handle our problems. The better we know the Lord, the more we feel His loving-kindness. Knowing Christ helps us rely on His sovereign control and gives us confidence in His wisdom and timing. As we trust Him more often, we will feel the security of His presence more often. Knowing Him leads to trusting in His perfect will for all the details of our life. A life dependent on Christ and the security of His character is true Christian living.

The better you know Christ the more satisfied you become.

Reflection Questions

Wherever possible support your answers with Scripture verses.

1. List evidences that God always wants His best for you.

2. How will trusting God's magnificent love change the way you cope with trials?

3. What did you learn about God's "loving-kindness" that you can apply to your life?

4. Give examples of how leaning on Christ's character helps you trust Him.

CHAPTER 4 PREVIEW

↬ Understanding God's Providence
↬ God Charts All Circumstances
↬ Sovereignty over Life and Death
↬ Submitting to God's Sovereignty
↬ God, the Perfect Matchmaker

CHAPTER 4

Confidence in God's Sovereign Providence

Do You Understand God's Providence?

I suspect many believers don't think about God's providence—His sovereignty. They may not understand, recognize, or understand it. People associate providence with uncontrolled destiny, fate, or luck. Our Lord's providence is unlike the implications of those terms. There is no luck or fate since our sovereign God manages everything.

God's providence is part of His nature. The word providence means to care, to prepare in advance, or foresee. The sovereignty of God refers to His supreme rule, power, and authority above all things in the universe. As supreme ruler, God has complete independence and authority over all. Divine providence indicates God's management and supervision of the world. Our heavenly Father manages everything—even the details in our lives—for the good of His perfect plan.

Four Characteristics of God's Sovereignty:

1. Authority—He is in control of the universe.
2. Predestination—He controls all developments and results.
3. Wisdom—He makes no mistakes.
4. Perfection—He does everything right and in our best interest.

Five Statements about God's Sovereign Providence:

1. He sustains everything.
2. He controls all events.
3. He supervises everything—all events to their appointed end.
4. He supervises and manages the timing of every circumstance or trial.
5. He does everything for His own glory or magnificence.

> *God alone is fit to take the universe's throne.*

Sovereignty Demonstrates Important Truths

God cares about the smallest details of your life. Nothing escapes His notice, from the sparrow that falls to the number of hairs on your head. He keeps the stars and planets on course and sustains the smallest microbe. The Lord Jesus determines the day of your birth, your death day, and He guides all the days between them (Ps. 139:16; Acts 17:26).

Everything belongs to God and He manages all things perfectly. Though we may think of them as senseless tragedies, there are no accidents with God only incidences. God directs and coordinates every detail flawlessly.

God's objective is to mold His children into the likeness of Jesus Christ (Rom. 8:29). God manages and supervises difficult times and lifequakes to accomplish this objective.

Verses that demonstrate these truths of God's sovereignty are:

- *"In Him we live and move and have our being"* (Acts 17:28).
- *"And He is before all things, and in Him all things consist"* (Col. 1:17).
- *"And upholding all things by the word of His power"* (Heb. 1:3).
- *"A man's heart plans his way, But the LORD directs his steps"* (Prov. 16:9).
- *"Our God is in heaven; He does whatever He pleases"* (Ps. 115:3).

In summary, God's sovereign providence controls, sustains, supervises, directs, coordinates, and manages everything according to His perfect wisdom, will, and plan. Trusting in the Lord's sovereign providence is essential to the believer's peace and sense of security.

As you read the real life stories in this chapter, keep in mind the truths about God's sovereign providence.

A Faith Adventure
God's Sovereignty over Adoption

We make plans, but God has the final word in our plans. Because He has all things under His matchless management on His flawless schedule, we have no reason to worry. The next illustration demonstrates God's control of the developments and results of an adoption case. Hannah explains God's providential guidance in her son's adoption story.

> My husband and I were unbelievers when we got married. In our third year of marriage, a co-worker invited me to his Bible-oriented church and I heard a clear salvation message. I was searching for truth about God, so when I heard the gospel I was receptive to it and I professed Christ as my Savior. I was excited and shared the gospel with my husband and he accepted Christ. How wonderful we were both believers from the beginning of our marriage.
>
> In the early years of our marriage, we didn't want to be parents, but sometime after we were saved, we wanted children. Years passed and we were saddened to learn we couldn't have children. Even so, my yearning for a child grew stronger and thoughts about being a parent consumed me.
>
> I volunteered in the church nursery so I could hold babies. Because I longed for a baby of my own, I often became tearful as I held the newborn babies. A woman from my adult Bible study group gave me a book about adoption and I started to think about adoption as an alternative. Although adoption was an option for me, my husband thought differently. He felt we couldn't afford to adopt—newborn domestic adoptions cost about $10,000 and international about $20,000.
>
> The Lord's sovereign will included a change of location and jobs before we adopted. We lived in the Southwest the first five years of our marriage, but we weren't happy because of the intense desert heat and we missed the changing seasons. We debated for about a year where to live, but we couldn't agree. We decided to delay any adoption until we could agree on a location. Through prayer, the Lord led us to move back to our home

state. We trusted God to provide employment, which He did. He also provided a local church and the people prayed with us about our adoption plan.

We started the adoption process by visiting Christian agencies. I was certain God would fulfill my desire for parenthood through the adoption process. However, my husband was resistant because of the cost. I reluctantly submitted to his decision and we put the adoption on hold.

I recall one worship service when I was longing for a child and the Lord reassured me through some children. The pastor's three children were sitting in the pew ahead of me and the organist began playing a hymn. With angelic voices, they began to sing, "In His time, in His Time. He makes all things beautiful in His time..." I knew the Lord was speaking to me and tears of emotion ran down my face. I knew that He eventually would bless us with a child.

The Lord is always available to help in time of need and He wants us to ask Him (Ps. 46; 50:15; 1 Peter 5:7). One night while my husband was at work, I was crying in despair and thinking I couldn't endure being childless one more day. I sobbed in prayer and pleaded with the Lord to change my husband's heart about adoption. After I had cried many tears, the phone rang. My husband was calling from work to say, "I have been thinking about this adoption and we should go ahead with it. The Lord will provide the money somehow." I was thrilled. When I saw the Lord change my husband's heart in direct answer to my prayers, I was more certain this was part of God's plan.

As we advanced through the phases of the adoption, the Lord provided the exact amount of each payment. The Lord supplied the funds in various ways—a tax refund, an insurance settlement, and a bonus at work. We never needed to borrow money for the adoption.

After only a two-year wait, a teenage birth mother chose us to be the parents of her baby. Four days before Christmas, we brought home our newborn son—the most wonderful day of our lives! The Lord had led us through the adoption process as we followed His will. The adoption had gone smoothly under God's perfect management and supervision. The Lord had arranged the adoption for us according to His perfect will and timing.

> *"A man's heart plans his way, but the Lord directs his steps"* (Prov. 16:9).

God's grace is the continuous waterfall of spiritual blessings that flow into your life. An excellent expression of God's grace is illustrated in one of my favorite hymns, "The Solid Rock." The words so vividly portray Christ, our Rock for eternal salvation. Descriptive word pictures portray His sufficiency and faithfulness. When I sing the last stanza, my soul soars as I imagine myself in His presence. Take time now to meditate on His matchless grace depicted in this hymn.

THE SOLID ROCK

My hope is built on nothing less
Than Jesus' blood and righteousness.
I dare not trust the sweetest frame,
But wholly trust in Jesus' Name.

REFRAIN: On Christ the solid Rock I stand,
All other ground is sinking sand,
All other ground is sinking sand.

When darkness seems to hide His face,
I rest on His unchanging grace.
In every high and stormy gale,
My anchor holds within the veil.

His oath, His covenant, His blood,
Support me in the whelming flood.
When all around my soul gives way,
He then is all my Hope and Stay.

When He shall come with trumpet sound,
O then in Him I shall be found.
Dressed in His righteousness alone,
Faultless to stand before the throne.

~ Edward Mote, 1797-1874 ~

Rely on His Sovereign Grip of Grace

Where will you turn the next time a lifequake strikes or you have a difficult decision to make? Will you run to the refuge of God's infinite love? Will you seek the security of the Lord's perfect management of your life? As the Savior's precious child redeemed with the blood of Christ, His sovereign grace shields and supports you.

Because of His grace, Christ cares about you. Therefore, He never tires of thinking of you, *"Yet I will not forget you. See, I have inscribed you on the palms of My hands"* (Isa. 49:15c-16). The Lord Jesus is upholding you in His arms of love, *"and underneath are the everlasting arms"* (Deut. 33:27). Because your Savior holds you securely in His grip of grace, you are never in a spiritual free-fall.

No matter what circumstance you face, you can always depend on the Lord to hold your hand and support you with His everlasting arms. The next hymn comforts us with the principle of God's grace in supporting His children.

Over a hundred years ago, two believers wrote the hymn "Leaning on the Everlasting Arms" to express the truths of this verse in Deuteronomy.

> The story behind the song "Leaning on the Everlasting Arms" is an interesting one. The theme of the song is Deut. 33:27: *"The eternal God is your refuge, And underneath are the everlasting arms."* Anthony J. Showalter chose this verse for letters sent to two men who had then just recently lost their wives in death. Showalter had conducted a singing school in South Carolina a few weeks earlier and both of these men had been students there.
>
> Showalter expressed his sympathy and love in response to their tragic losses. Lowell Mason was the father of the 'singing school movement' in America. Started in Boston around 1830, the movement would spread into the south. The teachers taught the masses to sing the hymns line-by-line and note by note. By 1888, native Virginian Anthony Showalter had become one of the best teachers of the movement.
>
> On a night in 1888, he sent a third letter containing the lines of a refrain and the melody of a song. Showalter wanted to express in song the truths of Deut. 33:27, but as hard as he tried,

he could not complete the stanzas for the hymn. He sent the letter to Elisha Hoffman in Pennsylvania asking for assistance in completing the song. Rev. Hoffman, author of "I Must Tell Jesus" and "Glory to His Name" and two thousand other hymn-poems, wrote three stanzas and sent them back to Professor Showalter in Alabama.

The experiences of attending "singing classes" under the singing master are lost memories now. Hymnals and overheads have taken their place, but the name of Showalter is etched in the pages of hymn history because of a song about the truths of His everlasting "Word" and "arms."

www.songtime.org/hymn/hymn0601.htm
Audio version: *www. hymntime.com/tch/htm/l/o/lotearms.htm*

This exceptional hymn has word pictures to remind us that our caring Lord continuously supports His beloved children.

LEANING ON THE EVERLASTING ARMS

"The eternal God is your refuge, And underneath are the everlasting arms." (Deut. 33:27).

What a fellowship, what a joy divine,
　Leaning on the everlasting arms;
What a blessedness, what a peace is mine,
　Leaning on the everlasting arms.

REFRAIN: Leaning, leaning, safe and secure from all alarms;
　Leaning, leaning, leaning on the everlasting arms.

Oh, how sweet to walk in this pilgrim way,
　Leaning on the everlasting arms;
Oh, how bright the path grows from day to day,
　Leaning on the everlasting arms.

What have I to dread, what have I to fear,
　Leaning on the everlasting arms?
I have blessed peace with my Lord so near,
　Leaning on the everlasting arms.

~ Elisha A. Hoffman, 1839-1929, Music: Anthony J. Showalter 1858-1924 ~

God Charts All Circumstances

God knows everything from eternity past and arranges everything to unfold according to His plan. Thinking again about the life of Joseph, God knew and directed all the details from the beginning to the end of his life. The Lord of all caused everything to transpire as He had intended. In addition, in His perfect providence, our Lord God never violated anyone's free will. He never manipulates people as He arranges events and circumstances to fulfill His purposes.

Years passed before God revealed His purposes to Joseph for positioning him in Egypt away from his family for many years. At God's appointed time, He reunited Joseph with his family. Understanding God's sovereign management, Joseph forgave his brothers and said, *"Do not be afraid, for am I in the place of God? But as for you, you meant evil against me; but God meant it for good, in order to bring it about as it is this day, to save many people alive"* (Gen. 50:19-20). In essence, Joseph told them that though their motives were wrong, God's motives were good. *"To save many people alive"* referred to the day when Joseph's father and family would journey to Egypt—sheltered under the rulership of Joseph.

God's sovereign design and coordination of the events of Joseph's life help us to understand the meaning of, *"And we know that God causes all things to work together for good to those who love God [believers], to those who are called according to His purpose"* (Rom. 8:28 NASB). In Joseph's trial, God's sovereignty managed every detail causing everything to occur at just the right moment and in just the right way. The sovereign Lord designed the right people to be in the right place to accomplish His purposes. How will you apply those principles to your life?

> *God's providence in action is His organizing all things together for our good and His purposes.*

God's Finest Choice for Your Future

The Lord Jesus guides your life on His perfect schedule. Our capable God manages and supervises every detail of your life—the good times and the difficult moments. Whether life's troubles are brutal lifequakes or just ordinary tremors such as work overload or concerns about the future, our Lord manages them all.

> *Believing that God's hand is in everything*
> *allows us to leave everything in His hands.*

"God Leads Us Along" by George Young is a meditative hymn reminding us of God's sovereignty through trials. Young, the author and composer, was an obscure preacher and carpenter who spent a lifetime humbly serving God in small rural areas. Often the salary was meager and life was difficult for his family. Through it all, Young and his wife never wavered in their loyalty to God and His service. The background of this hymn follows here.

> The story reveals that after much struggle and effort, the George Young family was finally able to move into their own small home, which they had built themselves. Their joy seemed complete until Young was away holding meetings in another area when hoodlums who disliked the preacher's gospel message set fire to the house, leaving nothing but a heap of ashes. Out of that tragic experience, George Young completed this hymn, which reaffirms so well the words of Job 35:10, *"God my Maker, Who gives songs in the night."*
>
> Hymn Pod *www.hymnpod.com/2009/01/09/god-leads-us-along*

> **GOD LEADS US ALONG**
> *"I am the LORD your God, Who teaches you...*
> *Who leads you by the way you should go"* (Isa. 48:17).
>
> In shady green pastures, so rich and so sweet,
> God leads His dear children along;
> Where the water's cool flow bathes the weary feet,
> God leads his children along.
>
> REFRAIN: Some through the waters, some through the flood,
> Some through the fire, but all through the blood;
> Some through great sorrow, but God gives a song,
> In the night season and all the day long.
>
> Sometimes, on the mount where the sun shines so bright,
> God leads his children along;
> Sometimes in the valley, in darkest of night,
> God leads his children along.
>
> Though sorrows befall us and Satan oppose,
> God leads his children along;
> Through grace we can conquer, defeat all our foes,
> God leads his children along.
>
> ~ G. A Young, 1903 ~

God's Sovereignty over Life and Death

Do you worry about safety, health, and the future? Are you willing to entrust Him with your life and the life of your loved ones? We need not worry because the Lord has everything under His management. Perhaps the next two stories will help you trust Christ, the ruler over everything including life and death.

A Soldier's Testimony

In a radio interview, a soldier on leave from active duty in Iraq, confirmed God's control or sovereignty in the war zone. Duke reported that roadside bombs often struck their trucks. He recalled a roadside bomb that exploded killing all the soldiers in the truck, yet the truck was undamaged. On another occasion, a truck was completely demolished, but the soldiers in it were unharmed. Duke stated that these incidences, inexplicable to us, were evidence of God's management of circumstances.

Another account of God's sovereignty is the preservation of George Washington during battles.

"Bulletproof" George Washington
The French and Indian War: Account of a British Officer – July 9, 1755

> The American Indian chief looked scornfully at the soldiers on the field before him. How foolish it was to fight as they did, forming their perfect battle lines out in the open, and standing shoulder to shoulder in their bright red uniforms. The British solders—trained for European war—did not break rank, even when braves fired at them from under the safe cover of the forest. The slaughter continued for two hours. By then 1,000 of 1,459 British soldiers were killed or wounded, and only 30 of the French and Indian warriors firing at them were injured.
>
> Not only were the solders foolish, but their officers were just as thoughtless. Riding on horseback, fully exposed above the men on the ground, they made perfect targets. One by one, the chief's marksmen shot the mounted British officers until only one remained. "Quick, let your aim be certain and he dies," the chief commanded. The warriors leveled their rifles at the last officer on horseback. Round after round was aimed at this one man. Twice the officer's horse was shot out from under him. Twice he grabbed a horse left idle when a fellow officer had been shot down. The sharpshooters fired ten, twelve, thirteen rounds. Still, the officer remained unhurt.
>
> The native warriors stared at him in disbelief. Their rifles seldom missed their mark. The chief suddenly realized that

a mighty power must be shielding this man. "Stop firing!" he commanded. "This one is under the special protection of the Great Spirit." A brave standing nearby added, "I had seventeen clear shots at him...and after all that could not bring him to the ground. This man was not born to be killed by a bullet."

As the firing slowed, the lieutenant colonel gathered the remaining troops and led the retreat to safety. That evening, as the last of the wounded were being cared for, the officer noticed an odd tear in his coat. It was a bullet hole! He rolled up his sleeve and looked at his arm directly under the hole. There was no mark on his skin. Amazed, He took off his coat and found three more holes where bullet had passed through his coat, but stopped before they reached his body. Nine days after the battle, having heard a rumor of his own death, the young lieutenant colonel wrote his brother to confirm that he was still very much alive.

> 'As I have heard since my arrival at this place, a circumstantial account of my death and dying speech, I take this early opportunity of contradicting the first and of assuring you that I have not yet composed the latter. But by the all-powerful dispensations of Providence I have been protected beyond all human probability or expectation; for I had four bullets through my coat, and two horses shot under me yet escaped unhurt, although death was leveling my companions on every side of me!'

This battle, part of the French and Indian War, was fought on July 9, 1755, near Fort Duquesne, now the city of Pittsburgh. The twenty-three-year-old officer became the commander in chief of the Continental Army and the first president of the United States. In all the years that followed in his long career, this man, George Washington, was never wounded in battle. Fifteen years later, in 1770, George Washington returned to the same Pennsylvanian woods. A respected Indian chief, having heard that Washington was in the area, traveled a long way to meet with him.

He sat down with Washington face to face over a council fire. The chief told Washington the following,

> I am the chief and ruler over my tribes. My influence extends to the waters of the great lakes and to the far blue mountains. I have traveled a long and weary path that I might see the young warrior of the great battle. It was on the day when the white man's blood mixed with the streams of our forests that I first beheld this chief [Washington].
>
> I called to my young men and said, "Mark yon tall and daring warrior? He is not of the redcoat tribe—he hath an Indian's wisdom and his warriors fight as we do—himself alone exposed. Quick, let your aim be certain, and he dies."
>
> Our rifles were leveled, rifles which, but for you, knew not how to miss—'twas all in vain, a power mightier far than we shielded you. Seeing you were under the special guardianship of the Great Spirit, we immediately ceased to fire at you. I am old and shall soon be gathered to the great council fire of my fathers in the land of the shades, but ere I go, there is something bids me speak in the voice of prophecy,
>
> Listen! The Great Spirit protected that man (pointing at Washington) and guided his destiny. He will become the chief of nations, and a people yet unborn will hail him as the founder of a mighty empire. I am come to pay homage to the man who is the particular favorite of Heaven, who can never die in battle.

Washington often recalled, this dramatic event helped shape his character and confirm God's call on his life. This story of God's divine protection and of Washington's open gratitude could be found in almost all school textbooks until 1934. Now few Americans have read it.

Under God, www.undergodthebook.com/story01.cfm

> *"A thousand may fall at your side, And ten thousand at your right hand; But it shall not come near you"* (Ps. 91:7).

Understanding God's Sovereignty

Because four of my family members died in the span of eleven months, I became overprotective of my infant son. My anxiety over his safety caused my overzealous supervision, which continued for years. One day my son, then four, and I went walking with a neighbor and her children. Her preteen son asked to take my son to the shallow creek just a block from where we were walking. My friend questioned my hesitancy and over protectiveness, so with some embarrassment, I explained the family deaths. She reassured me my son would be safe, so I reluctantly let him go. At that time, I didn't know how to trust God about death, so I worried.

About a year or two later, I heard a pastor's message on Bible tapes about God's perfect timing for death. Wherever we are, whether in an airplane or walking around the block, the moment God calls, "Time's up," it is His perfect time. God wouldn't remove us one second too soon or hold us here one second too long. Knowing about God's sovereignty over life and death gave me peace. We have no control over God's timing for death, but we can choose whether we worry or leave the matter in God's hands.

In His permissive will, God allows us to act contrary to His will. However, His timing is still sovereign over our misguided choices.

God Sovereignty over Marriage or Singleness

In His sovereignty, God knows everything and does all things well. God knew you before you were born. He knew what you would look like, your personality traits, and every detail of your life. The Lord knows the course of your life; He knows your decisions, your hopes and dreams, and your career choices. Although He knows everything about you, He wants you to depend on Him for guidance in all matters, including the selection of a marriage partner.

For those whom He intends marriage, He has designed the best suitable person. Since God determines whether you will marry and whom you will marry, why worry about it? Do you believe God will provide a suitable mate for you just as He did when He presented Eve to Adam? Since the Lord will bring His choice into your life, why go hunting for a mate?

Prior to the 20th century, courtship involved one man and one woman spending time together getting to know each other for the potential of marriage. Courting was done in the woman's home in the presence of and under the watchful eye of her family. Courtship is still considered the process of seeking a marriage partner, but the term has become ambiguous and includes "the date."

Between the late 1800s and the first few decades of the 1900s dating was the new layer added to courtship. An obvious change was the multiplication of partners (from serious to casual) a person was likely to have before marriage. Another difference was that courtship moved from public conduct in private places (front porches or the family parlor) to private acts conducted in public places, primarily in the entertainment world.

The rise of dating was also influenced by an explosion of information offering advice about courtship, marriage, and the relationship between the sexes. Before the 20th century, "normal" courtship was determined within families and their communities. Then the new authority for courtship became the "experts" who made a living writing books and articles offering their own viewpoint on matters of courtship, marriage, and sex. Added to this was the sexual revolution; having sex and being married were no longer linked together. New beliefs and attitudes developed which were often contrary to family and biblical values.

Dating evolved from these new values, opinions and customs. Many who aren't ready for marriage or aren't interested in marriage view dating as the practice of finding someone to spend time with, someone with whom to have fun. Unfortunately, most individuals begin dating in their teen years, long before they are prepared to marry. The foolishness of this dating practice is like an eight-year-old test-driving one car after another.

This new practice invites many singles in our culture to date casually with no intention of marriage. The social custom of casual dating often includes casual sexual activity. For many couples in America's dating scene, getting to know the other person—his standards, beliefs, and interests—seems less important than getting one's own needs met. With a self-centered focus, a lack of respect for the other person, the absence of communication to get to know one another, and the failure to seek God's will, dating remains merely physical often leading to promiscuity.

When physical attraction and fun become the focus, dating often follows the repeated pattern of involvement and breaking up. Another misfortune of dating is the string of broken hearts, the disappointments, and emotional scars that may carry into marriage. When expectations fail in the dating relationship, it is time to move on to someone new. This pattern of connecting and separating often transfers into marriage—thus our high divorce rate.

For many couples dating is self-serving, focusing on how good the other person makes one feel, what he does to please me; much of the focus is on self. Many couples, including believers, marry to fulfill their needs. They want to be served instead of seeking to serve one another as Christ serves us, His bride. Instead of waiting and relying on the Lord to provide his best, many singles enter the dating game—drifting from one relationship to another.

Often wise believers, who are ready for marriage, seek to know a possible marriage partner in public situations such as group activities, with family and with friends. As they become acquainted with each other's values, standards, beliefs, and interests, they may become attracted to each other and pray specifically for God's direction. At this point, the couple will engage in courtship, which is the act, period, or art of seeking the love of someone with intent to marry. The Lord will not disappoint believers who seek His guidance. Instead of hunting for a mate, call upon the sovereign Matchmaker to provide in His time.

A Faith Adventure
God, the Perfect Matchmaker

Singles will be encouraged by God's sovereign work in Dan's life as he waited on the Lord for a wife. Dan writes,

> I was thirty years old and on my way to the mission field in Albania. I had resolved in my mind that I probably would never get married. Since I had made wrong selections in the past, I had no desire to ever date again. I felt if the Lord wanted me to get married, He was going to have to make it happen. Since God's ways are certainly higher than our ways, I left the matter in His capable hands.
>
> As I did ministry, God positioned a believer named Bruni as my interpreter. Time passed and I began to wonder if the Lord wanted Bruni to be my wife. When I returned to the U.S., I began praying that Bruni and I know the Lord's will for us. We stayed in contact through email. When I returned to Albania, I expressed my feelings for her and we agreed to pray for the Lord to make us certain about His will. We did missionary work together but never once dated, and we remained pure (1Cor. 6:18) during this time. We didn't want anything to hinder us from knowing the Lord's will.
>
> After six months we were convinced the Lord's will for us was marriage. Even during our engagement, we decided to limit physical contact so our courtship and marriage would honor the Lord (Prov. 119:11). We decided only to hold hands during our engagement. This idea of limited physical contact sounds ridiculous by today's immoral standards, but this was our conviction. After our two-month engagement, we married and had our first kiss during our wedding ceremony. We had our first child, Esther, about nine months and one week later.

The Lord directed my path as He promised He would if I trusted Him. *"Trust in the LORD with all your heart, And lean not on your own understanding; In all your ways acknowledge Him, And He shall direct your paths"* (Prov. 3:5-6). When I look back at how our relationship began, I have no regrets. I thank the Lord Jesus Christ for my wife, Bruni and our four children. I have learned it's always best to wait for God's plan and timing.

God always gives His best to those who leave the choice to Him.

Surrendering to God's Sovereignty over Singleness

Ruth obeyed God's command not to marry an unbeliever (2 Cor. 6:14). Although she loved and wanted to marry the unbeliever who proposed marriage to her, Ruth's desire to be in God's plan and receive His blessings was greater. Ruth believed trusting and obeying God was the way to joy in the Lord. Although the Lord didn't remove Ruth's singleness, she continued to have confidence in God's wisdom for her life. In her singleness, Ruth depends on the sufficiency of Christ and finds fulfillment in Him, her spiritual Bridegroom.

Confidence in God's providence provides contentment.

The following hymn "The Will of God Is Always Best" suggests truths about God and His presence in trials. See how many you can find.

THE WILL OF GOD IS ALWAYS BEST

The will of God is always best
And shall be done forever;
And they who trust in Him are blest,
He will forsake them never.
He helps indeed in time of need,
He chastens with forbearing;
They who depend on God, their Friend,
Shall not be left despairing.

God is my Comfort and my Trust,
My Hope and life abiding;
And to His counsel wise and just,
I yield in Him confiding.
The very hairs, His Word declares,
Upon my head He numbers.
By night and day God is my Stay,
He never sleeps nor slumbers.

Lord Jesus, this I ask of Thee,
Deny me not this favor:
When Satan sorely troubles me,
Then do not let me waver.
Keep watch and ward, O gracious Lord,
Fulfill Thy faithful saying:
Who doth believe He shall receive
An answer to His praying.

When life's brief course on earth is run
And I this world am leaving,
Grant me to say: "Thy will be done."
By faith to Thee still cleaving.
My heavenly Friend, I now commend
My soul into Thy keeping,
O'er sin and hell, And death as well,
Through Thee the victory reaping.

~ Credited to Albrecht von Brandenburg, c.1554 ~

Reflection Questions

Wherever possible support your answers with Scripture verses.

1. Name five things that describe God's sovereignty.

    1.

    2.

    3.

    4.

    5.

2. Name the characteristics of God's sovereignty.

3. Give three examples of God's sovereignty in ordinary circumstances (your own if possible).

    1.

    2.

    3.

4. Apply God's sovereignty to a lifequake, tremor, or decision-making circumstances you are currently experiencing.

CHAPTER 5 PREVIEW
❧ Perspectives on Lifequakes
❧ Tremors and Lifequakes of Christ
❧ Thriving in Our Lifequakes

CHAPTER 5

The Ultimate Lifequake—God's Rescue Plan

Perspectives on Lifequakes

No matter how difficult life's trials are, no matter how much we suffer, our troubles pale in comparison to Christ's sufferings. Trials of all people combined can't compare to the horrific nature of our Savior's sufferings on the cross. Yes, our trials hurt, our disappointments break our hearts, and we may feel like giving up. However, when we reflect on our Savior's lifequakes, we can gain a proper perspective on our suffering.

Old Testament Scriptures reveal Christ's suffering in Isaiah chapter 53 (written seven hundred years before the birth of Christ) which gives an exact forecast of Christ's suffering. We read a descriptive portion from Isaiah. *"He is despised and rejected by men, A Man of sorrows and acquainted with grief. And we hid, as it were, our faces from Him; He was despised, and we did not esteem Him. Surely He has borne our griefs And carried our sorrows; Yet we esteemed Him stricken, Smitten by God, and afflicted"* (Isa. 53:3-4).

As you look at the tremors and lifequakes of Christ throughout His life, keep in mind some questions. How did Jesus handle His lifequakes? What can I learn from Jesus' response to His trials that I can use to thrive in my trials?

Christ's Sufferings as a Youth

A great preacher once said that Jesus, in essence, made a pledge to God His Father as He peered down from the edge of heaven. He vowed, "I will go where you want me to go, I will be what you want me to be, and I will do what you want me to do." God the Son left the riches of heaven to live in poverty in a sinful world. Jesus was born in a stable — a shelter for farm animals; He grew up in a small town where He helped His foster father, Joseph, with carpentry work.

Town's people poked fun of Jesus and sang scornful songs (Ps. 69: 12). Psalm 69, written about 1000 years before Christ, predicted details of ridicule. *"I have become a stranger to my brothers and an alien to my mother's children; Because zeal for Your house has eaten me up, and the reproaches of those who reproach you have fallen on me. When I wept and chastened my soul with fasting, That became my reproach. I also made sackcloth my garment; I became a byword to them. Those who sit in the gate speak against me, And I am the song of the drunkard"* (Ps. 69: 8-12). Jesus endured ridicule for you and me.

The reference to Jesus' siblings in Psalm 69:8 states, "my mother's children" suggests that Mary did not remain a virgin but had children with Joseph. Also in Matthew 13, we read about the half brothers and sisters of Jesus. *"Is this not the carpenter's son? Is not His mother called Mary? And His brothers James, Joses, Simon, and Judas? And His sisters, are they not all with us?"* (13:55-56a).

Living as God in human form must have been difficult for Jesus. Imagine how challenging life must have been for Jesus, a perfect child who never did anything wrong. He could never be guilty of any blame and as a result, His sinful siblings probably felt hostility towards Him. As a man in a world of sinful people, He had trials and temptations from people and Satan (Luke 4:1-13). Since He had no sin nature, he could not sin. How did Jesus in His humanity respond to this? Jesus grew in grace and wisdom (Luke 2:40, 52). He learned to trust His Father's love and depend on the power of the Holy Spirit.

The Bible speaks of Jesus as a Man of sorrows who experienced grief (Isa. 53:3). Through experience, He learned about sorrow, heartaches, and rejection. Throughout Jesus' life, men rejected and loathed Him as despicable, vile, and worthless. How difficult life must have been for Jesus who willingly subjected Himself to abuse from those He came to save.

Understanding the Hypostatic Union

Hypostatic describes the person of Jesus in which His human and divine natures are united. Jesus is one hundred percent man and He is one hundred percent God at the same time. Thus He is the God-Man (John 1:14). The Son of God took the form of a human with limitations of time and space. God took on human physical nature not our sinful disposition. Jesus the name of his humanity means Savior. Christ refers to His role as Messiah. This union of God and man in the person of Jesus is called the incarnation of Christ.

Scriptures set the two characters in perfect balance. Jesus said, *"I thirst"* (John 19:28) signifying His humanity. Jesus said, *"Your sins are forgiven,"* (Mark 2:5; Luke 5:23) indicating His deity since only God can forgive sins. Jesus weariness depicts His humanity. His raising Lazarus from the grave proved His deity. At times Jesus prayed to His Father for divine powers to come on Him.

The limits of the incarnate Christ on earth were the veiling of His preincarnate glory, His subordination in taking the likeness of sinful human flesh, and the voluntary suspension of certain qualities during His earthly life. The Greek word *kenōsis* means emptying, that is, He set aside continuous use of divine qualities. For example, He set aside His power, but He never suspended His deity (Phil. 2:5-8).

We can't imagine the difficulty of perfect God (deity of Jesus) being subjected to life among sinners. Seeing and hearing sin around Him must have caused misery to His righteous soul.

Christ's Trials in His Ministry

Jesus suffered in His humanity (Matt. 4:2; John 4:6; 11:35; 19:28). Jesus Christ, the God-Man was made a little lower than the angels were (Heb. 2:9). In His humanity, Jesus became hungry (Matt. 4:2), thirsty (John 19:28), and He grew tired (John 4:6). He wept (John 11:35). He was tested (Heb. 4:15).

Jesus suffered because of Satan (Matt. 4:1-11; Mark 1:12-13; Luke 4:1-13; Gen. 3:15). Christ was tempted just like we are; He experienced testing through trials yet without sin (Heb. 4:15). Because Christ Jesus was Satan's number one target, he must have tempted Him often. As part of Satan's anti-salvation plan, he intended to prevent Jesus from redeeming the world. Scripture records only a few times when Satan tempted Jesus, history's most important person and Satan's rival. He made a concerted effort at the beginning of Christ's ministry to tempt Him to avoid the cross and then Satan left Him *"for a season"* (Luke 4:13). When did Satan return? He probably returned many times. At the end of the Lord's ministry, Satan most likely harassed Jesus in the Garden and at Calvary tempting Him to abandon the Father's plan. Satan has no use for the cross of Christ. Why don't we read about more of Satan's temptations of Christ? Apparently, the Holy Spirit's wisdom is emphasizing God's rescue plan and not Satan's efforts to prevent Christ's cross work.

Jesus suffered physically because of the Pharisees (Matt. 12:14; 26:59; Mark 14:55; John 8:39-41, 48-49, 59; 10:31, 39; 11:47-53). The Pharisees, (Jewish religious leaders) who knew the Old Testament prophecies better than anyone, should have been directing people to Christ. Instead of lovingly welcoming Jesus, the Messiah, they constantly rejected Him and turned the people against Him. Jesus repeatedly experienced the unbelief of the Pharisees and His people, Israel. Since Jesus challenged their distinguished seats in the temple and marketplace, the Pharisees plotted how they might destroy Jesus.

Jesus suffered in anticipation of the horrors of the cross (Matt. 26:36-46; Mark 14:32-42; Luke 22:39-46; John 12:23-27). Jesus experienced great distress when He thought about His approaching suffering for the sins of all people.

Jesus understood the scope and ramifications of His approaching lifequake, which would take place in just a few hours. Despite His anguish, He gave time and attention to His disciples and celebrated one last Passover meal with them. Some background is needed here about the Passover and its connection with the cross.

The celebration of the Passover was a memorial to Israel's deliverance from Egypt. In review, the Israelites had moved to Egypt to avoid the famine in their land during the time that Joseph rose to a high position there. In time, a new Pharaoh rose to power and he enslaved the children of Israel (Ex. 1:8-14). As well as their deliverance from bondage/slavery, the Passover commemorated Israel's protection from the last plague that God visited upon Egypt (the death of the firstborn) (Ex. 11-13). They gave thanks to God for saving them from death and delivering them from slavery.

God had sent plague judgments on Egypt to persuade Pharaoh to let the Israelites go free. As the tenth and final plague, God sent an angel of death to strike dead every first-born child. No one could escape this plague unless there was blood from a perfect lamb on the lintel and the doorposts. They couldn't be saved because they were descendents of Abraham. No one could be saved by doing the best he could or because he was a good person. The Lord's angel of death wasn't looking for good behavior or rituals; he was looking for the blood of the lamb on the doorposts. Nothing needed to be added to God's plan. God said, *"When I see the blood, I will pass over you"* (Ex. 12:13). This was the Lord's Passover. God spared those who trusted in Him and the blood of the perfect lamb.

The blood is not a mystical sign. Throughout the Word of God is the principle that without the shedding of blood, there is no remission of sins (Lev. 17:11; Heb. 9:22). Since God takes sin seriously, He can't overlook it and do nothing about it. God says, *"The person who sins, shall die"* (Ezek. 18:20 NASB). However, God in His grace determined that an innocent life may be substituted for the guilty. Until Christ came, an unblemished lamb was offered. In the Father's time, He sent Jesus to be *"the lamb of God, which takes away the sin of the world"* (John 1:29). Those who believe in Jesus, God's Lamb sacrificed for their sin, will be "passed over" and not be condemned. God the Judge will not cast them into hell. Passover anticipated the future Lamb of God, Jesus Christ, slain to cover the sins of all people.

At their last Passover meal, Jesus gave His disciples a new metaphorical picture of Himself as the Savior when He replaced the Passover with His Supper. In this upper room, Jesus used a metaphor to communicate new truth—truth that pointed to His redemptive work. When Jesus said, *"this **is** my body"* (Mark 14:22) and *"this **is** my blood,"* (Mark 14:24) "is" means represents. He was speaking figuratively, not literally. Jesus often used metaphors to teach such as when He said, *"I am the door"* (John 10:9); *"I am the vine"* (John 15). The bread and the wine used in the Lord's Supper represent Christ's body and blood given and shed for the forgiveness of sins. Celebration of the Lord's Supper (communion) is a reflection on the cross work of the Lamb of God. The Lord's Supper is our Passover remembrance of God who passes over our sins because we believe in His Lamb who died in our place.

Following the first Lord's Supper, Jesus predicted events surrounding His impending death. Even in this distressful time, our loving Savior was thinking of those He loved. He offered His disciples encouragement, comforted them (John 14), and promised He would return for them. Ignoring His own feelings, Jesus washed the feet of His disciples, and then prayed for them and for all believers (John 17).

After supper, Jesus and His disciples took their last walk together to the Mount of Olives—a difficult walk considering what pressed on His soul. In the garden of Gethsemane, Jesus expressed His feelings of anguish and pleaded with His Father to remove the approaching lifequake (Luke 22:42).

Jesus knew Scripture prophecy such as Isaiah 53, thus He knew about the horrible coming events. More than the thought of agonizing physical torture, He dreaded His spiritual death.* Scripture says, *"The wages of sin is death"* (Rom. 6:23a); sin would separate Him from His Father. The thought of separation from His Father as the object of God's wrath caused Jesus enormous anguish. Both physical and spiritual deaths were necessary for completing the work of salvation.

---

* Death always indicates separation—physical death is separation of soul from the body; spiritual death is separation from God. Death does not mean non-existence.

In the garden, Satan was probably tempting Jesus to abandon the Father's rescue plan for the world and save Himself. Perhaps the temptations from Satan along with Jesus' intense emotions caused Him to fall to the ground as He prayed for deliverance from His approaching lifequake. As intense anguish continued, it caused hematidrosis (hemidrosis)—a condition in which tiny blood vessels or capillaries in sweat glands break resulting in mingled sweat and blood—which could have caused death. God the Father supported Jesus by sending an angel to strengthen Him. Despite His grief-stricken emotions, our faithful Savior never wavered from His commitment to God's rescue plan—the purpose for which He came (Luke 22:42).

Jesus was born to die so that we might live.

A hymn written by James Montgomery, "Go to Gethsemane" based on verses from Lamentations reminds us to look to Jesus—to the cross—and depend on Him. *"Remember my affliction and roaming...My soul still remembers And sinks within me...Therefore I have hope. Through the* LORD's *mercies we are not consumed, Because His compassions fail not"* (Lam. 3:19-22).

GO TO DARK GETHSEMANE

Go to dark Gethsemane,
You that feel the tempter's power;
Your Redeemer's conflicts see,
Watch with Him one bitter hour;
Turn not from His griefs away,
Learn of Jesus Christ to pray.

Jesus suffered because of His close friends (Matt. 6:30; 8:26; 14:31; 16:8; 17:16-17; John 20:25). He constantly dealt with the weak faith of His disciples. In His darkest hour, Jesus faced his disciples' denial and abandonment (Matt. 26:14-16, 47-50, 56, 69-75). Judas, a friend of three years, betrayed Him for thirty pieces of silver. When soldiers captured

Jesus, His disciples deserted Him. Peter, another close friend, denied Him three times. For three years Jesus and His disciples had spent most of their time together—sharing good times, disappointments, and travels. Besides, Jesus had been preparing them for their future ministry of spreading the good news of God's rescue plan.

Jesus suffered at the hands of the Romans. Innocent Jesus, the God-Man, suffered great injustices and abuses by the Romans. After Roman soldiers captured Jesus in the garden, they bound His hands (John 18:12). The binding of the hands was a painful act of tying hands behind the back and then pulling the arms up to the middle of the shoulder blades. Jesus willingly endured the prophetic fulfillment of God's perfect Lamb led to the slaughter (Isa. 53:7).

The tortures the Romans inflicted on Jesus were extraordinary. After removing Jesus clothing, Roman soldiers ruthlessly beat Him (Matt. 27:26; John 19:1). Roman whips were strips of leather with sharp pieces of bone and metal (used for shredding the flesh) fastened to the ends of each strip. Since the Romans had no limits on the number of lashes, most victims didn't survive the severe whipping. Because Roman soldiers were so experienced at their work, they could flog deeper and deeper into the flesh, exposing the nerves without disemboweling the victim. These severe beatings caused Jesus to lose an enormous quantity of blood, become exhausted, and dehydrated. Adding insults, the soldiers put a purple robe (representing royalty) on Jesus, pressed a crown of thorns into His head, stuck a reed in His hand, and then ridiculed and mocked Him (Matt. 27:28-30). Our Savior wore a of crown thorns—the "crown of the curse." Remember God had cursed the ground with thorns after the fall of Adam and Eve. The soldiers further abused Him by spitting on Him, punching Him, and plucking out His beard. Christ suffered disfigurement like no other, probably the result of bearing the weight of trillions of sins. *"His visage was marred more than any man, And His form more than the sons of men"* (Isa. 52:14).

Despite all these torturous injustices, Jesus never complained or demanded His rights. He never opened his mouth (Isa. 53:7-8). Keep in in mind Satan was probably tempting Jesus to give up and disregard His Father's will. Despite everything, our Savior Lamb chose not to escape by using His divine powers.

In addition, the innocent Lamb of God suffered numerous injustices under six unlawful trials of the Jewish religious leaders. Roman courts hired false witnesses to accuse Him. No matter how hard they tried to smear and discredit Jesus, He remained innocent of any crime. Despite this, the Jewish leaders and the crowd rallied for His death. Because of His commitment to the Father's will and His love for humanity, Jesus drank the "bitter cup of suffering."

Christ Drank Bitter Wormwood

Wormwood is a nonpoisonous but bitter plant common to the Middle East. The word wormwood occurs often in the Bible, and in a metaphorical sense. In Jeremiah 9:15; 23:15 and Lamentations 3:15 and 19, wormwood is symbolic of bitter calamity and sorrow, affliction, remorse, or punitive suffering. *Absinthian*, the Greek word for "wormwood," means "undrinkable." In addition, the Old Testament prophets pictured wormwood as the opposite of justice and righteousness. Therefore, wormwood is an accurate description of a bitter, sorrowful, unjust, and undrinkable "cup of suffering." By praying, *"Father, if it is Your will, take this cup away from Me; nevertheless not My will, but Yours, be done"* (Luke 22:42), Jesus expressed His willingness to "drink" this bitter cup.

James Montgomery uses the words wormwood and gall to describe Christ's suffering in stanza two of "Go to Dark Gethsemane." The last two lines of this stanza encourage us to think of His suffering as we bear our trials.

GO TO DARK GETHSEMANE

Follow to the judgment hall,
View the Lord of life arraigned;
Oh, the wormwood and gall!
Oh, the pangs his soul sustained!
Shun not suffering, shame, or loss;
Learn of Him to bear the cross.

Are you willing to suffer shame and loss because you share the gospel with others? Will you bear your "cross," that is, crucify your will and exchange it for God's will?

The Stroke of Injustice

In the Roman Empire crucifixion (death on a cross) was punishment for violent offenders, those guilty of high treason, detested enemies, deserters, slaves, and foreigners. Crucifixion, the most excruciating and shameful form of death, was the most dreaded execution in the ancient world.

The word "excruciating" originated about 1570 A.D. Excruciate comes from the classical Latin word *cruciare* (torture; torment). Using the Latin prefix *ex* (out), *cruciare* (torment, torture; cause grief), and the Latin *crux* (cross; hanging tree; impaling stake) we have "excruciate" or "torment out of the cross." Hence, crucifixion describes the most torturous, agonizing death on a cross.

Previously, you read about the Roman soldiers' abuse of sinless Jesus. Next, the soldiers replaced the purple robe (now soaked with His blood) with Jesus' own clothes. As you know, when you have a cloth bandage on open wounds, the cloth starts to adhere or stick to bloody wounds. As the soldiers took off the purple robe, the clotting wounds most likely ruptured once again and started to bleed.

On the road to Calvary, which was about 650 feet away, Jesus displayed unexpected physical strength and emotional control as He walked to His death. Christ carried either the large crossbeam weighing about 125 pounds or the entire cross until He collapsed and Simon of Cyrene carried it the rest of the way.

At the crucifixion site, soldiers removed Jesus' clothes—a further humiliation to those sentenced to death. Soldiers nailed prisoners to the cross through the hands—identified as any part of the forearm from wrists to elbows. The metal spikes irritated open nerve endings in the wrists. Next, soldiers pounded a spike through the feet to prolong agony. Our substitute, God's perfect Lamb, willingly yielded and proved His unparalleled love for us.

The crucified stretched-out position made breathing difficult. The desire to survive overcame the pain in the hands and feet. Therefore, despite the pain, the crucified person struggled for air using his feet to push himself up allowing air into the lungs. Despite His weakened and sleep deprived condition, it is surprising Jesus could even speak. Yet, He spoke seven sentences while He was on the cross. What were His first words? *"Father, forgive them"* (Luke 23:34). He was speaking of the men who had beaten and crucified Him. How humbling, my sins pinned Jesus on a cross.

Psalm 22, written about a thousand years before His crucifixion, predicted and described the crucifixion agonies suffered by our Savior. Verses 14-16 prophetically describe crucifixion—excruciating physical pain, extreme thirst, suffocation, and mental anguish. The bones of His hands, arms, shoulders, and pelvis became dislocated from hanging. Crucifixion produced profuse perspiration caused by intense suffering and induced heart failure. The scorn and ridicule continued (vv. 6-8, 12-13), yet Jesus trusted and prayed to His Father (vv. 4-5, 9-11).

Jesus didn't defend Himself or call for help. Jesus wasn't a victim; He willingly yielded to death. *"No one takes it from Me, but I lay it down of Myself. I have power to lay it down, and I have power to take it again. This command I have received from My Father"* (John 10:18). Because of His tremendous love for you, Christ surrendered to crucifixion.

> *God took the worst thing man could do to His Son and transformed it into the best thing He could do for man.*

Thomas Kelly's powerful hymn, "Stricken, Smitten, and Afflicted" pictures vivid images of Christ's physical and spiritual suffering on the cross. Kelly balances the suffering of Christ with comforting assurances of His victory—our salvation.

STRICKEN, SMITTEN, AND AFFLICTED

*"He is despised and rejected by men...He has borne our griefs
And carried our sorrows...Smitten by God, and afflicted"* (Isa. 53:3-4).

Stricken, smitten, and afflicted,
See Him dying on the tree!
'Tis the Christ by man rejected;
Yes, my soul, 'tis He, 'tis He!
'Tis a long expected Prophet,
David's son, yet David's Lord;
Proofs I see sufficient of it:
'Tis the true and faithful Word.

Tell me, You who hear Him groaning,
Was there ever grief, like His?
Friends through fear His cause disowning,
Foes insulting His distress;
Many hands were raised to wound Him,
None would interpose to save;
But the deepest stroke that pierced Him
Was not stroke that justice gave.

You who think of sin but lightly,
Nor suppose the evil great
Here may view its nature rightly,
Here its guilt may estimate.
Mark the Sacrifice appointed,
See who bears the awful load;
'Tis the Word, the Lord's Anointed,
Son of man, and Son of God.

Here we have a firm foundation,
Here the refuge of the lost;
Christ's the Rock of our salvation,
His the name of which we boast.
Lamb of God, for sinners wounded,
Sacrifice to cancel guilt!
None shall ever be confounded,
Who on Him their hope have built.

~ Thomas Kelly, 1769-1854 ~
Audio at: *www.hymntime.com*

> *We must take God's wrath against sin seriously!*

The Greatest Blow—God's Justice

Punishing Christ instead of us was an unimaginable display of our Father's grace and love for sinful people. Although Jesus never was a sinner and never became a sinner, God the righteous Judge transferred the sins of the entire world—past, present, and future—to Christ, the perfect Lamb. The sin-soaked Christ suffered for six hours under the wrath of God. At midpoint, at the brightest time of day, the Judge blocked out the sun. During those last three darkest hours, God judged Jesus, the Lamb of God, in our place. The Bible doesn't tell us why God caused the darkness. Perhaps God hid Jesus in the dark to conceal the consequences of His rage against sin; the horrible penalty for sin is a sight too horrendous for people to see. Maybe God darkened the sky so people, especially Christ's enemies, wouldn't misinterpret, distort, or minimize it. The immensity of God's wrath poured out on Christ is beyond our comprehension.

As God blocked out the sun in the sky, He blocked out His Son on the cross—abandoned Him. Perfect God could have nothing to do with a sin-soiled Christ. As Judge, God regarded Christ with contempt, considering Him repulsive and despicable. As Jesus experienced the full measure of God's wrath against sin, He groaned and roared (Ps. 22:1 KJV). Since God the Judge could have nothing to do with Jesus, He couldn't send angels to comfort Jesus as He had done in the garden. Jesus suffered alone in dark silence for you and for me.

Have you ever experienced the "silent treatment" when someone ignored you? If so, then you know how unbearable rejection feels. Even if we magnified those feelings a trillion times, we couldn't comprehend how Christ felt when His Father abandoned Him. God the Judge abandoned Christ when He needed comfort the most. Jesus had no one to turn to for comfort or support—no disciples, no friends, no angels, and no Father. He was alone—except for His greatest enemy, Satan. No doubt, the cunning Satan was there, relentlessly tempting Jesus to flee the cross. The penalty for sin cost Christ everything, but cost you nothing.

Despite all this, our sacrificing Savior refrained from calling ten thousands angels to rescue Him from this indescribable agony. Jesus didn't draw on His divine power to save Himself. Because of His love, Jesus chose to stay nailed on that cross to spare you and me from God's fury against sin. Jesus endured to the end to rescue us from living in the fires of hell—eternity without Him.

As the object of God's wrath, Christ experienced the greatest lifequake in history—a quake customized for Jesus Christ alone. The greatest man suffered the maximum lifequake for the highest gain to all people. Only the perfect Lamb of God could satisfy the righteousness and justice of God.

> *God's wrath towards Christ transfers His grace to us.*

Victories of Christ

Christ's death wasn't a tragedy, but the solution God implemented to save the world from the punishment it deserves. His sacrifice fulfilled God's rescue plan when He became God's offering for sin and our sin bearer (Isa. 53:5-6, 10-12; John 1:29; Luke 19:10; 1 John 2:2), defeated Satan and his fallen angels (Col. 2:14-15; 1 John 2: 8b), and defeated the sin nature's ruling power in the believer's life (Rom. 6:6-7; 8:1-4; Gal. 5:16, 24).

Christ's lifequake tested His reliance on His Father and His commitment to His Father's rescue plan. The lifequake of Jesus tested His love for every person and He proved His love for us.

At the cross, we see God's immeasurable grace poured out. We see the expensive value our loving God places on each soul. Did you know that if you were the only person in the world, Christ would still surrender Himself to God's judgment for your sins? How much more do you need to convince you of His high-priced love for you? How much more will it take to convince you to trust Him in everyday tremors and in lifequakes?

> *The imprint on your soul reads, "Cleaned with the Lamb's blood."*

Jesus is the lover of my soul. Oh, how wide, how high, and how deep is God's love for me! I can rejoice in the extravagance of His love—Jesus finished the Father's rescue plan for me.

The words of the hymn "And Can It Be" by Charles Wesley depict the magnitude of grace and love of Christ. I can't sing "And Can It Be" without misty eyes of joy and appreciation—He did it all for me!

AND CAN IT BE
"Oh, the depth of the riches . . . of God" (Rom. 11:33a)

And can it be, that I should gain
An interest in the Savior's blood?
Died He for me who caused his pain?
For me who Him to death pursued?
Amazing love! How can it be
That Thou my God, shouldst die for me?
Amazing love! How can it be,
That Thou, my God, shouldst die for me?

He left his father's throne above,
So free, so infinite His grace!
Humbled Himself and came in love,
And bled for Adams helpless race!
'Tis mercy all, immense and free!
For O my God, it found out me.
'Tis mercy all, immense and free!
For O my God, it found out me.

Long my imprisoned spirit lay
Fast bound in sin and nature's night.
Thine eye diffused a quickening ray;
I woke- the dungeon flamed with light!
My chains fell off, my heart was free;
I rose, went forth, and followed Thee.
My chains fell off, my heart was free;
I rose, went forth, and followed Thee. (continued)

> No condemnation now I dread:
> Jesus and all in Him is mine!
> Alive in Him, my living Head,
> And clothed in righteousness divine,
> Bold I approach the eternal throne,
> And claimed the crown, through Christ my own.
> Bold I approach the eternal throne,
> And claimed the crown, through Christ my own.
>
> ~ Charles Wesley, 1707-1788 ~

The Significance of His Resurrection

The resurrection of Christ is the focal point of our Christian faith. Because He rose from the dead as He promised, we can believe what He says is true—for He is God! His resurrection certifies God the Father accepted Christ's death as payment for our sins. Our risen Savior represents us to God the Father. Christ's resurrection proves He defeated death; therefore, we can be certain He will raise us to eternal life.

Christ's resurrection is the central fact of Christian history and His resurrection is the heart of the Christian's belief. The truth of Christ's resurrection makes Christianity distinctive and unlike religions that emphasize strong morals and traditional writings of men. Only Christianity has a God who took on human flesh, died for His people, rose from the dead, and now reigns in power and glory forever.

When God the Judge finished judging trillions of sins, the people heard Christ's victory shout, *"It is finished!"* God the Judge had judged Jesus for everyone's sins. Jesus succeeded in enduring the punishment to its conclusion; He stayed under God's wrath to the end for you and me. Therefore, God awarded His stamp of approval on Christ's cross work by raising Him from the dead. He is not the dead God-Man who failed His mission; He lives as the Savior with victory over sin, the world, and death.

Our Victory Cheer

As you may know, Easter has its origins in pagan religions. Easter originated in heathen symbols, from Ishtar, the ancient goddess, and evolved into celebrations with eggs and the Easter bunny. These pagan Easter traditions overlapped with celebrations of the beginning of spring and symbolized the coming of new life. In time, pagan and Christian traditions became interwoven. Some Christians began to celebrate Christ's resurrection on Easter—the pagan holiday—hoping to suppress the heathen holiday. Today many people (including many believers) associate Easter with secular celebrations of spring and new life. Many Christians today join in these rituals and fail to give a second thought to Christ's resurrection and its significance.

Have you given any thought to the "Happy Easter" greeting? Did you know Christian churches of the past had a wonderful greeting on Easter? The pastor would greet the congregation with "Allelujah! Christ is risen!" and the people would respond, "He is risen indeed! Allelujah!" In our day, this victory cheer would be a vast improvement on "Happy Easter!" Share your joy in His victory by greeting others with the traditional "He is risen!"

How Did Jesus Respond to His Lifequake?

Jesus chose to focus on future rewards, *"who for the joy that was set before Him endured the cross, despising the shame"* (Heb. 12:2). What was His joy? Christ Jesus looked forward to being honored as Savior of the world—victor over sin, death, and the devil. Christ Jesus anticipated calling you and me His own, redeemed by His blood. He rejoiced, knowing God the Father would give Him an inheritance, which He would eagerly share with His own. He eagerly anticipated living and reigning with us forever. What will you focus on in your next lifequake?

Thrive by Looking to the Cross

Christ's victory gives life meaning and a guaranteed future life with

Him. The same divine power that raised Christ is available to us for overcoming sin, the world, and Satan. When we walk by faith, we have His power to overcome sin. His resurrection is our source of stability and comfort to help us thrive in any trial.

In addition, unless we measure our problems against the immeasurable love of God displayed at the cross, we will continue to focus on our problems. When we reflect on what happened to Christ and why it happened, we gain a new perspective on suffering. Our Savior did it all for you, so you won't suffer punishment in hell for your own sins. What we suffer in lifequakes is like a grain of sand compared to the enormity of His suffering.

How we think about lifequakes, tremors, and our emotional responses to them usually needs adjustment. What difference would it make in your life if Jesus had failed His rescue mission? How would you face tomorrow or even think about eternity without confidence in Christ's victory? If Jesus had deserted God's rescue plan, how would you respond to your lifequakes? Are you living and responding to your lifequakes as if Jesus had failed?

Remember, unless we consider our lifequakes against the backdrop of the cross, we will fail to see our Father's big picture—His magnificent grace plan to mold us into Christ-likeness! Are you learning to let Christ's likeness shine through you by responding in faith to lifequakes as He did?

> *A Cross-centered perspective will enable you to thrive in your trials.*

Considering Christ's lifequake puts ours into perspective as Paul Gerhardt so adequately expressed in stanzas three, four, and five of "Awake, My Heart, with Gladness." These stanzas provide a victory perspective in trials.

AWAKE, MY HEART, WITH GLADNESS

"Having disarmed principalities and powers, He made a public spectacle of them, triumphing over them in it" (Col. 2:15).

This is a sight that gladdens
What peace it does impart!
Now nothing ever saddens
The joy within my heart.
No gloom shall ever shake,
No foe shall ever take
The hope which God's own
Son in love for me has won.

Now hell, its prince, the devil,
Of all their pow'r are shorn;
Now I am safe from evil,
And sin I laugh to scorn.
Grim death with all its might
Cannot my soul cause fright;
It is a pow'rless form,
However it rave and storm

The world against me rages,
Its fury I disdain;
Though bitter war it wages,
Its work is all in vain.
My heart from care is free,
No trouble troubles me.
Misfortune now is play,
And night is bright as day.

~ Paul Gerhardt (1607-1676) ~

Reflection Questions

Supply Scripture verses wherever possible to support your answers.

1. God the Father rejected and abandoned Jesus on the cross. How do you know He will never do that to you?

2. Why was Christ's spiritual death important?

3. How does Christ's perspective during His ultimate lifequake encourage you to carry your cross (yield to God's will)?

4. Describe the consequences of failure to view lifequakes against the backdrop of the cross.

CHAPTER 6 PREVIEW

༂ Overview of Trial Fundamentals
༂ Basics of Trials
༂ God Causes Good from Trials

CHAPTER 6

Why Do We Have Trials?

Since nothing was going well, Pete was ready to give up. His family rejected him when he announced he had accepted Jesus Christ as his personal Savior. His father showed his displeasure by refusing to pay Pete's school tuition. Is this what it's like being a Christian, Pete wondered? Since Pete is a new believer in Christ, he hasn't learned about Christ and His plans for him. As Pete grows in the Word of God, he will learn that Christ will never desert him. He will learn to depend on Christ, who supplies his needs. In time, Pete will discover that trials are from his loving heavenly Father to help him draw closer to Jesus, his best Friend.

Jesus is a one-of-a-kind friend. As you meditate on the next hymn, count the reasons that Jesus is your best friend.

> **NO, NOT ONE!**
> *"I have called you friends"* (John 15:15b)
>
> There's not a friend like the lowly Jesus—
> No, not one! No, not one!
> None else could heal all our diseases—
> No, not one! No, not one!
>
> REFRAIN: Jesus knows all about our struggles,
> He will guide till the day is done;
> There's not a friend like the lowly Jesus—
> No, not one! No, not one!
>
> There's not an hour that He is not near us—
> No, not one! No, not one!
> No night so dark but His love can cheer us—
> No, not one! No, not one!
>
> Was ever a gift like the Savior given?—
> No, not one! No, not one!
> Will He refuse us a home in heaven?—
> No, not one! No, not one!
>
> ~ Johnson Oatman, Jr. 1856–1922 ~

Trials Challenge Our Faith

When life's shock waves jolt you and you hurt, trust the truths about God, not your feelings. You may not agree with the trial God has selected, but your wise Father knows best what trial to send to challenge your faith to make it more consistent. When pain, anger, worry, and confusion cause you to doubt God, remember His comforting words: *"For I know the thoughts that I think toward you, says the* LORD*, thoughts of peace and not of evil, to give you a future and a hope"* (Jer. 29:11). Find peace believing your loving Father desires your faith to grow; therefore, He designs trials to stretch it.

The Fundamentals of Trials Overview (1 Peter 1:3-9)

Three general reasons for trials are Adam's sin and its consequences (Gen. 2–4), the sins of an individual (Gal. 6:7-8; Heb. 12:15), and God's training through trials (Rom. 8:18-19).

Knowing the basics of trials helps prepare us to rely on the Lord during our trials. The following overview highlights the facts about trials, which I will expand throughout the book.

1. **Trials are for believers** (1 Peter 1:3-6a; James 1:2a).
2. **Trials need not discourage a believer.** We can rejoice in the Lord when we consider our blessings in Christ (1 Peter1:6a).
3. **Trials are temporary** (1 Peter 1:6b). *"After you have suffered a while"* (1 Peter 5:10c). Ecclesiastes 3:1-8 tells us about seasons—a time for everything.
4. **Trials are necessary and unavoidable** (1 Peter 1:6c).
   "My brethren, count it all joy when you fall into various trials" (James 1:2). Consider the trials of the heroes of faith in Hebrews 11. If we want to grow spiritually, we need trials.
5. **Trials cause great stress in your life** (1 Peter 1:6d).
6. **Trials vary** (1 Peter 1:6e; James 1:2c). God varies trials because He knows best what area or from what angle we need help to grow in faith.
7. **Trials are designed to refine your faith** (1 Peter 1:7a). The Lord designs them to polish your faith (Rom. 8:28).

8. **Trials are tests and are different from temptations.** Temptations are from Satan, the world, or our flesh; they are attractions to evil (James 1:13-14).
9. **Trials will result in praise, honor, and glory to the Lord when He returns, if we respond correctly to them** (1 Peter 1:7b).
10. **Trials can either be passed or failed** (1 Peter 1:7c).
11. **Trials should not surprise us** (1 Peter 4:12a).
12. **Trials do not mean that God is displeased with us** (1 Peter 4:12-16). Although God disciplines us to correct us, to restore us, to turn us around, He also uses trials to mold us to be like His Son. *"He knows the way that I take; When He has tested me, I shall come forth as gold"* (Job 23:10).
13. **Trials are designed to increase patience** (James 1:3, 4, 12). They may help us learn to rely on God's wisdom and wait for His timing.
14. **Trials reveal the God of all comfort** (2 Cor. 1:3-4). There is no trial too great for God's comfort.
15. **Trials that we bear may comfort others** (2 Cor. 1:4b). Our trust and joy in Christ Jesus during difficult times can encourage others to look to the Lord.
16. **Trials can cause us to rely on God.** They can teach us to redirect our focus from troubles toward the Lord (2 Cor. 1:8-9).
17. **Trials may be a result of individual sin.** Like the discipline of the Prodigal Son (Luke 15), God disciplined unfaithful Israel. God disciplines us with trials to draw us back to Himself.

Is Satan Involved in Trials and Discipline?

Scripture provides examples of Satan's role in trials or discipline. The apostle Paul had a thorn in the flesh from Satan, to keep him from becoming prideful because of all he knew (2 Cor. 12:7). The Bible reveals Satan's involvement in Job's trial, which God used to show Job the condition of his faith and to stretch it. A Corinthian believer was disciplined for his ongoing sin when He removed him from the spiritual support of the church at Corinth. This man was left alone with his sin and Satan in the hope that this emptiness would drive him to confess his sin and return to the church (1 Cor. 5:5). All discipline from the Lord has restoration of fellowship as it ultimate goal.

God disciplined Jonah for disobedience when He allowed a great fish to swallow him alive. When we have a trial, we should examine our life and our actions to determine if the trial is God's discipline. We can pray that God would show us our sin because the trial could be the consequences of sin (Ps. 139:23-24).

You may be experiencing a continuing trial that is overwhelming you. Take time to meditate on the comforting words of three stanzas of this hymn.

WHAT GOD ORDAINS IS ALWAYS GOOD
"He is the Rock, His work is perfect; For all His ways are justice, A God of truth and without injustice; Righteous and upright is He" (Deut. 32:4).

What God ordains is always good.
He is my Friend and Father;
He suffers naught to do me harm,
Though many storms may gather.
Now I may know both joy and woe,
Someday I shall see clearly
That He hath loved me dearly.

What God ordains is always good.
Though I the cup am drinking
Which savors now of bitterness,
I take it without shrinking.
For after grief God grants relief,
My heart with comfort filling
And all my sorrow stilling.

What God ordains is always good.
This truth remains unshaken.
Though sorrow, need, or death be mine,
I shall not be forsaken.
I fear no harm, For with His arm
He shall embrace and shield me;
So to my God I yield me.

~ Samuel Rodigast, 1649-1708 ~

God Causes Good from Quakes

We rarely consider the gains that result from natural earthquakes. The same forces that cause earthquakes produce large amounts of our fuel reserves, concentrate reserves, and make searching for fuel more accessible and less expensive. Scientists also tell us that earthquakes create natural beauty such as the spectacular Wasatch Mountains, formed on an active fault above Salt Lake City, Utah. Earthquakes remain a potential danger for Salt Lake City, but its mountains are the prize. In the same way, our caring Father plans good to come from our lifequakes.

Often we fail to see the Lord's blessings that come from our trials. During trials, some believers become bitter, continue to linger on the losses, and fail to see the good God sends. Can you identify with the bitter believer in the next story?

Thank You, Lord, for the Thorns—Adapted

Sandra felt as low as the heels of her Birkenstocks as she pushed against a November gust and the florist shop door. Her life had been easy, like a spring breeze. Then in the fourth month of her second pregnancy, a minor automobile accident stole her happiness. During this Thanksgiving week, she would have delivered a son. She grieved over her loss. As if that weren't enough, her husband's company threatened a transfer. Then her sister, whose holiday visit she coveted, called to say she could not come. What is worse, Sandra's friend angered her by suggesting her grief was a Lord-given path to maturity to help her to empathize with others who suffer. Has she lost a child? No, she has no idea what I'm feeling, Sandra shuddered. Thanksgiving? Thankful for what, she wondered. Why would she be thankful for a careless driver whose truck was hardly scratched when he rear-ended her, thankful for an airbag that saved her life but took the life of her child?

"Good afternoon, may I help you?" The approach of the clerk at the flower shop startled her.

"Sorry," said Jenny, "I just didn't want you to think I was ignoring you." "I...I need an arrangement."

Why Do We Have Trials?

"For Thanksgiving?" Sandra nodded. "Do you want beautiful but ordinary or would you like to challenge the day with a customer favorite I call the 'Thanksgiving Special'?" Jenny saw Sandra's curiosity and continued, "I'm convinced that flowers tell stories, that each arrangement conveys a particular feeling. Are you looking for something that conveys gratitude this Thanksgiving?"

"Not exactly! Sorry, but in the last five months everything that could go wrong has" Sandra blurted. Sandra regretted her outburst but was surprised when Jenny said, "I have the perfect arrangement for you."

The door's small bell suddenly rang. "Barbara! Hi!" Jenny said. She politely excused herself from Sandra and walked toward a modest workroom. She quickly reappeared carrying a massive arrangement of green bows and long-stemmed thorns.

The ends of the rose stems were neatly snipped—no flowers. "Want this in a box?" Jenny asked. Sandra watched for Barbara's response. Was this a joke? Who would want rose stems and no flowers! She waited for laughter, for someone to notice the absence of flowers on top the thorny stems but neither woman did. "Yes, please. It's exquisite!" said Barbara. "You'd think after three years of buying the Special I wouldn't be motivated by its significance, but it's happening again. My family will love this one. Thanks."

Sandra stared. Why is this normal conversation about such a peculiar arrangement, she wondered. "Uh," said Sandra, pointing. "That lady just left with...uh..." "Yes?" "Well, she had no flowers!" "Yep. That's the Special. I call it the Thanksgiving Thorns Bouquet."

"But, why do people pay for that?"

Despite herself, she chuckled. "Do you really want to know?"

"I couldn't leave this shop without knowing. I'd think about nothing else!"

"That might be good," said Jenny. "Well," she continued, "Barbara came into the shop three years ago with feelings similar to those you feel today. She thought she had very little to be thankful for. She had lost her father to cancer, the family business was failing, her son was into drugs, and she faced major surgery. That same year I lost my husband. I assumed complete responsibility for the shop and for the first time, spent the holidays alone. I had no children, no husband, no family nearby, and too great a debt to allow any travel."

"What did you do?"

"I learned to be thankful for thorns."

Sandra's eyebrows lifted. "Thorns?"

"I'm a Christian, Sandra. I have always thanked the Lord for good things in life and I never thought to ask Him why good things happened to me. However, when awful stuff hit, did I ever ask! It took time to learn that dark times are important. I always enjoyed the flowers of life but it took thorns to show me the beauty of the Lord's comfort. You know, the Bible says the Lord comforts us when we are afflicted and from His consolation we learn to comfort others."

Sandra gasped. "A friend read that passage to me and I was furious! I guess the truth is I don't want comfort. I've lost a baby and I'm angry with the Lord." She started to ask Jenny to "go on" when the door's bell diverted their attention.

"Hey, Phil!" shouted Jenny as a balding, rotund man entered the shop. She softly touched Sandra's arm and moved to him. He tucked her under his side for a warm hug. "I'm here for twelve thorny long-stemmed stems!" Phil laughed heartily.

"I figured as much," said Jenny. "I've got them ready." She lifted a tissue-wrapped arrangement from the refrigerated cabinet.

"Beautiful," said Phil. "My wife will love them."

Sandra could not resist asking, "These are for your wife?"

Phil saw that Sandra's curiosity matched his when he first heard of a Thorn Bouquet.

"Do you mind me asking, "Why thorns?"

"No, in fact, I'm glad you asked," he said. "Four years ago my wife and I nearly divorced. After forty years, we were in a real mess, but we but we slugged through problem by rotten problem. We rescued our marriage—our love. Last year at Thanksgiving, I stopped in here for flowers. I must have mentioned surviving a tough process because Jenny told me that for a long time she kept a vase of rose stems—yes, STEMS—as a reminder of what she learned from 'thorny' times. That was good enough for me. I took home stems. My wife and I decided to label each one for a specific thorny situation and give thanks for what the difficulties taught us. I am sure this stem review is becoming a tradition." Phil paid Jenny, thanked her again, and as he left, said to Sandra, "I recommend the Special!"

"I don't know if I can be thankful for thorns in my life," Sandra said to Jenny.

"Well, my experience says thorns make roses precious. We treasure the Lord's providential care more during trouble than at any other time. Remember, Sandra, Jesus wore a crown of thorns so we might know His love. Don't resent the thorns."

Tears rolled down Sandra's cheeks. For the first time since the accident, she loosened her grip on resentment. "I'll take twelve long-stemmed thorns, please."

"I hoped you would," Jenny said. "I'll have them ready in a minute. Then, every time you see them, remember to appreciate both good and tough times. We grow through both."

"Thank you. What do I owe you?"

"Nothing. The first year's arrangement is always on me." Jenny handed a card to Sandra. "I'll attach a card like this to your arrangement, but maybe you'd like to read it first. Go ahead, read it."

The card read, "My Lord, I have never thanked You for my thorns! I have thanked You a thousand times for my roses but never once for my thorns. Teach me the value of thorns. Show me that I may draw closer to You by the path of pain."—Jenny L.

http://living4jesus.net/dynamic/in.thankyouthorns.htm

We may feel cheated looking at what we have lost or what others have. How often do we fail to see God's roses of grace because of preoccupation with thorny problems or pain? The next hymn reminds us to look to our Lord Jesus and count His blessings to us.

COUNT YOUR BLESSINGS
"Many, o LORD my God, are Your wonderful works" (Ps. 40:5).

When upon life's billows you are tempest tossed,
When you are discouraged, thinking all is lost,
Count your many blessings, name them one by one,
And it will surprise you what the Lord hath done.

REFRAIN: Count your blessings, name them one by one,
Count your blessings, see what God hath done!
Count your blessings, name them one by one,
And it will surprise you what the Lord hath done.
Are you ever burdened with a load of care?
Does the cross seem heavy you are called to bear?
Count your many blessings, every doubt will fly,
And you will keep singing as the days go by.

When you look at others with their lands and gold,
Think that Christ has promised you His wealth untold;
Count your many blessings. Wealth can never buy
Your reward in heaven, nor your home on high.

So, amid the conflict whether great or small,
Do not be disheartened, God is over all;
Count your many blessings, angels will attend,
Help and comfort give you to your journey's end.

~ Johnson Oatman, Jr., 1856-1922 ~

www.hymntime.com

The Refining Pot of Faith

Other beneficial reasons for trials include God's refining of our faith, His revealing something to us and His giving rewards and opportunities to us through trials.

Trials Are Designed to Refine:

1. *Our faith* (James 1:3-4; 1 Peter 1:7). Our Father desires that we claim His promises. Christ wants our dependency on Him; therefore, He permits repeated trials to develop a consistent reliance on Him and His promises.
2. *Our knowledge of God's Word* (Ps. 119:71-72, 75). God can use trials to turn our attention to Him and His Word.
3. *Our application of God's Word* (Ps. 119:67). We need the Word of God to advance our faith (Rom. 10:17; Heb. 4:2). Trials can redirect our will toward obedience to His will. For example, Jonah wouldn't obey God's command to travel to Nineveh, instead he tried to run from God. Therefore, God redirected Jonah's will through a trial—an enormous fish swallowed him, and in the dark, stinking, slimy stomach with digestive juices swirling about, Jonah chose to rethink his decision. He repented (changed his mind) and after being vomited on the shore, he obeyed God.

Note the wisdom of the psalmist, *"Before I was afflicted I went astray, But now I keep Your word"* (Ps. 119:67). Sometimes God sends us a trial to push us to reconsider a foolish decision.

> *God's refining breaks down every barrier that hinders reliance on Him.*

Trials Are Designed to Reveal:

1. *Our motives* (Ps. 16:2; 66:10; Prov. 16:2; 17:3). God looks at our intentions to see if they are pure. God may use suffering to humble us

and teach us about our motives such as pride and self-centeredness. Do I rely on myself to succeed and to serve God? Am I seeking to please people with my life and service instead of living and serving as unto the Lord? Do I disregard God's will in favor of my own?

2. *Our insufficiency* (Prov. 24:10; 2 Cor. 1:8-10; 3:5-6). Do I consider myself able to handle my troubles without God or do I recognize my inadequacies and admit them to Him? Do I believe that God is capable and trust Him in tremors and lifequakes?

3. *Our love for the Lord* (Deut. 13:1-4). The degree of love we have for God's Word reveals the extent of our love for Lord Jesus. We don't love God if we don't spend time in His Word. God may permit a trial to test the quality of our love for Him.

Trials Are Designed to Reward Us:

1. *With spiritual development* (Ps. 66:10-12). Lifequakes show us our need to trust God's promises (Ps. 119:92, 153; Isa. 30:20-21). Through trials we learn to rely on Christ instead of ourselves (2 Cor. 1:8-10). God loves us too much to allow us to remain the way we are—proud, impatient, and self-reliant. Trials can also benefit us by preventing pride (2 Cor. 12:6-7). Our Lord uses lifequakes and tremors to direct us to a Christ-centered life (Heb. 12:6-11). In addition, trials offer the opportunity to rely on the adequacy of God's grace (2 Cor. 12:8-10). Another blessing of trials is the option to experience God's comfort (2 Cor. 1:3-4a).

2. *With privileges in our Christian life.* Through trials we have the privilege of giving Him glory (Ps. 50:14-15, 23; 1 Peter 4:14, 16). *"I will sing of the mercies of the LORD forever; With my mouth will I make known Your faithfulness to all generations"* (Ps. 89:1). Our Father allows our trials to give us an opportunity to shine glory back on Him by trusting Him. When we depend on our Savior

during our adversities, we give evidence of the character of God, which gives Him glory. Praising God for His grace, love, faithfulness, and for all His characteristics is a privilege of living by faith.

3. **With opportunities to witness for Christ** (1 Peter 3:14-17). Instead of giving attention to our circumstances, we can turn the conversation away from ourselves and point others to Christ. We can use our trial to talk about our confidence in our future heavenly home, and then engage others in conversation about salvation. Through our response to the trial, we can show how faith in Him is the key to contentment even in a trial.

4. **With future, heavenly rewards** (Matt. 5:10-12; James 1:12). Our loving Father allows us to experience the heat of trials to purify us. Someone said, "Crowns are formed in crucibles (severe tests)." Our champion Jesus Christ first endured the cross and then received His crown of glory. When we reach heaven, our Father will present us with the crown (rewards), which we earned by trusting Him.

In addition, our heavenly Father uses suffering to prepare His children for future lifequakes. Are you preparing daily for lifequakes by reading, believing, and memorizing God's Word? The next story is about a believer who learned to depend on God and His sufficiency before his tragic accident.

A Faith Adventure
Keeping the Faith Focus

Vince reports,

On November 16, 2007, my twelve-year-old son Zeke and I were deer hunting in the woods in northern Wisconsin. I was in the tree lowering my son's deer stand, when the branch I was holding onto broke off. I fell 25 feet, landing on my back on the forest floor. The vertebra in the middle of my back separated, crushed my spinal cord causing instant, permanent paralysis in the lower half of my body from my chest down.

I am thankful that my son and my friend, Bill, were with me that day in the woods. My friend used a cell phone to call the rescue squad and then left the woods to meet the rescuers. I was in excruciating pain as I lie in the woods. I spoke with my son and shared with him valuable truths from the Word of God that I wanted him to remember.

I thought the Lord was taking me home that day. Despite the pain and uncertainties, I had peace in my heart because I have confidence my Lord Jesus loves me and died to pay the penalty for every sin I had ever committed. I knew I would go to heaven based on the merits of Christ's shed blood on the cross and His resurrection from the dead. My son and I prayed together and after our prayer, we "sang" a gospel hymn, "How Great Thou Art."

I submitted my life to my heavenly Father's hand. He would either take me home to Him or grant me more time to raise my son, and be a witness for His grace and glorious gospel. I told the Lord I would accept His will. If I never used my legs again, I would accept that as His will.

I was 41 years old at the time and had been a Christian for 29 years. I had been through tough times and that day the Lord made me aware of something. Lying on the ground I had the presence of mind (by God's grace) to realize that leaning on the faithfulness of God through past difficulties had prepared me for this. The Lord had taught me that He doesn't leave His children lost and adrift in the sea of the troubles.

I knew my God loved me and had a plan and a purpose for me as the Word of God reveals. *"'For I know the plans that I have for you,' declares the LORD, plans for welfare and not for calamity to give you a future and a hope"* (Jer. 29:11 NASB). Through my rehab and recovery, I kept this perspective about His plan for my life.

I went through difficult days—physically, emotionally, and

spiritually. The prospect that I would never use my legs again was overwhelming. I realized my career as a construction worker was over. I would never walk in the woods or participate in life as I had.

The long list of negatives you can think about during a trial can cause sadness or severe depression. The lonely, heavy hand of anxiety and doubt was constantly knocking at my door, calling me to doubt the love and care of my God. Yet, God says, *"If you do well, will not your countenance be lifted up? And if you do not do well, sin is crouching at the door; and its desire is for you, but you must master it"* (Gen. 4:7 NASB). The Lord will not allow temptation beyond what we can overcome by applying His Word through the power of the Holy Spirit (1 Cor. 10:13).

The faithfulness of God is strong and true. The Lord strengthened me through encouragements from brothers and sisters in Christ who called me and visited me in the hospital and at home. I received comfort through the love of my wife and children as we read the Scriptures, prayed and shared together. I read encouraging books, similar to the one you are reading and gained a proper understanding of trials—to draw us near to God.

In addition, we have trials so He can draw us closer. As Jesus said in John 12:32, *"And I, if I am lifted up from the earth, will draw all peoples to Myself."* Through adversity, we have the chance to proclaim the faithfulness of God and to exalt Him as Savior and Creator.

Because we are believers, the trials we face work together for our benefit (Rom. 8:28). Keeping my focus on the Lord sustained me.

> *As sure as God puts His children in the furnace*
> *He will be in the furnace with them.* —Charles Spurgeon

Even though I no longer have the use of my legs, in a spiritual sense I can still walk, stand, run, jump, leap, and kneel.

WALK (live, behave, think)

- *"for we **walk** by faith, not by sight"* (2 Cor. 5:7 NASB).

- *"But I say, **walk** by the Spirit, and you will not carry out the desire of the flesh"* (Gal. 5:16 NASB).

- *"Therefore we have been buried with Him through baptism into death, so that as Christ was raised from the dead through the glory of the Father, so we too might **walk** in newness of life"* (Rom. 6:4 NASB).

- *"For we are His workmanship, created in Christ Jesus for good works, which God prepared beforehand so that we would **walk** in them"* (Eph. 2:10 NASB).

- *"Therefore I, the prisoner of the Lord, implore you to **walk** in a manner worthy of the calling with which you have been called"* (Eph. 4:1 NASB).

- *"And **walk** in love, just as Christ also loved you and gave Himself up for us, an offering and a sacrifice to God as a fragrant aroma"* (Eph. 5:2 NASB).

- *"Therefore be careful how you **walk**, not as unwise men but as wise"* (Eph. 5:2 NASB).

- *"So that you may **walk** in a manner worthy of the LORD, to please Him in all respects, bearing fruit in every good work and increasing in the knowledge of God"* (Col. 1:10 NASB).

STAND

- *"Be on the alert, **stand** firm in the faith, act like men, be strong"* (1 Cor. 16:13 NASB).

- *"Put on the full armor of God, that you may be able to **stand** firm against the schemes of the devil"* (Eph. 6:11 NASB).

- "Therefore, my beloved brethren whom I long to see, my joy and crown, so **stand** firm in the Lord, my beloved" (Phil. 4:1 NASB).

- "Through Silvanus, our faithful brother (for so I regard him), I have written to you briefly, exhorting and testifying that this is the true grace of God. **Stand** firm in it!" (1 Peter 5:12 NASB).

RUN

- "Do you not know that those who **run** in a race all **run**, but only one receives the prize? **Run** in such a way that you may win" (1 Cor. 9:24 NASB).

- "Holding fast the word of life, so that in the day of Christ I may have cause to glory because I did not **run** in vain nor toil in vain" (Phil. 2:16 NASB).

- "Therefore, since we have so great a cloud of witnesses surrounding us, let us also lay aside every encumbrance and the sin which so easily entangles us, and let us **run** with endurance the race that is set before us" (Heb. 12:1 NASB).

LEAP

- "Be glad in that day and **leap** for joy, for behold, your reward is great in heaven. For in the same way their fathers used to treat the prophets" (Luke 6:23 NASB).

KNEEL

- "For this reason I bow my **knees** before the Father" (Eph. 3:14 NASB).

- "Therefore, strengthen the hands that are weak and the **knees** that are feeble" (Heb. 12:12 NASB).

Be strengthened and encouraged as you ponder God's Word in the following verses.

"I can do all things through Him who strengthens me" (Phil. 4:13 NASB).

> "Yet those who wait for the LORD will gain new strength; They will mount up with wings like eagles, They will run and not get tired, They will walk and not become weary" (Isa. 40:31 NASB).

As I considered the faithfulness of the Lord working in and through my paralysis, I realized important and encouraging truths, which I have shared with you. May my comments and perspective be encouraging for believers as they go through trials.

How to Have Joy during Trials

The Lord instructs us to count it joy when we suffer: *"My brethren, count it all joy when you fall into various trials"* (James 1:2a). But, you ask, when I am suffering how can I be joyful? About what should we be joyful? Is happiness the same as joy? No. Happiness is an emotional response to pleasant circumstances.

Our feelings rise and fall depending on our circumstances. When we have financial security or receive a job promotion, we are happy. When we are at peace with a loved one, we are happy. Receiving an "A" on a test makes us happy. Our children make us happy when they obey us. Our happiness fades when we lose our job, a friend betrays us, or we become ill. Emotions are like a roller coaster—when things are going well we are happy; when we have trouble we are sad or depressed. We can trade the roller coaster of emotional highs and lows for joy through God's plan. His word directs us to have joy (inner contentment) amid trials.

God's rescue plan in hard times offers joy in trials. How is that possible? We gain joy from thinking about Christ and thinking from His viewpoint amid sorrows. For example, we can claim, *"Do not sorrow, for the joy of the LORD is your strength"* (Neh. 8:10b). After meditating on this verse, we see the key words are *"joy of the Lord."* What does this verse mean to you?

When you think of the Lord, what gives you joy, that is, inner contentment? I find joy thinking about Jesus Christ—what He did for me at Calvary, how He keeps praying for me, or how He is with me. I consider joy to be my position in Christ. I belong to the family of God, with Christ as my Savior, my spiritual Bridegroom, and my best Friend. Knowing He supplies me with His love, peace, confidence, endurance, and security, fills me with joy. Thinking about my loving, faithful Lord Jesus gives me strength to endure the tests in life. He provides everything I need; He is my all in all. When I consider my trials against the backdrop of the cross, I count it all joy that Christ took my place. My trials can't compare with the lifequake He took in my place, therefore, I rejoice with a song in my heart. When I ponder those truths, I rise up on eagles wings; I soar with His strength.

I don't need to like my trial or be happy about it, but I can count it joy. I regard it joy to know the Lord desires to mold me into the likeness of Christ. My Father cares enough to send the best trials, customized to benefit me by drawing me closer to Himself.

Joy comes from Christ, not circumstances.

Another believer who learned the secret of joy in trials was Fanny Crosby. Physically blind from birth, Fanny Crosby could "see" her Lord with spiritual eyes. Her faith-based hymns have comforted Christians for over a hundred years. As you meditate on the following Scripture verse and Crosby's hymn, "Never Give Up," be aware of principles to apply to your life.

NEVER GIVE UP

"My brethren, count it all joy when you fall into various trials, knowing that the testing of your faith produces patience. But let patience have its perfect work, that you may be perfect and complete, lacking nothing" (James 1:2-4).

Never be sad or desponding,
If thou hast faith to believe.
Grace, for the duties before thee,
Ask of thy God and receive.

> REFRAIN: Never give up, never give up,
> Never give up to thy sorrows,
> Jesus will bid them depart.
> Trust in the Lord, trust in the Lord,
> Sing when your trials are greatest,
> Trust in the Lord and take heart.
>
> What if thy burdens oppress thee;
> What though thy life may be drear;
> Look on the side that is brightest,
> Pray, and thy path will be clear.
>
> Never be sad or desponding,
> There is a morrow for thee;
> Soon thou shall dwell in its brightness,
> There with the Lord thou shall be.
>
> Never be sad or desponding,
> Lean on the arm of thy Lord;
> Dwell in the depths of His mercy,
> Thou shalt receive thy reward.
> ~ Words: Fanny Crosby, 1903 Music: Ira Allan Sankey ~

> *Look to Jesus for joy during trials.*

Thinking about Him

Dependency on the Lord is the key to peace as He promises, *"You will keep him in perfect peace, Whose mind is stayed on You, Because he trusts in You"* (Isa. 26:3). To have your mind stayed on the Lord doesn't mean thinking about Him continually; instead, it means leaning on or trusting Him.

Depend on Him for everything, spiritual and physical, and believe He does what is best for us. I am confident the Lord will heal me from health difficulties; I just don't know the "when" of His perfect timing. He could heal me while I live on earth. One day, He will heal me with my resurrection body. Either way it is a win-win solution since He always delivers us. Leaving the "when" and "how" solution in His hands offers us peace during our trials.

Hudson Taylor is an example of a believer's steadfast faith in the Lord for everything. Taylor realized that if God wanted the gospel spread, He would have to provide the means. Financial concerns were always present in the missionary work in China. At one point Taylor affirmed,

> I am indeed proving the truth of that word, *"You will keep him in perfect peace, Whose mind is stayed on You, Because he trusts in You"* (Isa. 26:3). My mind is quite as much at rest as, nay, more than, it would be if I had a hundred pounds in my pocket. May He keep me ever thus, simply depending on Him for every blessing, temporal as well as spiritual *(Hudson Taylor's Spiritual Secret, p. 44)*.

> *God's perfect peace is part of His rescue plan.*

Whether our trials are severe or moderate in nature, a mind stayed on Christ always brings God's blessings. The next faith adventure also illustrates the peace we have "keeping our mind on Him."

A Faith Adventure
Promises Fulfilled beyond Expectations

Ian testifies to the reliability of God's promises and writes,

> One of my favorite verses is Psalm 32:8, *"I will instruct you and teach you in the way you should go; I will guide you with My eye."* The Lord has taught me in recent years that when He makes a promise, I can trust Him to fulfill it to the fullest application. Because the Lord gave His Word, and because He is, by nature, truth, He can't fail to fulfill it.
>
> I was looking for a job in my field just before graduation from college. All my friends had already found employment and I didn't have much time left to find steady income before

my wedding. However, I took the Lord at His word and applied for many jobs knowing that He would make His perfect will clear in His perfect timing.

Four days before graduation, God fulfilled His promise of guidance in a greater way than I thought possible. During my senior year of college, I was unsure how I would like to apply my new skills as a mechanical engineer. I thought that perhaps I would enjoy working as a design engineer in a small company. Instead, the Lord put me in a large company working as a product quality engineer—a position I enjoy much more than design engineering. The Lord knew the perfect fit for me. We must cling to, *"Now to Him who is able to do exceedingly abundantly above all that we ask or think, according to the power that works in us"* (Eph. 3:20).

> *Those who declare independence from the Lord become dependent on changing circumstances. However, those who depend on the Lord live independent of their circumstances.*

In summary, when we experience inevitable lifequakes, we must remember the fundamentals of trials and reasons for them. God allows trials to refine our faith, our motives, our knowledge, and application of His Word. Trials reveal whether we have wavering or consistent faith. They reveal our self-sufficiency or dependence on the Lord. God plans specific lifequakes to draw us into a deeper relationship with Him. He uses lifequakes to mold us to be like Christ. Trials also reveal the degree of our love for the Lord and His Word. God uses trials to give us occasions to share the gospel with others.

> *Trials are God's building blocks of faith.*

Reflection Questions

Where possible support your answers with Scripture.

1. Name three things trials are designed to refine.

    1.

    2.

    3.

2. Name three things trials are designed to reveal.

    1.

    2.

    3.

3. Name four things trials provide as rewards.

    1.

    2.

    3.

    4.

4. We should consider trials as opportunities to…

5. How can you experience "joy" during a trial?

6. Name reasons why God designs lifequakes.

7. How will knowing the reasons for trials help you deal with them?

CHAPTER 7 PREVIEW

↬ Living by Faith is a Choice
↬ Saved by Faith, Live by Faith
↬ Family of God vs. Fellowship with God
↬ The Importance of Fellowship with God

CHAPTER 7

What Kind of Faith Does God Seek?

What God Do You Trust?

Do you believe in yourself and your self-sufficiency to handle your problems? Do you believe in the thought of god or ideas of faith? Someone with an obscure faith says, "My faith got me through this trial," suggesting no object of faith. Before John trusted in Christ, he didn't know who God was, he just believed in the impression of god. Whenever he felt the need, he would think, god will help me. Do you have faith in a vague version of god, a generic "Higher Power," or the true God of the Bible?

Many people these days view faith as a collection of thoughts for living; thoughts easily shattered defending themselves against competing thoughts. Views such as, love conquers all, wisdom comes through academics, or self-discipline is the key to success are popular beliefs in our day.

Often, religions co-exist within Christianity when people mix believing in Christ as their Savior with these heathen practices. They practice astrology, Karma, or some other heathen worldviews with their Christianity. Christians see nothing wrong with Yoga—a Hindu discipline of exercise practiced to promote control of the body and the mind. They excuse their participation stating they don't believe the Hindu part, they just attend for the exercise. Would you attend a Buddhist temple so you could say you went to church? God commands that Christians be set apart unto God, separated (be different) from the world (anything that opposes God). Christians should not even give a hint of tolerance or acceptance of the gods of this world—things to distract us from Christ. God says we are either for Him or against Him, and combining Christianity with heathen religion signals a mutated, unbiblical faith that opposes Him.

Pagan religions such as Hinduism and Buddhism are becoming more prevalent among Americans. Hinduism teaches reincarnation, a supreme being of many forms and natures, and seeks freedom from evils of the world. Buddhism teaches that desire causes suffering, that suffering stops when desire ceases, and that understanding earned through right conduct, wisdom, and meditation releases one from desire, suffering, and rebirth. These religions embrace the idea of fate and destiny and that a person's actions and conduct during successive phases of life control them. Followers speak about Karma (the effect of a person's actions and conduct) which, they believe, determine the person's destiny.

Other faiths in America's melting pot of religions include Spiritism, which believes the dead communicate with the living (spiritualism). Spirituality, another popular religion, is a preoccupation with the concerns of human inner nature, especially ethical or ideological values. Astrology is the study of heavenly bodies in the belief that they influence the course of natural earthly occurrences and human affairs. New Age covers themes from spiritualism and reincarnation to approaches to health and ecology. Numerology is the study of occult meanings of numbers and their supposed influence on our life.

Besides those listed above, beware of mysticism and Christian mysticism. Mystics hold to the belief in or experience of a reality beyond normal human understanding or experience, especially a reality perceived as essential to the nature of life. The religion of mysticism employs contemplative prayer and spirituality aimed at achieving a direct experience with the divine. Mysticism is obscure or confused belief or thought and has many variations. Christian mysticism is the pursuit of communion with, identity with, or conscious awareness of God through direct experience, intuition, instinct, or insight. Christian mysticism centers on the habitual practice of "deep prayer" involving the person of Jesus Christ and the Holy Spirit. Mysticism attempts to achieve unity with the divine apart from the Scriptures.

In contrast, biblical Christianity is based on the teachings and work of a perfect person, Jesus Christ. Believers in Christ have a secure bond with Jesus Christ, which is far superior to man's idea of a god. A religious life based on a faith of thoughts, an idea of a god, or false gods is a useless substitute for a life-changing bond with Jesus Christ. Besides, man's faulty views of faith or false creeds offer no help during trials. What a privilege to have a relationship with the true God through our position in Christ!

Living by Faith Is a Choice

Our decisions influence us negatively if they conflict with God's master plan. Decisions made contrary to God's will often have devastating results for us, others, and future generations. Either we use free will to live God's truth by trusting Him or we choose our way.

The Cost of Abraham's Wrong Decision

The Lord promised Abraham a son and descendants as countless as the stars (Gen. 12:1-3; 15:5; 18:19). God asked Abraham and Sarah to trust Him for a son even though she was past childbearing age. Time passed and they were still childless. Therefore, choosing not to trust God, they decided on a human solution. Sarah directed Abraham to father a son with her maidservant and Abraham agreed (Gen. 16). Abraham's wrong decision with the maidservant, Hagar, resulted in the birth of Ishmael, the son who became the father of the Arab nation. In His perfect timing God, the faithful promise keeper, kept His promise to Abraham and Sarah and blessed them with Isaac. Through their son Isaac, God fulfilled His promise of countless descendants—the Jews (Israel). Abraham's decision of disbelief resulted in conflict between the Arabs (Ishmael's descendants) and Israel (Isaac's descendants) that continues to this day.

Israel's Wrong Decision at Kadesh-Barnea

Another part of God's promise to Abraham was land for his descendants (Gen. 12:7; 13:17; 15:18-19). Time passed, Abraham's descendants (now called Israelites) were slaves in Egypt, and God was ready to deliver them and give them the Promised Land of Canaan. But were they ready to trust and obey?

As we look at events leading to Israel's opportunity to enter the land of promise, we first meet Moses whom God chose to lead His captive people (over two million) out of Egypt. God called Moses from shepherding to leading Israel to the Promised Land flowing with milk and honey (Ex. 3).

We read in Numbers 13-14 about the second year after God rescued the Israelites from Egyptian bondage. Israel had seen the mighty power of God displayed when He delivered them from slavery, leaving no question of His sovereignty and power. They watched God's discipline of the mighty Egyptians with plague after plague. They witnessed Him defeat the armies of Pharaoh by burying them in the Red Sea. Israel experienced God's daily protection leading through the pillar of cloud by day and the pillar of fire by night. In the desert, Jehovah God distributed daily provisions of manna and water for them. They feared God's thundering voice when He presented His commandments to Moses. Israel had already experienced God's mighty power, His faithful protection, and His loving care, but now they chose to doubt Him.

Israel's Choice Not to Trust God

God had promised a land for the nation of Israel and now He wanted to present the land to them. Two years after God delivered Abraham's descendants from bondage in Egypt they arrived at the edge of the land in the southern region of Canaan called Kadesh-Barnea. God's appointed time for Israel to seize and occupy the land had come. The time had come for them to claim the heritage that He had promised to their fathers. Now was their one-time opportunity to seize the land—their land. Therefore, God told Moses to send spies to explore the land (Num. 13:1-3). Moses sent a leader from every tribe—twelve men—into the land (Num. 13:17b-20).

The twelve men assessed the land and returned to Kadesh-Barnea with stories about the prosperity in the land. As proof of the land's abundance, two men carried back an enormous cluster of grapes on a pole. Twelve spies agreed the land was fertile, *"it truly flows with milk and honey"* (Num. 13:27). The excited spies reported the land was just as God said. What fertile real estate God was giving them! God, the true owner was giving it to them; He guaranteed the victory.

Israel Feared the Giants

Ten spies brought back a discouraging report about the inhabitants in the land of Canaan. They obsessed on the people and reported that they were strong giants. The more they thought about the inhabitants, the larger they seemed (Num. 13: 28-29, 31-32). This Promised Land was a terrifying place. How could they conquer giants that lived in the land? Who would want to live there? Perhaps they had misunderstood what God told them; how did God get it so wrong?

They refused to believe God's obvious statement, *"the land of Canaan, which I am giving to the children of Israel"* (Num. 13:2). They failed to trust the all-knowing, all-powerful, promise-keeping God. What was their underlying sin? In their arrogance, they believed they knew better than Jehovah God, so they opposed Him.

However, two faithful men—Joshua from the tribe of Ephraim and Caleb from the tribe of Judah—trusted Jehovah and opposed the ten spies. Caleb urged the Israelites to follow God's will and confiscate their land. *"Let us go up at once and take possession, for we are well able to overcome it"* (Num. 13:30). Joshua and Caleb believed God was superior to the giants.

Israel Perceived Giant Men and a Little God

The ten spies resisted Caleb's appeal and obsessed about how humanly impossible it would be to conquer these Canaanites. In their minds, the "giants" grew bigger and Jehovah God grew smaller.

> But the men who had gone up with him said, "We are not able to go up against the people, for they are stronger than we. And they gave the

> *children of Israel a bad report of the land which they had spied out, saying, "The land through which we have gone as spies is a land that devours its inhabitants, and all the people whom we saw in it are men of great stature. There we saw the giants (the descendants of Anak came from the giants); and we were like grasshoppers in our own sight, and so we were in their sight"* (Num. 13:31-33).

Although the time to take the Promised Land had come, Israel failed to act because they let fear instead of faith direct them. Israel focused on people instead of God. They thought about the size of the inhabitants and forgot the mighty deeds God had performed for them the past two years. They decided not to trust God—as if God failed to consider the land was filled with Canaanites. Israel chose to believe men instead of God.

Ten spies incited Israel to rebel against God and reject the chance to seize the land. Imagine, a four-hundred year old promise God was ready to keep, but Israel balked. Unfortunately, God's people accepted the majority viewpoint of rebellious disbelief. Israel complained and blamed God for their self-induced misery and spent the night weeping (Num. 14:1).

In the morning, God's people complained bitterly in the presence of God—the same mighty God who had delivered them from Egyptian bondage.

> *And all the children of Israel complained against Moses and Aaron, and the whole congregation said to them, "If only we had died in the land of Egypt! Or if only we had died in this wilderness! Why has the* LORD *brought us to this land to fall by the sword, that our wives and children should become victims? Would it not be better for us to return to Egypt?" So they said to one another, "Let us select a leader and return to Egypt"* (Num. 14:2-4).

Standing firm in their wrong decision, stubborn Israel refused to listen to Moses. Aaron pleaded with them to trust God. Joshua and Caleb tore their clothes (a sign of great anguish) and appealed to them to take the land. Instead, the unbelieving generation threatened to stone them to death.

> *Some minds are like concrete, thoroughly mixed up and permanently set.*

Additional conversation occurred between God and Moses. God told Moses He would start a nation from Moses' descendants. *"Then the LORD said to Moses: 'How long will these people reject Me? And how long will they not believe Me, with all the signs which I have performed among them? I will strike them with the pestilence and disinherit them, and I will make of you a nation greater and mightier than they'"* (Num. 14:11-12).

Amazingly, Moses disagreed and petitioned God pleading for mercy for Israel. *"Pardon the iniquity of this people, I pray, according to the greatness of Your mercy, just as You have forgiven this people, from Egypt even until now"* (v. 19). God did pardon them (v. 20), but they would suffer consequences for their sinful unbelief. God records their penalty in Numbers 14:26-33:

> 26 *And the LORD spoke to Moses and Aaron, saying,*
> 27 *"How long shall I bear with this evil congregation who complain against Me? I have heard the complaints which the children of Israel make against Me.*
> 28 *Say to them, 'As I live,' says the LORD, 'just as you have spoken in My hearing, so I will do to you:*
> 29 *The carcasses of you who have complained against Me shall fall in this wilderness, all of you who were numbered, according to your entire number, from twenty years old and above.*
> 30 *Except for Caleb the son of Jephunneh and Joshua the son of Nun, you shall by no means enter the land which I swore I would make you dwell in.*
> 31 *But your little ones, whom you said would be victims, I will bring in, and they shall know the land which you have despised.*

> 32 *But as for you, your carcasses shall fall in this wilderness.*
> 33 *And your sons shall be shepherds in the wilderness forty years, and bear the brunt of your infidelity, until your carcasses are consumed in the wilderness.'*

After Moses warned the children of Israel of God's judgment on them, they mourned. Now because of fear they decided to obey, but it was too late—obedience must be on God's terms and immediate. Moses warned them not to advance because the Lord wouldn't give them the victory. In defiance, Israel attacked the Canaanites and lost the battle (Num. 14:39-45).

> *Opportunity may knock once,*
> *but temptation bangs on your door forever.*

Although God kept His promises of land, He delayed its fulfillment. By making wrong choices, the first generation lost their chance to enjoy the land. God sentenced Israel to wander in the desert for forty years, a journey which they easily could have traveled through in eleven days. God gave these prideful people what they wanted—they thought dying would be better than taking the land. Israel didn't want to enter the land by faith and obedience, so they would never enter it. God sentenced them to meander in circles forty years until their rebellious generation died off. Their children plus Joshua and Caleb would occupy the land. The ten spies who gave an evil report died of a plague before the Lord (Num. 14:36-38).

Not only did the wrong decision cause them to lose the land, it caused the death of their generation (about two million people) in the desert. Is fighting God worth it?

> *When we choose to sin, we choose to have sin's consequences.*

When we make a wrong decision apart from God's will, we may miss an opportunity God provided. When choosing a career or a job offer, do you fail to seek God's guidance and miss His best? If you marry outside God's will, you will miss the Lord's handpicked selection. Our wrong decisions not only cause us suffering, but they cause pain to others. Our wrong use of free will detours us from living by faith.

Striving to Keep "The Ten" Is Failure

Betty believed a good Christian must keep the Ten Commandments. She was discouraged because no matter how hard she tried, she couldn't keep them. The more we *try* to keep the Commandments the more we fail; sinful people can't keep His perfect standards (Rom. 7:18).

Unfortunately, the majority of believers think the rule of life rests in the Ten Commandments (the moral law) given at Mount Sinai. The majority think keeping the Law means the Ten Commandments. They don't know that the Ten are part of 613 commandments which God says must be kept to be saved. The Law exposes our failure to keep God's standards by showing us our sin (Rom. 3:20) and reveals our need for a Savior.

> *As sinners, the law revealed our need of deliverance from the penalty of sin; as believers, the law reveals our need of deliverance from the power of sin.* —Miles Stanford

However, like Betty, many are unaware how to live the Christian life without striving to keep the Ten Commandments. Most people mistakenly believe the Christian life is a moral life—an outward performance of doing good deeds and avoiding bad behavior. Since unsaved people can live moral lives, morality isn't the Christian life. Since the Ten Commandments show us our sin and need for a Savior, keeping them can't be the Christian way of life as the next quote aptly explains.

> *The Ten Commandments require no life of prayer, no Christian service, no evangelism, no missionary outreach, no Gospel preaching, no life and walk in the Spirit, no union with the Lord Jesus, no fellowship of saints, no hope of salvation, and no hope of heaven.* —L.S. Chafer

Therefore, if keeping the Ten Commandments isn't the Christian life, then what is Christian living?

If Not Mount Sinai, then Where?

Aren't we under grace, not the Law? Paul declares, *"For sin shall not have dominion over you, for you are not under law but under grace"* (Rom. 6:14). Since we live under grace, we look in the New Testament letters for living the Christian life.

The Lord Jesus gave us His commandments for Christian living. When Christ said, *"If you love Me, keep My commandments"* (John 14:15), He wasn't referring to the Ten Commandments. His commandments are instructions for living the Christian life, which include the "one another" commands and various other principles. Here are a few of Christ's commandments.

> *"This is My commandment, that you love one another as I have loved you"* (John 15:12).
>
> *"And be kind to one another, tenderhearted, forgiving one another, just as God in Christ forgave you"* (Eph. 4:32).
>
> *"Abide in Him* (1 John 2:28) *or be filled with the Spirit"* (Eph. 5:18).
>
> *"Walk in the Spirit, and you shall not fulfill the lust of the flesh"* (Gal. 5:16).

By faith, not striving, we keep Christ's commandments. When we trust Him, He enables us to obey and live by His commandments. Christian living revolves around Christ and His works through us, not around our performance. Law keeping, striving to please God through good deeds, following church standards and traditions describe religion—a practice of behaviors or service to appease God. Trusting Christ as your Savior and adding performance is false Christianity. In religion, the emphasis is on "doing" for God from your flesh—your own ability—and it excludes Jesus Christ.

> *Few believers know how to live by faith and instead, live by law.*

Living by law (religion) keeps the focus on self instead of Christ. In contrast, believers who live by faith experience a deep bond with Christ.

CONTRAST RELIGION vs. CHRISTIANITY	
RELIGION	**CHRISTIANITY**
Man's Way	God's Way
Work of Man	Work of God
Reward	Gift
Works	Grace
Christ Plus	Christ Alone
Do	Done
Achieve	Accomplished
Try	Trust
Hope So	Know So
You Need Us	You Need Christ
Sin	Son
Fear	Faith
Law	Love
External	Internal
Religious	Regenerate
Horizontal	Vertical
Actions	Attitude
Performance	Personal Relationship

When we live by grace and not by law, Jesus Christ becomes our motivating force; the law is no longer the motive or rule for living. A person, Jesus Christ, who loved you and gave Himself for you, replaces the Law. Jesus Christ is the new center and source for your life replacing self-centered (what I must do) living with Christ-centered living—allowing Him to live through you.

> *The Christian life is a relationship with Christ, living dependently on Him and pointing people to Him.*

Saved by Faith, Now Live by Faith

At one time I lived by the standards of false Christianity—"do this and don't do that." Although I accepted Christ as my Savior, my focus centered on me, on being good, how I was doing. I knew how to live by rules (law), not by faith. I had saving faith, but I didn't understand how to apply this faith to life, how to overcome the power of sin by faith. Gradually, the Lord led me to truths for living genuine Christianity—living by faith. Oh, the joy and peace I found in the meaning of *"saved by faith, live by faith"* (Col. 2:6).

Perhaps you think that your saving faith is lost if you can't believe God during a trial. Saving faith and living by faith is the same faith, only applied differently. The faith that saves believes one time on Christ's finished work at Calvary. After salvation, we use that same faith *repeatedly* to trust the Lord moment by moment in daily life, including during trials and in overcoming sin.

I will use the terms dependent faith, living faith, or consistent faith to refer to "living by faith" after salvation. To clarify further, both the faith that saves from the power of sin and faith for living are *dependent* faith—both depend on God's grace and Christ's work. Salvation can't be lost even when you can't apply faith to life's pressures. Your application of faith after salvation doesn't keep you saved, God keeps you saved unto eternal life (John 10:27-30; 1 Peter 1:3-5).

> *Christian living is trusting not trying!*

Live by Faith, Not by Works

In review, God makes two offers, one to the unsaved and one to the believer. To the unsaved, He offers salvation from the penalty of sin (phase one). To the believer, He offers salvation from the power of sin (phase two). Both phases of God's rescue plan include the same essentials: God's grace, Christ's work, and our trust. Both have the same terms: accept the offer by allowing Him to do the work.

Every believer accepted the first offer, but too many believers fail to accept the second one. Often believers mistakenly think they must strive to overcome the power of sin in their life. They believe they must ask God to help them in their determination to do better. However, God's Word states the Christian life is lived by faith, not performance. *"As you have therefore received Christ Jesus the Lord, so walk in Him"* (Col. 2:6). We trusted our Father's salvation plan from sin's penalty; now, as believers, we must trust that He saved us from the *power* of sin in our daily life (Rom. 6:11*). Until we walk in dependence on the Spirit, we can't defeat the lust of the flesh (Gal. 5:16).

A believer may wonder why he had difficulty understanding his salvation was by trust, not by works. Now after salvation he again struggles to be good; he believes the Christian life is a life of good behavior, of following rules. He thinks living by faith is too effortless; thus, he seeks to please God by following rules. Therefore, he places himself under the bondage of law and he remains under the power of sin from which Christ freed him. Instead of living by faith and claiming the resurrection power to overcome sin, he continues to work. He continues trying—he tries to solve his problems and defeat sin by himself. The believer who fails to rely on the Lord fails to advance spiritually. Believers must trust in Christ's finished work—for spiritual birth and for spiritual growth.

> *Living under law places rules above a relationship with Christ.*

Spiritual development is the work of the Holy Spirit. Our Lord Jesus revealed, *"He* [the Spirit of Truth] *will glorify Me, for He will take* [draw upon, receive] *of what is Mine and declare* [transmit, disclose] *it to you"* (John 16:14). The Spirit's work of displaying Christ-like nature in us happens when we yield to Him by faith. We yield when we trust the Lord, when we surrender our will to His will. Only then can the Sprit teach us and mold us to the likeness of Christ.

---

* For an in-depth explanation about overcoming sin, see Rom. 6:11 in chapter nine.

> *Christian living isn't overwork by striving;*
> *it's the overflow of Christ's life through us.*

The hymn, "My Faith Looks Up to Thee" pictures saving faith and a desire to live by faith. This hymn has comforted generations around the world as the following account of one incident describes.

> Mrs. Layyah Barakat, a native of Syria, was educated in Beirut and taught for a time in Egypt. Driven out in 1882 by the insurrection of Arabi Pasha, she (with her husband and child) came to America by way of Malta and Marseilles. Her past is a strange illustration of God's providential care, since they were without any direction or friends in Philadelphia when they landed. But the Lord took them into His own keeping, and brought them to those who had known of her in Syria. While in this country she frequently addressed large audiences, to whom her deep earnestness and broken but piquant English proved unusually attractive. Among other incidents, she related she had seen the conversion of her whole family. Her mother, sixty-two years of age, had been taught, "My Faith Looks Up to Thee" in Arabic. They would sit on the house roof and repeat it together. When the news came back to Syria that the daughter was safe in America, the mother could send her no better proof of her faith and love than in the beautiful words of this hymn, assuring her that her faith still looked up to Christ.
>
> *http://www.hymntime.com*

As you meditate on this prayer-like hymn look for examples of both saving faith in Christ our Savior and living by faith in Him.

> **MY FAITH LOOKS UP TO THEE**
> *"Looking unto Jesus, the author and finisher of our faith"* (Heb. 12:2).
>
> My faith looks up to Thee,
> Thou Lamb of Calvary, Savior divine!
> Now hear me while I pray, take all my guilt away,
> O let me from this day be wholly Thine!
>
> May Thy rich grace impart
> Strength to my fainting heart, my zeal inspire!
> As Thou hast died for me, O may my love to Thee,
> Pure warm, and changeless be, a living fire!
>
> While life's dark maze I tread,
> And griefs around me spread, be Thou my Guide;
> Bid darkness turn to day, wipe sorrow's tears away,
> Nor let me ever stray from Thee aside.
>
> When ends life's transient dream,
> When death's cold sullen stream over me roll;
> Blest Savior, then in love, fear and distrust remove;
> O bear me safe above, a ransomed soul!
>
> ~ Ray Palmer, 1808-1887 ~

Living by Faith Is a Choice

We can use our free will to live our way or God's way by faith. Learning to live by faith happens gradually when we stay connected to Christ. Trust is a decision to stay-connected to (abide in) Christ like a branch to a vine. Just as a vine produces fruit through the limb that stays connected, so also, God produces the fruit of the Spirit (Gal. 5:22-23) as we stay connected to Christ. Staying connected to Christ, our vine, means reliance on Him (John 15:1-5). A dependent connection on Jesus Christ is the means for growing in faith.

> *By faith, I choose to allow Christ to shine through my life.*

The Family of God

When you believed in Christ, God the Holy Spirit placed you in the family of God (1 Cor. 12:13). The Spirit's placement into God's family is called the baptism of the Spirit. Our English word "baptize" is a transliteration of the Greek word *baptizō.* A transliteration differs from a translation, which gives the word an English equivalent. In transliteration, the translators simply carry over the Greek letters. The Greek word *baptizō* means, "to put into, to identify with, to immerse." Therefore, the Spirit identified you in Christ and in the family of God at the moment your placed your faith in Christ.

Biblical writers and other writers used the Greek word *baptizō* in various contexts. For example, Xenophon, a Greek soldier and writer in the fourth century B.C., wrote that Spartan soldiers dipped their spears into pigs' blood before engaging in battle. They believed that by identifying their spears with blood, the spear's nature changed from a hunting spear to a warrior spear. Soldiers referred to the dipping into the blood as *baptizō*.

In the fifth century B.C., Euripides, a Greek dramatist, used *baptizō* to describe a sinking ship, thus identified baptized or immersed with the water, so it no longer floats.

In ancient Greek literature, the term *baptizō* was connected with the phrase "over head and ears in debt." The concept is identification, placed in union with, or drowned in debt.

The moment someone believes in Jesus Christ, the Holy Spirit baptizes, that is, identifies the new believer with the death, burial, and resurrection of Christ. God identifies the new believer with Christ; the believer is hidden (submersed) in union with Christ (Col. 3:3).

What Is Fellowship?

Fellowship is from the Greek word *koinōnia*, and means, "sharing or having in common, communion." *Koinōnia* is Christian fellowship or communion with God or with fellow Christians. It is said in particular of the early Christian community—an association of people who shared common beliefs or activities. Christian fellowship is a key aspect of the Christian life. Believers in Christ should come together in love, faith, and encouragement—the essence of koinonia. To have fellowship also means to have agreement with each other. *"Can two walk together, unless they are agreed?"* (Amos 3:3). If we are disagreeing, we can't have fellowship.

Fellowship is a close association, a joint participation, or friendship based on a condition of sharing similar interests, ideas, or experiences. An association of fellowship must include honesty, humility, and communication. If someone you know lies, you can't trust him and dishonesty is damaging to the relationship. Humility is the willingness to admit we are wrong, being able to take correction, and being teachable. We are good communicators when we share our opinions and thoughts, speak in a loving way, and show interest in the thoughts and opinions of another.

Can you have fellowship with your spouse if you are fighting? Teen, if your friends criticize one of your teachers, and you know that is wrong, can you fellowship with them? When co-workers degrade your boss, you can't agree and honor the Lord, so you can't have fellowship.

Fellowship includes love, unity, encouragement, enjoyment, trust, friendship, and warmth. Fellowship connects with people and isn't about connecting through deeds. Performance connects deeds to rewards; for example, study hard and get a good grade, work and earn a paycheck. Religion connects performing with pleasing God, but Christianity emphasizes fellowship or sharing in common with God through the person of Jesus Christ.

God intends we have fellowship with Him. The result of fellowship with the Lord is fullness of joy (1 John 1:4). His joy comes from sharing the mind of Christ, agreeing with His viewpoint. When we know the Lord, we can have joy in our fellowship with Him.

Our heavenly Father wants you to have fellowship with brothers and sisters in the family of faith (1 John 1:1-4). True Christian fellowship must have a common belief in Jesus Christ with agreement about who Jesus is, what He taught, and a belief that Jesus Christ is the Savior (1 John 1:3a). We please our Father when we enjoy fellowship with other like-minded Christians.

Christian fellowship means sharing about Christ; we talk about Christ and His importance. The apostle John writes about fellowship. *"That which we have seen and heard we declare to you, that you also may have fellowship with us; and truly our fellowship is with the Father and with His Son Jesus Christ"* (1 John 1:3). How often do we share truths about our Lord Jesus and His Word when we gather with other believers?

The Difference between Family and Fellowship

Although all believers are in the family of God, not all believers have "fellowship" with God.

FAMILY OF GOD vs. FELLOWSHIP WITH GOD	
FAMILY OF GOD	**FELLOWSHIP WITH GOD**
1. Entered at a *point in time when born again* (John 1:12-13, 3:1-18, 1 John 3:2)	1. Enjoyed in the *present* if a believer *walks in the light* (1 John 1:3-7)
2. True of *all* genuine believers in Christ (Gal. 3:26; 1 John 5:1)	2. *Not* true of all believers…"if" (1 John 1:5-10)
3. Sins are *positionally/judicially* forgiven (Eph. 1:7; Col. 2:13; 1 John 2:12)	3. Sins may be *parentally* forgiven (1 John 1:9)
4. *Faith* alone required (John 1:12; Gal. 3:26)	4. *Faith* and *confession of sin* is required (1 John 1:9; Heb. 11:6)
5. Evidenced by a *new nature* (2 Peter 1:3-4), God's *chastisement* (Heb. 12:6-8), becoming a *new creation* (2 Cor. 5:17)	5. Evidenced by *obedience* to God's will (1 John 2:3-6) and *love* for other believers (1 John 2:7-11)

We read 1 John 1:1–2:2 which describes the biblical experience of fellowship, our next topic.

1 John 1:1-10:
1 *That which was from the beginning, which we have heard, which we have seen with our eyes, which we have looked upon, and our hands have handled, concerning the Word of life–*
2 *the life was manifested, and we have seen, and bear witness, and declare to you that eternal life which was with the Father and was manifested to us–*
3 *that which we have seen and heard we declare to you, that you also may have fellowship with us; and truly our fellowship is with the Father and with His Son Jesus Christ.*
4 *And these things we write to you that your joy may be full.*
5 *This is the message which we have heard from Him and declare to you, that God is light and in Him is no darkness at all.*
6 *If we say that we have fellowship with Him, and walk in darkness, we lie and do not practice the truth.*
7 *But if we walk in the light as He is in the light, we have fellowship with one another, and the blood of Jesus Christ His Son cleanses us from all sin.*
8 *If we say that we have no sin, we deceive ourselves, and the truth is not in us.*
9 *If we confess our sins, He is faithful and just to forgive us our sins and to cleanse us from all unrighteousness.*
10 *If we say that we have not sinned, we make Him a liar, and His word is not in us.*

1 John 2:1-2:
1 *My little children, these things I write to you, so that you may not sin. And if anyone sins, we have an Advocate with the Father, Jesus Christ the righteous.*
2 *And He Himself is the propitiation for our sins, and not for ours only but also for the whole world.*

What is the Basis for Fellowship with God? (1 John 1:5).

God is light (righteousness) and with Him there is no darkness (sin), which is a principle for fellowship with Him. Because He can't have anything to do with sin, we can't have fellowship with God if we have unconfessed sin. We must regularly admit our sin to Him (1 John 1:9) and resume our trust in Him, which restores us to fellowship.

We must be honest, humble, and communicate with our perfect God. Your relationship with Him must be honest since you can't pretend with God. Outwardly, you can hide hypocrisy, but God sees the heart—the center or core of life; the inner being (1 Sam. 16:7; 1 Kings 8:39). Don't take fellowship with God for granted.

How do you know if you are in fellowship with God?

The test for fellowship is recorded in 1 John 1:6-10.

1. *"If we say that we have fellowship with Him, and walk in darkness, we lie and do not practice the truth"* (v. 6). Whenever we lie or behave in a deceitful way, we sin and aren't in fellowship. We don't have agreement, honesty, humility or right communication, thus we don't have fellowship.

2. *"But if we walk in the light as He is in the light, we have fellowship with one another, and the blood of Jesus Christ His Son cleanses us from all sin"* (v. 7). To walk in the light means living by God's truth, following His will. When we walk in the light of God's truth, we have fellowship with Him and with other believers.

3. *"If we say that we have no sin, we deceive ourselves, and the truth is not in us"* (v. 8). To have fellowship we must agree with the truth that we have a sin nature, which manifests sins. If we deny our sin nature, we deceive ourselves.

4. *"If we confess our sins, He is faithful and just to forgive us our sins and to cleanse us from all unrighteousness"* (v. 9). Sin breaks fellowship

with the Lord. Confession of sin restores fellowship and immediate admission of sin keeps fellowship intact.

5. *"If we say that we have not sinned, we make Him a liar, and His word is not in us"* (v. 10). God calls us a liar when we say we haven't sinned or we excuse sin, and He tells us this attitude indicates His truth isn't in us. Therefore, we don't have agreement, honesty, humility, and right communication, hence, there is no fellowship. When we deceive ourselves, we pretend to be something we aren't. A Christian is miserable in his choice to hide his sin. A believer who chooses to excuse sin misses fellowship with Christ, which hinders his relationship with Him.

6. *"My little children, these things I write to you, so that you may not sin. And if anyone sins, we have an Advocate with the Father, Jesus Christ the righteous"* (1 John 2:1). But if you do sin, remember you have an advocate with the Father. Jesus is with you and pleads for you at God's throne (Rom. 8:34). Your heavenly Father forgives your sins every time you confess them to Him.

Living in Fellowship—The Spirit-filled Believer

Fellowship with God is another term for being filled with the Holy Spirit, the biblical meaning of spirituality. God commands us to be filled with the Spirit (Acts 2:4; 4:31; Eph. 5:18). The filling of the Spirit is synonymous with being under the Spirit's control (Eph. 5:18), with surrendering your will to God's (Rom 12:1-2), and with allowing the Spirit to guide you (Rom. 8:14). Being Spirit controlled doesn't mean the loss of free will. Instead, the Spirit controlled believer exercises his free will to follow the will of the Spirit. In other words, being filled with the Spirit (walking in the Spirit) is living by faith.

How can you live by the Spirit? Many are deceived into thinking that they must restrain the sin nature, at least in some degree, and then they can live by the Spirit. That is backwards since it is impossible to tame or control the sin nature. Instead, we live in the Spirit, that is, we trust Christ's finished work over sin. Only by faith can we subdue the lusts of the flesh. A Spirit-controlled believer gains victory over sin because the Spirit enables the defeat of temptation. *"Walk in the Spirit, and you shall not fulfill the lust of the flesh"* (Gal. 5:16). The Spirit desires dependency on Him to overcome sin. He is grieved by our sin (Eph. 4:30) since sin indicates failure to trust Him in overcoming temptation.

Why is it so necessary to be a Spirit-filled Christian? What benefits result from the filling of the Spirit? When we trust Him, the Spirit produces Christ-likeness (Gal. 5:22-23) in and through us. Victory over sin occurs when we respond to the Word of God (walk in the Light) in faith (1 John 1:7). Finally, the Spirit-filled believer yields acts of worship and praise (Eph. 5:18-20), compliance to God (Eph. 5:21), and service (Rom. 12:1; Eph. 6:7; Phil. 2:17). By faith, you trust the Spirit of the Lord to produce the character of Christ in and through you.

Family Position and Fellowship Condition

As a believer your status with God, based on your position in Christ, is unbreakable. You are in the family of God as His child forever (1 John 5:13; Rom. 8:39-39).

Consider a modern illustration of fellowship and family position. Since young Jack placed his trust in his parents for his needs and obeyed them, he was in a right relationship with his father and mother. In fellowship with his family, Jack enjoyed blessings associated with a harmonious relationship. However, when Jack disobeyed his father, although he remained a member of the family, he caused disharmony in their relationship and lost privileges. After Jack took responsibility for sin by admitting it, his father forgave him and restored him to fellowship.

The most miserable people are carnal believers—those out of fellowship with the Lord. To please themselves, they live independent lives outside God's will as did the son in the following parable.

A biblical parable is a short story with a spiritual lesson. The parable of the prodigal son (Luke 15) helps us understand our position in the family of God and our fellowship condition with God.

Dissatisfied living at home, the son asked his father for his inheritance. Although the father knew this was a poor decision, he allowed his son to exercise his free will. The son left his father's love and the security of home to indulge in sinful pleasures and enticements of the world. Sin delighted him because sin deceives. The foolish son exhausted his inheritance on pleasures. With no food or shelter, he accepted a job feeding swine; in his desperate state, he probably considered the pig's slop a food alternative. Coming to the end of himself, he reflected on the pleasant life he had left. Living in sin, he had given up the security and privileges of his father's house.

Miserable, hungry, and humbled, the Prodigal Son returned to his father and confessed his sins. His father received him (a picture of God's grace). Although the Prodigal Son temporarily lost the joys of fellowship with his father, he never lost his position in the family.

While sin has momentary pleasure, it enslaves us. Believers adrift in sin are under sin's domination, but walking by faith guards us from giving into temptations. *"Walk in the Spirit, and you shall not fulfill the lust of the flesh"* (Gal. 5:16). The pleasure of sin deceives us into thinking it will satisfy us, fill the emptiness in our soul—needs only satisfied by the Lord Jesus.

When we trust, we center our life on Christ. Our faith must depend on God's Word alone—not on others or ourselves. When we allow anything to distract us from Him, we toss aside our faith. David stop trusting God when he lusted after beautiful Bathsheba (2 Sam. 11). If David would have kept his faith focused on the Lord (faith dependence), he wouldn't have looked. The moment we become occupied with what we see, we forsake Him whom we can't see.

In summary, you may fall out of fellowship with God but you will never lose your position in the family of God. The Lord alone keeps you secure in His family no matter what you do or don't do, so you may rest or relax in His hand (John 10:27-28; Rom. 8:38-39). When you confess your sin and resume trusting, God restores you to fellowship. Trusting in the Lord keeps you in fellowship.

Living Contrary to God's Will

Moving forward without considering God's plan and timing may have unfavorable results for individuals and organizations. After praying, people often think that what they want, God also wants. Individuals fool themselves into believing they need something, so it must be God's will. They fail to follow God's guidance and leading.

Often pastors fail to heed God's guidance and leading. Because pastors and their congregations so desperately want a church building or a building addition, they believe God wants it for them. The church may not have the financial means so they hold fundraisers and pressure members to pledge contributions. Pastors or leaders who direct their congregations to overextend financially not only set a poor financial example but also ignore God's will.

Succeeding on our terms is a failure to live by faith. When a church does achieve its goal in their strength and determination, they failed to allow God to direct and orchestrate matters to provide His best. Moving independently of the Lord may shift attention from the Lord to the project. In addition, striving without the Lord may cause divisions in the church. Financial strain can cause members to leave the church, which further increases the burden. Because of these problems, some churches eventually have few members left and subsequently disband.

Moving independently of God's will is always a mistake because we will never know what God's best might have been. Trusting the Lord and waiting for His timing will result in His best provision.

> *Waiting on God's leading and timing always reaps His best.*

A Faith Adventure
Benefits of Seeking God's Will

The following is a present-day example of believers who chose to follow God's leading and how He honored their trust beyond their expectations.

Word of Grace Bible Church (WGBC) started meeting in peoples' homes in 1997. Every other weekend the pastor and his wife traveled from Duluth, Minnesota to Milwaukee, Wisconsin to minister to a small group of believers who met in homes. As the attendance grew, we began renting a meeting room. We continued to grow and rented various facilities. In 1999, WGBC became an official church.

The rental expenses of a meeting room twice a week plus an office for the pastor was the best use of money entrusted to the Lord's work since He wasn't providing anything else. Therefore, we prayed for a building so we could be better stewards of the funds entrusted to us. We believed it is biblical to purchase within our financial means and not ask for pledges from members based on their future unknown earnings. Furthermore, God wants us to give freely out of appreciation, not grudgingly from a sense of duty (2 Cor. 9:7). The Lord wants us to pray for guidance in the amount we should give in our worship offering. He desires we commit everything to Him, letting Him work out details according to His purpose and schedule.

God's Perfect Will and Timing

We looked at numerous buildings and each time a building didn't match our needs or our financial resources, we believed the Lord had something better in His time. Years passed and we still had no building, so we continued to pray and trust the Lord for a suitable building. Although we couldn't see it, our faithful Lord was indeed working behind the scenes, as He always does.

On Thursday June 12, 2008, a friend called to inform me of a church building for sale. Pastor and the deacon viewed it and confirmed it would suit our needs. We prayed for the Lord's will and direction as we moved forward. By Monday, we put in an offer along with the other bidders. Although we were becoming increasingly confident the Lord was directing us to this church building, we continued praying that His will be done. We prayed and trusted the Lord to work out the details if He wanted this building for us. By Wednesday June 18, the sellers accepted our offer above the other bids.

Shortly after we moved into the building, a pastor of the church that had formerly rented the building stopped in to talk with pastor. He indicated that in February, his congregation had offered to buy the building, but the owners had refused the offer. This pastor expressed his belief that God had indeed purposed to give us the building.

In addition, the Lord accomplished the financial details. In today's real estate market the asking price for this building could easily have been much higher. For adequate space and other good features, this building was an exceptional opportunity. Because it was well within our financial means, we were able to make a sizable down payment and easily manage mortgage payments. Banks and loan companies have tight regulations and restrictions for loaning to churches and wouldn't loan us money because we didn't meet their criteria. Again the Lord intervened and resolved our financial need when He motivated our sister church to give us the remaining balance in an interest free loan for three years.

We were delighted to see how the Lord orchestrated the proceedings. *"Blessed be the Lord, Who daily loads us with benefits, The God of our salvation!"* (Ps. 68:19). We knew and believed our Lord could do all the work, yet it was exciting to see it happen before our eyes. Just as He says, *"You will not need to fight in this battle. Position yourselves, stand still and see the salvation of the LORD, who is with you, O Judah and Jerusalem!' Do not fear or be dismayed; tomorrow go out against them, for the LORD is with you."* (2 Chron. 20:17). The Lord did the work of arranging the details as we waited in faith.

God Answered All the Facets of Our Prayer

We had prayed
- for God's direction and His will to be done.
- for a building that was centrally located to serve local communities.
- for a building within our financial means.
- that we would be pleasing to God.
- for God to receive the glory.

The Lord provided in excess of our expectations (Eph. 3:20). God enabled us to keep our thoughts on Him and do things His way. Not only did the Lord provide a furnished building (not just a suitable commercial building) with beautiful landscaping, it was a "turn-key" church building within our financial means. The church He provided is centrally located near the pastor's residence. In His perfect time, God worked out all details including the finances. The Lord showered us with more than we thought or expected just as He promised. To God alone be the glory for giving us His best (Eph. 3:21).

> *"Stand still and consider the wondrous works of God"* (Job 37:14).

Reflection Questions

Support your answers with Scripture verses and/or principles where possible.

1. Christianity is a _____ with the person of _____.

2. Biblical spirituality means "being filled with the Spirit" and occurs when we are _____ God.

3. When a believer sins indicating a _____ to trust, he breaks _____ with God but he remains in the _____ of God.

4. Give Bible verses and principles that prove you are secure in the family of God.

5. Both phases of God's rescue plan include the same essentials: God's _____, Christ's _____, and our _____; both have the same terms: accept the offer by allowing Him to do the _____.

6. What have you learned that you will apply to your life of faith?

CHAPTER 8 PREVIEW

∽ How Long Must We Suffer?
∽ When Suffering Lingers, Does God Care?
∽ God's Grace and Sovereignty Set Trial Clocks
∽ Spiritual Victory, More than Trial Removal

CHAPTER 8

God's Trial Clocks Are Precise?

Lord, How Long Must I Suffer?

Chuck suffered severe burns to his face, neck, arms, hands, and upper body in an industrial explosion. Although Chuck endured numerous surgeries before he could return to his routine, reconstructive surgery left him disfigured and horribly scarred. He was difficult to look at, yet people often gawked at him. Once while he was driving his car, the driver in another car stared at him, kept driving, and plowed into a utility pole. "I can't take it anymore," Chuck muttered. Miserable and frustrated, Chuck decided to stop at a nearby church.

Alone in church, Chuck grumbled about the scars and disfigurement. "Years of suffering are long enough to bear the scars," Chuck protested as he earnestly begged God to remove them. He waited a couple minutes and then raced to the mirror in the rest room. Disappointed to see the scars, he scurried back to the altar to insist that God remove the scars. Again, he checked the mirror—still no healing. In despair, Chuck crawled back and forth on his hands and knees in front of the altar as he repeatedly pressed God to erase the scars. Surely now God would answer yes, so he eagerly dashed to check the mirror but still no change. Chuck became furious and ordered God to remove the scars, then hurried to the mirror—still disfigured.

Didn't God care how intensely he had suffered? Now Chuck resorted to threatening God to remove these scars or else! Although he didn't know what "else" could mean toward the almighty God, he was determined. Chuck lingered to give God extra time to "obey" as he strolled to check the mirror but still no change. Now Chuck was fuming! He slowly drifted toward the church door and raising his fist toward the ceiling, he demanded that God remove the scars.

On the way to the door, he continued to pester God as he shuffled his feet to give God additional time to comply. Now outside he walked and "prayed," and as he looked upward he stumbled, fell, and injured his pride. Quickly he sprang to his feet and peeked around, hoping no one saw him. The fall broke his concentration. He stopped pestering God, and humbly walked back into church.

Finally, he realized harassing God was ineffective. He sat quietly in a pew. His spirit had begun to break preparing his heart to accept what God wanted him to understand.

God reminded Chuck of the sufferings of Christ Jesus. Three times in the garden, Jesus asked His Father to *"take this cup from Me"* (Matt. 26:39). The Father didn't remove it and Jesus accepted the will of His Father. Christ willingly suffered for *me*, Chuck reflected. As Chuck thought about Christ's submission to His Father, and the love of Christ for him, he recalled how much Jesus cares. He remembered His Savior bares scars, too—crucifixion scars for eternity. These thoughts humbled Chuck. His loving Father had brought Chuck to his spiritual knees. Now he was ready to accept God's plan for his life.

> *We can go through trials fighting and complaining, or God's way—in humble dependency.*

God's Plan for Chuck

In His perfect time, the Lord directed his servant, Chuck into teen ministry. Since many teens have hidden or suppressed emotional scars and hurts, Chuck had common ground with them. Chuck's physical scars became the basis to direct them to Christ who alone can heal them from sin's penalty and then heal their emotional scars. Through Chuck, God encouraged teens that He is always available for them. The Lord also used Chuck to reassure teens that Christ loves them, accepts them, and has a plan for each precious life (Ps. 111:3-4; Rom. 8:28).

> *When we are dissatisfied with God's answer,*
> *we have difficulty surrendering to His will.*

Lessons from a Leper

Let us compare Chuck's prayer with the prayer of the man Jesus healed from leprosy. Here we see two suffering saints, each with different prayer approaches. The way we ask is as important as what we ask the Lord in prayer. Chuck's self-centered, demanding prayer is a sharp contrast with the humble leper's prayer. *"A leper came and worshiped Him, saying, 'Lord, if You are willing, You can make me clean.' Then Jesus put out His hand and touched him, saying, 'I am willing; be cleansed.' Immediately his leprosy was cleansed"* (Matt. 8:2-3).

Contrast Chuck's prayer with five marks of the leper's perspective.

1. Sometimes our pride prevents us from seeking the Lord, but the leper came in humility with his problems.
2. He worshiped the Lord. Adoration for the Lord filled his heart.
3. He recognized Jesus to be the Savior. Not only did the leper believe Jesus was his Savior and his Lord, he also honored Him as the holy God. He recognized the holiness of God's nature; therefore, he made no demands, and struck no deals (Isa. 6:1-7).
4. The leper subjected his will to the Lord by asking if He was willing to heal him.
5. The leper announced his faith saying, *"You, Lord, can make me clean."* He didn't expect Jesus had to heal him or would heal him, but he believed Jesus could heal him of leprosy, if He wanted. The Lord delighted in the leper's attitude and was willing to heal him.

Timing for Trials Are Always on Schedule

God's schedule for Chuck's industrial accident began at a specific time in his adulthood while he was at work. The Lord God scheduled Joseph's trials to begin when his jealous brothers sold him into slavery.

God's Trial Clocks Are Precise

God's timing of trials are His, *"For My thoughts are not your thoughts, Nor are your ways My ways," says the* LORD (Isa. 55:8). Even Jesus Christ was on the Father's scheduled timetable for rescuing people from the penalty of sin. The Lord's timing for our trials is on His perfect schedule.

In His perfect timing, God custom designed a lifequake for H.G. Spafford the writer of the hymn, "It is Well with My Soul." Spafford endured much grief in the trial that prompted the writing of this hymn as noted here in the history of the hymn.

> After two major traumas in Horatio G. Spafford's life, he wrote this hymn. The first was the great Chicago Fire of October 1871, which ruined him financially (he had been a wealthy businessman). Shortly after, while crossing the Atlantic, all four of Spafford's daughters died in a collision with another ship. Spafford's wife, Anna, survived and sent him the now famous telegram, "Saved alone." Several weeks later, as Spafford's own ship passed near the spot where his daughters died, the Holy Spirit motivated these words. The words articulate the eternal hope all believers have, no matter what pain and grief befall them on earth. Ironically, Bliss, who composed the music, died in a train wreck shortly after writing this music.
>
> *www.hymntime.com*

Notice Spafford found comfort "going back to the cross"—an example for us when we face lifequakes.

IT IS WELL WITH MY SOUL

"You have dealt well with Your servant, O LORD, *according to Your word"*
(Ps. 119:65).

When peace, like a river, attendeth my way,
When sorrows like sea billows roll;
Whatever my lot, You have taught me to say,
It is well, it is well, with my soul.

> REFRAIN: It is well, with my soul, It is well, with my soul,
> It is well, it is well, with my soul.
>
> Though Satan should buffet, though trials should come,
> Let this blest assurance control,
> That Christ has regarded my helpless estate,
> And has shed His own blood for my soul.
>
> My sin, oh, the bliss of this glorious thought!
> My sin, not in part but the whole,
> Is nailed to the cross, and I bear it no more,
> Praise the Lord, praise the Lord, O my soul!
>
> For me, be it Christ, be it Christ hence to live:
> If Jordan above me shall roll,
> No pang shall be mine, for in death as in life
> You will whisper Your peace to my soul.
>
> ~ Horatio G. Spafford, 1828-1888 ~

Scheduled Times for Trials Serve God's Purpose

How painful for Horatio and Mrs. Spafford who suffered four great losses at one time. God sets the trial clocks for specific dates and times and adjusts the clocks for all ages—for children, teens, and adults. When children suffer or die, we often wonder why. We must keep in mind God's reasons for trials are benefits in disguise.

Benefits of suffering are:
1. To purify your faith
2. To encourage a consistent dependency on Him
3. To enable you to gain a deeper intimacy with our Lord
4. To draw us into the Word of God, the fuel for faith
5. To confront our motives
6. To reveal our insufficiency; to keep us humble
7. To challenge the degree of our love for Christ
8. To offer a future heavenly reward for trusting
9. To glorify God with our trust
10. To give opportunities to serve the Lord
11. To testify to others of God's magnificent character
12. To draw people to Christ for salvation

> *Our loving Father managers all things, including trials, to serve His supreme objective of displaying the character of His Son in His redeemed ones.*

Whether we suffer directly or by association, we must remember why God allows trials. When you read the next story, check how many reasons for suffering you notice.

My Little Lamb for My Purpose
Author unknown—adapted for use here.

"Tomorrow morning," the surgeon began, "I'll open your chest."

"I'm not afraid because Jesus is with me," the boy interrupted.

The surgeon looked up, annoyed, "I'll cut your heart open," he continued, "to see how much damage has been done."

"But when you open my heart, Jesus will help you," said the boy.

The surgeon looked to the parents and then addressed the boy, "When I see how much damage has been done, I'll sew your heart and chest back up, and I'll plan what to do next."

The boy firmly spoke, "Jesus loves me and will always take care of me. The Bible says He loves me. The Bible says He will be with me forever."

The frustrated surgeon spoke sternly. "I'll tell you what I'll find in your heart. I'll find damaged muscle, low blood supply, and weakened vessels. And I'll find out if I can heal you."

"Jesus will help you, too. He died for your sins, too. He loves you. If you believe Jesus is your Savior from sin, then He will be with you and keep you safe, too," the boy advised.

The day after exploratory surgery, the surgeon, with a heavy heart, retreated to his office where he recorded his notes from the surgery—damaged aorta, damaged pulmonary vein, and widespread muscle degeneration. A heart transplant will not help—no hope for a cure—just therapy, painkillers, and bed rest. Prognosis was death within one year. He could say more, but he stopped the recorder. Why? He pleaded aloud. Why did You do this? You've put him here. You've put him in this pain and You've sentenced him to a premature death. Why? The surgeon's tears were hot, but his anger was hotter. You created that boy and You created that heart. He will be dead in months. Why? He questioned some unknown god.

Afterward the surgeon discussed the prognosis with the boy's parents. He explained his difficulty understanding the child's faith and understanding why God would do this. The parents used the occasion to explain to him the wonderful news of Jesus Christ. The grieved parents were not hopeless. "We will miss him, but we will be together again," they told the surgeon. The parents explained God's ways are not ours, but His ways are always the best. They explained to the doctor, "The boy became God's lamb when he accepted Jesus as his Savior. The Lord didn't intend our son to live long on earth with His flock, but he will live forever in heaven. In heaven with others in God's family, our son will feel no pain, suffer no tears, and he will live with His Savior and best Friend.

"One day we will join him and we will know greater peace and joy there. On earth, God's flock will continue to grow as believers tell others about Jesus, the Savior of humanity. When the Lord calls our son home, it will be because He has completed His purpose for our son, His little lamb. Perhaps God used our son to salvage just one soul and bring him into God's family." The surgeon left the room weeping.

Before long, the surgeon joined the boy's parents in the hospital room and sat near the boy. The boy awoke and whispered, "Did you cut open my heart?"

"Yes," said the surgeon. "What did you find?" asked the boy.

The surgeon responded in a calm and caring manner, "Just as I thought, you have many problems with your heart. I can't change that, but I must tell you some good news. I accepted Jesus as my Savior. He loves me and died for me, too." The boy's beaming eyes and big smile said it all.

> *We do not necessarily doubt that God will do the best for us;
> we wonder how painful the best will be.* —C.S. Lewis

David Questioned God, "How Long?"

Examine with me David's agonizing but outstanding prayer recorded in Psalm 13. David probably wrote this psalm while fleeing for his life — probably from King Saul. He may have been hiding in a cave while Philistines were hunting for him. Whatever the case, David was in a desperate situation. In his weariness of body and mind, David poured out his heart to God. He lamented over his distress, *"How long, O LORD? Will You forget me forever? How long will You hide Your face from me? How long shall I take counsel in my soul, Having sorrow in my heart daily? How long will my enemy be exalted over me?* "(Ps. 13:1-2).

We see David's self-centered perspective as he mournfully complained that God had not comforted him nor delivered him from his enemies. Four times David asked how long he must wait for deliverance, which suggests the depth of his distress. Because he felt God had forgotten him and was ignoring him, he told God how he spent each day agonizing about that. David complained to God that his enemies triumphed over him because they thought God had deserted him. Since David was reacting from his emotions and not responding by faith to God's truths, he was impatient with God's delay in responding to his prayers.

> *Patience carries much "wait."*

David Begged the Lord for Deliverance

In prayer, David pressed for rescue and asked for divine viewpoint when he said, "enlighten my eyes." He feared he would die and his enemies would rejoice in his death — the defeat of a believer who put his confidence in the Lord. David was concerned about the Lord's honor: *"Consider and answer me, O LORD my God; Enlighten my eyes, or I will sleep the sleep of death, And my enemy will say, 'I have overcome him,' And my adversaries will rejoice when I am shaken"* (Ps. 13:3-4 NASB).

Remembering, the Lord's loyal love changed his perspective. David regained confidence in the Lord's loving-kindness to deal with his enemies. He expressed his renewed trust in God's unfailing love, *"But I have trusted in Your lovingkindness"* (Ps. 13: 5a NASB). David praised God for salvation saying, *"My heart shall rejoice in Your salvation. I will sing to the LORD, because He has dealt bountifully with me"* (Ps. 13: 5b-6 NASB). David recalled his commitment to trust the strength of his faithful Lord.

Confident that God would defeat his enemies, David vowed to sing the Lord's praises before the people. Because David believed in God's deliverance, the Lord blessed him with peace and joy.

> *In His wisdom, God regulates the timing and duration of trials according to His precise timepiece.*

Is Praying for Removal of Suffering Acceptable?

Job, in his suffering, questioned how long he would have to suffer. *"Will You not look away from me, And let me alone till I swallow my saliva? Have I sinned? What have I done to You, O watcher of men? Why have You set me as Your target, So that I am a burden to myself? Why then do You not pardon my transgression, And take away my iniquity? For now I will lie down in the dust, And You will seek me diligently, But I will no longer be"* (Job 7:19-21).

In the Garden of Gethsemane, Jesus asked for removal of His suffering and we can, too. When the suffering remained, Jesus' prayer illustrates His acceptance of the Father's will. We can follow the example of Christ and express our feelings, confess discouragement and other painful emotions (Matt. 11:28; 1 Peter 5:7).

Asking for removal of suffering by begging God to end your life is giving up on the Lord. Pleading to die is failing to trust God's perfect will in His custom designed trial. Begging to die is not the same as longing to go home to be with the Lord; it is all about attitude. In addition, our heavenly Father doesn't want us to turn to Him just because we wish relief. Although asking God to remove suffering is acceptable and natural, we must keep in mind God's purposes for suffering. Praying and then trusting the Lord to walk with you through the trial is the attitude God seeks.

Our Father wants to shape you to the likeness of Christ, which takes time. Therefore, our Father's perfect love and wisdom will allow pain or suffering to persist only as long as necessary.

The Lord Jesus realizes exactly how long the trial must continue and how intense the suffering must be to complete His work. God commands us to *"Be still, and know that I am God"* (Ps. 46:10). "Be still" means, "take your hands-off." Stop worrying, He is God; let Him work. During the trial, God commands us to leave everything in His care as the next hymn, "Be Still My Soul," encourages.

BE STILL MY SOUL
"Be still, and know that I am God...I will be exalted in the earth" (Ps. 46:10).

Be still, my soul! the Lord is on thy side:
Bear patiently the cross of grief or pain;
Leave to thy God to order and provide;
In every change, He faithful will remain.
Be still, my soul! Thy best, thy heavenly Friend,
Thru thorny ways leads to a joyful end.

Be still, my soul! Thy God doth undertake
To guide the future as He has the past.
Thy hope, thy confidence let nothing shake;
All now mysterious shall be bright at last.
Be still, my soul! the waves and winds still know
His voice Who ruled them while He dwelt below.

Be still, my soul: when dearest friends depart,
And all is darkened in the vale of tears,
Then shall thou better know His love, His heart,
Who comes to soothe thy sorrow and thy fears.
Be still, my soul: thy Jesus can repay
From His own fullness all He takes away.

Be still, my soul! the hour is hastening on,
When we shall be forever with the Lord,
When disappointment, grief, and fear are gone,
Sorrow forgot, love's purest joys restored.
Be still, my soul! when change and tears are past;
All safe and blessed we shall meet at last.

~ Katharina von Schlegel, 1752   Music: Finlandia, Jean Sibelius, 1899 ~

Are You Trusting His Schedule?

Until God removes our suffering, we must wait patiently and rely on His grace. The following account describes a believer who waited on the Lord in a difficult work atmosphere.

A Faith Adventure
Nathan's Dependency Viewpoint

Nathan was a talented professional musician in an orchestra. His performance satisfied the previous conductor, but the current orchestra leader never appreciated his performance. Every day the conductor would criticize and ridicule his performance in front of the entire orchestra; obviously, the conductor didn't like him. Nathan understood this long trial of conflict between him and the conductor was part of spiritual warfare. He continuously gave the problem over to the Lord who provided strength to endure under pressure. Nathan was confident the Lord was allowing this trial for his spiritual growth.

Nathan relied on His Lord and faithfully fulfilled his responsibilities to please Him. In His perfect timing, God removed Nathan's employment pressures. Living by God's principles, Nathan remained in the orchestra until the Lord directed him to more fulfilling employment in another orchestra.

> *God arranges trials to increase dependency on Him.*

When Suffering Lingers, Does God Care?

We pray and pray yet the trial remains. What do you think when the trial persists? When you are overwhelmed because you have much to do, does He care? Does He care when He calls your dearest one away? Maybe you think, if God cared, He would end this trial because He knows I can't endure it any longer.

When God prolongs the pain and anguish for years, the believer may doubt whether God cares. We may identify with Job who despaired, *"For now I will lie down in the dust, And You will seek me diligently, But I will no longer be"* (Job 7:21b).

Again Job expressed his misery, *"For the thing I greatly feared has come upon me, And what I dreaded has happened to me. I am not at ease, nor am I quiet; I have no rest, for trouble comes"* (Job 3:25-26). Job complained about his misery, *"When I lie down, I say, 'When shall I arise, And the night be ended?' For I have had my fill of tossing till dawn. My flesh is caked with worms and dust, My skin is cracked and breaks out afresh"* (Job 7:4-5).

Yes, it's difficult to feel God cares when He doesn't respond the way we want or on our schedule. Remember the principle: we can't always trust our feelings, but we can always trust God's Word. *"Many are the afflictions of the righteous, But the* LORD *delivers him out of them all"* (Ps. 34:19).

We pray but the suffering lingers with no ending in sight, so we wonder if God cares. Our Father's "yes" answers aren't dependent on how many are praying, the amount of faith we have, how intensely and long we pray, or how long we suffered. Responses to prayers are solely dependent on God and His plan. *"The* LORD *is righteous in all His ways, Gracious in all His works. The* LORD *is near to all who call upon Him, To all who call upon Him in truth"* (Ps. 145:17-18). Our Father responds independently according to His perfect schedule.

> *God's trial clock is set to His time.*

The children of Israel complained that God didn't care about them (Isa. 40:27). Of course, they were wrong as Isaiah chapter forty pictures God's greatness, His power, and His sovereignty. Notice God isn't too superior to care for His children. He is the everlasting God, the Creator who never tires and His understanding is incomprehensible (v. 28). Take time to meditate on God's comfort recorded in Isaiah 40. Will you believe what He tells you about Himself?

How can we think our Father God doesn't care? If the Lord didn't care, He wouldn't send lifequakes to draw you nearer to see His attention and interest in you. Allowing lifequakes demonstrates His faithfulness in His desire to conform you to the likeness of His Son. *"I know, O LORD, that Your judgments are righteous, And that in faithfulness You have afflicted me"* (Ps. 119:75 NASB). What an honor, God wants to mold us to be like Christ and not leave us as we are.

He wants you to be aware of Him and His supreme power to take care of you. He watches over you in trials with His hand of protection. *"[We] who are protected by the power of God through faith for a salvation ready to be revealed in the last time. In this you greatly rejoice, even though now for a little while, if necessary, you have been distressed by various trials"* (1 Peter 1:5-6 NASB). Yes, we rejoice because He provides everything we need. He cares how we experience trials and wants us to have joy (inner contentment) in them, to rejoice in His plan to shape us through the trial to be more like Christ. In addition, through our varied trials, our caring Lord wants to hear about our troubles. He tells you to *"cast all your anxiety on Him, because He cares for you"* (1 Peter 5:7 NIV).

Are you still unconvinced your loving Lord cares about you in your suffering? Then go back to His cross for the answer. Christ gave His life for you because He considered your lost condition. His sacrifice on the cross demonstrates His passionate sensitivity and awareness of your need for deliverance from sin's penalty. If He cared enough to endure the cross to secure eternal life for you before you belonged to Him, don't you think He cares about your less significant trials now that you are His child?

> *How much did Christ care about me?*
> *He stayed on the cross!*

Our faithful Lord further soothes us with His caring words, *"Now may our Lord Jesus Christ Himself and God our Father, who has loved us and given us eternal comfort and good hope by grace, comfort and strengthen your hearts in every good work and word"* (2 Thess. 2:16-17 NASB). Will you believe what the Lord says about Himself and His love?

During difficult times, believers throughout the ages questioned whether God cared about them. Over a hundred years ago, the Lord gave Frank Graeff difficult trials. During this time, he suffered great despondency, doubt, and physical pain. When he turned to God's Word, 1 Peter 5:7 gave wonderful words of comfort, *"He cares for you."* After meditating on that truth, Graeff wrote these lyrics for "Does Jesus Care" with the resounding affirmation in the chorus, "O yes, He cares!"

Audio at: *http://www.hymnalaccompanist.com*

DOES JESUS CARE

"Cast all your anxiety on Him, because He cares for you" (1 Peter 5:7 NIV).

Does Jesus care when my heart is pained
Too deeply for mirth or song,
As the burdens press, and the cares distress
And the way grows weary and long?

REFRAIN: Oh yes, He cares, I know He cares,
His heart is touched with my grief;
When the days are weary, the long nights dreary,
I know my Savior cares.

Does Jesus care when my way is dark
With a nameless dread and fear?
As the daylight fades into deep night shades,
Does He care enough to be near?

Does Jesus care when I've tried and failed
To resist some temptation strong;
When for my deep grief there is no relief,
Though my tears flow all the night long?

Does Jesus care when I've said "goodbye"
To the dearest on earth to me,
And my sad heart aches till it nearly breaks,
Is it ought to Him? Does He see?

~ Frank Graeff (1866-1919) ~

God's Grace and Sovereignty Set Trial Clocks

We must consider the duration of trials as part of God's grace. His sovereign timetable stems from His grace and is always for our benefit.

Jesus was on His Father's timetable beginning with His entrance into the world (Gal. 4:4-5). All events before, during and after the lifequake of Christ at Calvary were on the Father's perfect timetable. On the cross, our suffering Savior's torments lingered until God judged the last sin. His grace set the precise timetable at Calvary that secured our freedom from the penalty and power of sin.

Consider the grace of God exemplified through sufferings of believers in the Bible. For example, God cared for the apostle Paul, so He permitted his suffering to linger. Why? So Paul would learn to trust the sufficiency of the grace of God. Oh, how that grace viewpoint, which Paul wrote about, has blessed believers for centuries!

Will you trust the wisdom of God's precise trial clock for your trials? His perfect management of your trial schedule is an action of His grace. Our Lord desires that your faith be attentive to His grace, which can carry you through any trial. His power gives us everything we need to live by faith. *"His divine power has granted to us everything pertaining to life and godliness, through the true knowledge of Him who called us by His own glory and excellence. For by these He has granted to us His precious and magnificent promises"* (2 Peter 1:3-4 NASB).

> *Many church members who sing "Standing on the Promises" are just sitting on the premises.*

What is keeping you from trusting His promises so you can thrive during trials? "Standing on the Promises" is an outstanding hymn based on a Scripture verse and reminds us of the strength of God's promises.

> **STANDING ON THE PROMISES**
> *"By these He has granted to us His precious and magnificent promises"*
> (2 Peter 1:4).
>
> Standing on the promises of Christ my King.
> Through eternal ages let His praises ring;
> Glory in the highest, I will shout and sing,
> Standing on the promises of God.
>
> Refrain: Standing, standing,
> Standing on the promises of God my Savior:
> Standing, standing,
> I'm standing on the promises of God.
>
> Standing on the promises that cannot fail,
> When the howling storms of doubt and fear assail,
> By the living Word of God I shall prevail,
> Standing on the promises of God.
>
> Standing on the promises of Christ the Lord,
> Bound to Him eternally by love's strong cord,
> Overcoming daily with the Spirit's sword,
> Standing on the promises of God.
>
> Standing on the promises I cannot fall,
> Listening every moment to the Spirit's call,
> Resting in my Savior, as my all in all,
> Standing on the promises of God.
>
> ~ R. Kelso Carter, 1859-1928 ~

God Controls the "Stopwatch" on Our Trials

After struggling with chronic fatigue for over twenty years, I was near collapse. Daily exhaustion hindered me from routine responsibilities. When my health declined, my husband considered moving me into a nursing home.

The Lord, in His mercy, arranged a series of events that led to improved health. My chiropractor took neck x-rays and noticed dark shadows in my jawbone. I saw my dentist who determined that poisons from a failed root canal were weakening my immune system and slowly killing me. An oral surgeon extracted the tooth and almost immediately I felt renewed life. On His accurate timetable, my Lord responded with "yes" to years of prayers for healing from fatigue. *"There is an appointed time for everything. And there is a time for every event under heaven...A time to kill and a time to heal"* (Eccl. 3:1, 3 NASB). Just as God causes earthquakes to stop shaking, He limits the quivering of our lifequakes.

Our sovereign Lord controls the trial buttons on His watch.

Perhaps the Lord is waiting for our trust so He can resolve the problem; thus, trusting quickly may result in the decreased duration of a trial. Possibly our Father has mercy on frail faith by giving a quick response to prayer. On the other hand, God may strengthen consistent faith or wavering faith by delaying resolutions. Lingering trials can offer opportunities to honor God with steadfast trust in Him. In addition, even when we are relying on God, He may delay His reply while He works out the details—everything for our advantage (Rom. 8:28). When His purposes are complete, our wise Father will end the suffering or trial.

> *God regulates the schedule, duration, and the end of trials.*

Suffering Fades When Compared to Heaven's Joy

When we are thinking according to God's principles, our hardships help us shift our perspective from the fleeting temporal to the eternal realm. Oh, the joys of a perspective like Paul's, *"For momentary, light affliction is producing for us an eternal weight of glory far beyond all comparison, while we look not at the things which are seen, but at the things which are not seen; for the things which are seen are temporal, but the things which are not seen are eternal"* (2 Cor. 4:17-18 NASB). He compared his pressures and hardships to momentary, light affliction.

Paul wrote in 2 Corinthians 1:8 that his trials were "far beyond" his ability to endure, so he focused on his coming *"glory far beyond all comparison."* What trials did Paul have? Consider Paul's list of trials.

> *Are they servants of Christ? —I speak as if insane—I more so; in far more labors, in far more imprisonments, beaten times without number, often in danger of death. Five times I received from the Jews thirty-nine lashes. Three times I was beaten with rods, once I was stoned, three times I was shipwrecked, a night and a day I have spent in the deep. I have been on frequent journeys, in dangers from rivers, dangers from robbers, dangers from my countrymen, dangers from the Gentiles, dangers in the city, dangers in the wilderness, dangers on the sea, dangers among false brethren; I have been in labor and hardship, through many sleepless nights, in hunger and thirst, often without food, in cold and exposure. Apart from such external things, there is the daily pressure on me of concern for all the churches. Who is weak without my being weak? Who is led into sin without my intense concern?*
>
> *In Damascus the ethnarch under Aretas the king was guarding the city of the Damascenes in order to seize me, and I was let down in a basket through a window in the wall, and so escaped his hands.* (2 Cor. 11:23-29, 32-33 NASB).

Despite these trials, Paul viewed his severe and continual burdens as "light" or easy to bear. In his view, they were nothing when compared to the riches of eternal glory in the presence of his Lord Jesus (2 Cor. 4:14) when he would be like Him (1 Cor. 15:49; Phil. 3:21; 1 John 3:2).

Paul's heavenly perspective and confidence in his heavenly future helped him spiritually thrive amid his trials. He reminded the Corinthian Christians that this world and its current problems are passing away (1 Cor. 7:31). Paul declared the material of this world, what we see, as temporary, but what we can't see, the spiritual, as eternal. God will replace the material goods with a *"glory that does not fade away"* (1 Peter 5:4), *"His eternal glory in Christ"* (1 Peter 5:10 NASB). Ironically, Paul said believers shouldn't look to what we can see but what we can't see.

Al is a present-day example of someone drawing on Paul's perspective. When his house and all his possessions burned to the ground, Al shifted his thoughts from his material loss to his eternal treasures. He focused on the Lord and testified that material belongings matter little compared with the riches of heaven. Al believed, compared with eternity, present sufferings are like a split second, *momentary, light*. His perspective modeled, *"For I consider that the sufferings of this present time are not worthy to be compared with the glory which shall be revealed in us"* (Rom. 8:18). Al's heavenly viewpoint believed in God's perfect plan for him, including blessings in eternity. Sufferings can't compare to the glory of living with Jesus Christ.

> *A heavenly perspective is a tribute to God's grace.*

Spiritual Victory, More than Trial Removal

People think spiritual victory is surviving the trial without cursing God or giving up. Others proudly think they successfully overcame the trial because they didn't have an emotional breakdown. Remaining intact emotionally or psychologically by your determination isn't the victory God seeks. Any carnal believer or an unsaved person can survive intact by his own will power.

Instead, the Lord Jesus looks for dependency on Him so He can work to carry you with stability and peace. Our working Shepherd Lord never wants us to go through anything alone. He always wants to work in our behalf. When we allow Him to uphold us with emotional and spiritual strength, He gets the glory, which belongs to Him. Surrendering our self-sufficiency and allowing Him to carry us in His arms reveals His power and loving care.

Our caring Lord Jesus places us in exactly the right lifequake to "burn up" the spiritual rubbish—anything that hinders or distracts us from fellowship with Him. Therefore, to insist that God remove your trial is asking Him to stop burning your spiritual rubbish, which halts your spiritual growth. Have you been insisting God smother the fire of your trial? Are you feeling sorry for yourself thinking God doesn't want you to be happy?

The Lord doesn't intend to rob His children of happiness. Instead, the Lord Jesus may pour the cup of sorrow into any happiness that hinders us from dependent attachment to Him. Fellowship with the Lord Jesus is, after all, the true joy in life.

> *Burning spiritual rubbish stinks, but*
> *the sight of new growth brings delight.*

Spiritual Thriving Produces Contentment

Are you as content at work as you are at a lovely resort or hunting lodge in the woods? Are you just as content when you live from paycheck to paycheck as when you have money in the savings account? Although our circumstances may cause discontent, we can choose to live above them in contentment. Changing circumstances didn't alter Paul's joy—inner contentment, which he expressed to fellow believers in Philippi:

> *But I rejoiced in the Lord greatly, that now at last you have revived your concern for me; indeed, you were concerned before, but you lacked opportunity. Not that I speak from want, for I have learned to be*

content in whatever circumstances I am. I know how to get along with humble means, and I also know how to live in prosperity; in any and every circumstance I have learned the secret of being filled and going hungry, both of having abundance and suffering need. I can do all things through Him who strengthens me (Phil. 4:10-13 NASB).

Paul states he could do everything—including living in poverty or living with plenty—through Christ who gave him endurance for any difficulty. He wasn't boasting in his abilities but affirming the strength Christ provided for contentment regardless of hardships.

We close this chapter with the last two stanzas of Horatio Spafford's hymn of contentment.

IT IS WELL WITH MY SOUL

"You have dealt well with Your servant,
O LORD, according to Your word" (Ps. 119:65).

But, Lord, 'tis for Thee, for Thy coming we wait,
The sky, not the grave, is our goal;
Oh trump of the angel! Oh voice of the Lord!
Blessed hope, blessed rest of my soul!

REFRAIN: It is well, with my soul, It is well, with my soul,
It is well, it is well, with my soul.

And Lord, haste the day when my faith shall be sight,
The clouds be rolled back as a scroll;
The trump shall resound, and the Lord shall descend,
Even so, it is well with my soul.

Reflection Questions

Wherever possible, support your responses with Scripture verses and principles.

1. List several principles you learned from the leper.

2. What are biblical principles you will apply to lingering trials?

3. Name truths you learned about God's timing and duration of trials.

4. List ways trials are connected with God's grace.

5. What constitutes victory in a trial?

6. How does God's perfect timetable encourage you?

CHAPTER 9 PREVIEW

- The Battle for the Mind
- Gaining the Mind-set of Christ
- Whom Does God Help?
- Does God Give Us More than We Can Handle?
- Recognizing Your Spiritual Liabilities and Assets
- Replacing Our Weakness with God's Strength

CHAPTER 9

Life Time Replacements

Throughout life, we make substitutions and exchanges by trading or replacing used or obsolete items. Tradeoffs usually refer to losing one feature in return for gaining another with full knowledge of pros and cons. We exchange thoughts in a mutual expression of views, ideas, and information and sometimes we express ourselves in bitter exchanges. Sometimes we give something in return for something received. For example, we give money for food. Tradeoffs may occur because of compromises. We faced a tradeoff between buying cookies and buying medicine. We exchanged an old truck for a new Buick.

In the spiritual realm, Christ made the supreme exchange. This great exchange is the heart of the gospel—Jesus took our sins and offered us His righteousness. On the cross He traded acceptance by the Father for the wrath of God so His righteousness could replace our sinfulness when we believe. In the exchange, Christ gave His life (He died) so we might live.

To clarify, God does the exchanging since we have nothing to trade. The Lord can't receive our thinking, emotions, weakness, or sin in an exchange. When we give something from our sin nature to God, He disposes of it because He considers it rubbish. We don't exchange something of ours, but by faith God replaces our feeble qualities with something magnificent of His. For example, when we admit our helplessness and trust Him, we gain His strength (Isa. 40:29-31; 41:10). Dear believer, God's rescue plan includes His replacement tools for living by faith—tools for winning spiritual battles.

We begin by looking at spiritual battles and then continue with keys for replacing our weaknesses with His strength.

The Battle for Our Mind

As believers, we have spiritual battles, conflicts from without and fears from within ourselves. From where do our internal conflicts stem? Inner conflicts occur between our two natures: our sin nature, which we received at physical birth and our new nature in Christ, which we received at salvation.

Our sinful nature is evil and opposes God and His will. The heart—inner control center, part of the mind—is the seat of sin. *"What comes out of a man that defiles a man. For from within, out of the heart of men, proceed evil thoughts, adulteries, fornications, murders, thefts, covetousness, wickedness, deceit, lewdness, an evil eye, blasphemy, pride, foolishness"* (Mark 7:20-22).

At salvation, we received a new nature. We were born again spiritually; we were made alive in Christ. *"I have been crucified with Christ; it is no longer I who live, but Christ lives in me"* (Gal. 2:20a). The new nature seeks to please the Lord. *"Therefore, if anyone is in Christ, he is a new creation; old things have passed away; behold, all things have become new"* (2 Cor. 5:17).

The conflict between these two natures is ongoing. When our sin nature is winning the conflict, we sin and when our new nature is winning we are trusting God. Since sin is always a choice, we can't blame Satan, the world, or our sin nature—our three enemies. We choose to sin when we listen to our sin nature. God holds us accountable and He expects us to take responsibility for our sins by admitting them to Him.

Paul speaks of this inner conflict as the battle for his mind, which affected his actions (Rom. 7). If our new nature doesn't win the battle in the mind, we won't win the battle in our attitude, thinking and actions.

A Christian friend stated that when he was twenty-one years old his actions were carnal—fleshly, worldly, self-willed—in nature. The struggle between his two natures gradually caused his conscience to became calloused to the guilt from sinning, causing the battle between the two natures to subside. Oddly, during this failure to live by faith, he witnessed for Christ and encouraged other believers to press on in the faith. Scripture principles, conviction from God's Word, and encouragement from his family and friends restored this carnal believer to fellowship with the Lord.

Winning the Daily Battles between the Two Natures

Many believers have an incomplete or inadequate understanding of the meaning of Christ's accomplishments at the cross, thus they are carnal or try to live for God out of themselves. They struggle to please or serve God out of the ever-present weakness and poverty of themselves, out of the flesh. Are you seeking to serve God by striving to control your sin nature? Do you struggle to defeat sin?

The key to defeating sin is believing what Christ achieved at Calvary. To defeat our sin nature we must understand Romans 6:11-14, specifically verse 11: *"Likewise you also, reckon yourselves to be dead indeed to sin, but alive to God in Christ Jesus our Lord."* We need to know and believe what happened to sin and the sin nature when Christ died on the cross. Reckon means to count on it, to reason through, to believe it as true. Reckoning is a faith response. To overcome sin, we need to know the facts of Romans 6:1-10 and count them to be true.

Romans 6:1-11 (below) gives us the facts we need to believe to have victory over sin. Following this text is a discussion about these facts.

1 *What shall we say then? Shall we continue in sin that grace may abound?*
2 *Certainly not! How shall we who died to sin live any longer in it?*
3 *Or do you not know that as many of us as were baptized into Christ Jesus were baptized into His death?*
4 *Therefore we were buried with Him through baptism into death, that just as Christ was raised from the dead by the glory of the Father, even so we also should walk in newness of life.*
5 *For if we have been united together in the likeness of His death, certainly we also shall be in the likeness of His resurrection,*
6 *knowing this, that our old man was crucified with Him, that the body of sin might be done away with, that we should no longer be slaves of sin.*
7 *For he who has died has been freed from sin.*
8 *Now if we died with Christ, we believe that we shall also live withHim,*
9 *knowing that Christ, having been raised from the dead, dies no more. Death no longer has dominion over Him.*
10 *For the death that He died, He died to sin once for all; but the life that He lives, He lives to God.*
11 *Likewise you also, reckon yourselves to be dead indeed to sin, but alive to God in Christ Jesus our Lord.*

Not only did Christ pay the penalty for sin, He defeated the sin nature at Calvary. Therefore, when we trusted Christ, our past master-slave relationship with the sin nature ceased to exist (Rom. 6:6b-7). We were separated legally from the sin nature. God nailed the old man (all that we were in Adam) to the cross with Christ. Now God sees us as crucified with Christ. Because of the cross work of Christ, we are no longer enslaved to the sin nature.

Although the sin nature is no longer our master, it has not changed. It is alive and well, and it will never improve. We will always have the sin nature with us until we lose it when we go home to be with the Lord. However, because of our identification with Christ's death, God freed us from our previous relationship to the sin nature (sin's power). We don't have to live according to the flesh. We now have the option to walk in newness of life—live by the Spirit. Although our new nature desires to please God, in and of itself, it has no power. The believer's power source is the Holy Spirit for defeating sin. We trust in Him to overcome temptation.

Remember this important fact: Christ died to sin once and for all, and He now lives to God. Not only did Christ die "for our sins," He also died "unto" the sin nature. He died to break the sin nature's power to reign in our lives. Christ's death condemned the sin nature (v. 10).

What is true of Christ is true of me because I am in Christ, in union with Him. God identifies me with Christ in His death, burial, and resurrection. Since I have been co-crucified with Christ, I am dead to sin. I died to sin and rebellion against God. I am no longer a slave to my sin nature. God, the Holy Spirit, gives us the power not to obey the sin nature when we count it as fact that we are dead to it. The Lord tells us to consider ourselves dead (lifeless) to sin. We should be unresponsive to sin. Just as a dead body can't respond to temptations, neither will we respond to them when we remember we are dead to them. Dying with Christ was the only way your sin nature can be set aside so the new nature can live through you.

Our identification with Christ should determine how we live our life. A summary chart of the facts of Romans 6:1-10 follows.

SUBSTITUTION TRUTH	IDENTIFICATION TRUTH
1. Christ died for our sins (1 Cor. 15:3).	1. Christ died unto sin (Rom. 6:10).
2. Christ died for you (Rom. 5:8).	2. You died with Christ (Gal. 2:20).
3. Christ was buried (1 Cor. 15:4).	3. You were buried with Christ (Col. 2:12).
4. Christ was raised for your justification (Rom. 4:25).	4. You have been raised with Christ for sanctification (Col. 3:1).
5. Christ ascended and is seated at God's right hand (Eph. 4:10; Col. 3:1).	5. You are seated in heaven in Christ. (Eph. 2:6).
6. Christ freed you from sin's penalty (Rom. 5:9-10).	6. Christ freed you from sin's power (Rom. 6:6-7).
7. God accepted Christ's work on your behalf (1 John 2:2; 4:10).	7. God accepts you in Christ (Eph. 1:6).

Applying these Truths to Defeat the Sin Nature

Most people think that they can conquer sin by praying about it, just doing the right thing or not doing the wrong thing. Many believe that striving or working at not sinning is the way to stop, but this only increases sin.

Instead, you can respond to the truths you've just learned. You don't have to let the sin nature rule in your life by obeying its lusts. Yield yourself to God as instruments of righteousness (Rom. 6:11-13). Submit yourself to the Lord and enjoy fellowship with Him.

These truths must be our constant mind-set. We must consciously choose to *think* this way. We can pray: "Thank You Father that I am dead to sin and alive to you. I am going to count on that fact, present myself to You by faith. I am going to depend upon You to give me victory in this temptation."

What you think determines how you will respond to temptation. Temptation is not sin, but yielding to temptation is. You can choose to follow the sin nature that puts "me" first or place Christ first. As believers *"we are not under law, but under grace,"* a great motivator for living in the Spirit (Rom. 6:14).

> *"Not by might, nor by power, but by My spirit,*
> *says the* LORD *of hosts"* (Zech. 6:6b).

Some Misconceptions about Sin

Is sin fun? Sin can be fun as the Bible says, *"enjoying the pleasures of sin for a season"* (Heb. 11:25 KJV). Teenagers often think their parents don't have a clue because what they (their parents) are telling them is contradictory with what they are experiencing. *"As a dog returns to his own vomit, So a fool repeats his folly"* (Prov. 26:11). The Prodigal Son (Luke 15) probably had a terrific time squandering his inheritance, but when he ran out of money and found himself in a pigpen eating pig slop, sin was no longer fun.

Sin can have hidden and unexpected consequences—killing someone while driving drunk or an out-of-wedlock pregnancy. While you may confess your sin and God will forgive you, the consequences for sin usually follow you through life.

Some people mistakenly believe since we are God's children through faith in Christ, we aren't responsible for our behavior. They believe they aren't responsible for their sins because God the Father punished Jesus for them. Yes, God judged and punished Jesus Christ for every sin; therefore, He won't judge our sins and condemn us to hell. We have passed from death to life (John 5:24). Our sins can no longer *condemn* us since we believe Christ suffered the punishment for sin. Christ satisfied the justice of God through payment for sin at the cross (Col. 2:14). This is positional forgiveness—we are forgiven because of our position or union in Christ. On the other hand, God, our Father forgives our sins every time we confess them (1 John 1:9). This parental forgiveness restores us to fellowship.

POSITIONAL vs. PARENTAL FORGIVENESS	
POSITIONAL FORGIVENESS	**PARENTAL FORGIVENESS**
1. Offered to all *sinners* (Luke 24:47)	1. Offered only to *God's children* (Ps. 32:5; James 5:15)
2. Associated with *entering* the family of God (Eph. 1:7; 4:32)	2. Associated with *enjoying fellowship* with God (1 Cor. 11:30-32; 1 John 1:3-10)
3. *Faith alone* required (Acts 10:43; 13:38-39; 26:18)	3. *Repentance / confession* of sin required (Luke 15:11-24; 1 John 1:9) received by *all* believers in Christ (Col. 1:14; 2:13; 3:13)
4. Received by *all* believers in Christ (Col. 1:14; 2:13; 3:13)	4. Received *only* by repentant/responsive believers (Prov. 28:13; Acts 8:22)
5. Needed to go to *heaven* in the *future* (1 Cor. 6:9-11)	5. Needed to have the *joy* of your salvation in the *present* (Ps. 51:10)
6. Frequency: *once* and for all (Ps. 103:10-12; Col. 2:13)	6. Frequency: *whenever* the believer sins and the Holy Spirit convicts (Ps. 32:3-5; 38:1-18; 1 John 1:9)

God holds us *accountable* for our choices because sin is never justifiable. Although we are no longer under eternal conviction, we will suffer consequences for our acts of sin. For example, imagine you are in a courtroom charged with speeding. The speeding resulted in an accident that wrecked your car and caused injury to your back. You admitted you broke the law and the judge fined you two thousand dollars. A man in the courtroom had mercy on you and used his own money to pay your fine; therefore, judicially, he paid your debt and you are free to leave. However, there are consequences for your behavior; you have car repair expenses, medical treatments for your back, and perhaps lifelong back pain.

God is just and He knows sin (even when it's fun) is always hurtful. Sin hurts us and causes harm to others who by association with us experience pain from the consequences of our sin. A biblical example of consequences is King David who committed adultery with Bathsheba, another man's wife who then became pregnant. With that discovery,

David strived to cover up one sin with another by having Uriah, Bathsheba's husband, placed in the front line of battle, which guaranteed his death (2 Sam. 11). Sin caused David to be miserable and hindered his relationship with God, the immediate results of his sin. Eventually, David confessed his sins and experienced God's parental forgiveness (2 Sam. 12:13). However, God held David accountable and he suffered the consequences of his sins (2 Sam. 12:14-18).

Our sin harms us because it breaks fellowship with God. When you are tempted to sin, remember there will be consequences. We reap what we sow!

> *Forbidden fruit produce jams.*

Satan Strives for Your Destruction

Temptations come mainly from our sin nature because we carry it with us. However, other enemies that struggle for control of our mind are Satan and his world. Temptations from our sin nature are similar to those from Satan. We can rarely be certain from whom the temptations come; the source of temptation isn't important.

Although God limits Satan's power as he rules the world, his goal remains to defeat and destroy the believer. Satan uses his worldly attractions to sway us away from trusting God. As a result, our choice not to trust smothers our testimony of faith in Christ. Through his world system, Satan indirectly tempts us with fear, worry, despair, anger, hatred, tension, stress, strife, and every damaging thought and deed that is in opposition to God and His program. Satan's anti-God worldview charms our sin nature and tempts us to compare ourselves with others, to complain, to feel sorry for ourselves, or to think God has abandoned us. Therefore, when we are miserable with worry, fear, or anxiety, we give Satan reason to rejoice. When we trust ourselves instead of the Lord, Satan cheers with excitement. If we give up, we display a lack of faith in the Lord and Satan celebrates. If a believer becomes so despondent that he takes his life,* Satan succeeded in suppressing the believer and his testimony of the Lord Jesus.

Satan may use a direct approach to wound or destroy the believer. If Satan calls your name, he targets you for his destructive purpose as he did Simon Peter. In the upper room the night before Jesus' crucifixion, He warned Peter about Satan's attack and then encouraged him, *"Simon, Simon! Indeed, Satan has asked for you, that he may sift you as wheat. But I have prayed for you, that your faith should not fail; and when you have returned to Me, strengthen your brethren"* (Luke 22:31-32).

> *When Satan calls your name, Jesus prays for you.*

It appears that Satan tempted me to renounce reliance on Christ because of my poor health. My relentless exhaustion made it difficult to get up in the morning, get my sons ready for school, and then drive them. One morning as I struggled to get ready, an uncanny, ominous presence, unlike I had ever experienced, overshadowed me. A forceful thought entered my mind—just give up Christ and life would be better. For a moment I thought about the implication. If I deny Christ, I would be alone. The Lord reminded me of what the apostle Peter said, *"To whom should we go?"* (John 6:68). I uttered, "I will never give up Christ, no matter how awful things become." The eerie sensation left and has never returned. God's Word was my source of strength to overcome.

When Satan calls your name, he will use his worldly schemes to tempt you to reject or deny Christ and to abandon the use of God's faith plan. By faith, you can rely on the power of Christ to overcome the temptation. As it is written, *"No temptation has overtaken you except such as is common to man; but God is faithful, who will not allow you to be tempted beyond what you are able, but with the temptation will also make the way of escape, that you may be able to bear it"* (1 Cor. 10:13).

---

*Although God judged Christ for the sin of suicide, this selfish sinful act reveals a lack of trust. God gives the believer eternal life and protects him forever; therefore, a believer who takes his own life will never lose his salvation (Rom. 8:31-32, 38-39; John 5:24; 6:37-40; 10:27-30; 1 Peter 1:3-5).

Always remember, Christ defeated the power of sin and as a believer, you have Christ's power to defeat sin. You have a choice to follow the sin nature or submit to God (James 4:7).

> *The sight of a joyful, trusting believer enrages Satan.*

Relying on Christ when attacked by Satan or our sin nature is the subject of the next hymn. James Montgomery's "In the Hour of Trial" is a prayer, which clings to Christ as it reflects His suffering.

> **IN THE HOUR OF TRIAL**
> *"Satan has asked for you, that he may sift you as wheat. But I have prayed for you, that your faith should not fail"* (Luke 22:31-32).
>
> In the hour of trial, Jesus, plead for me,
> Lest by base denial I depart from Thee.
> When Thou sees me waver with a look recall,
> Nor for fear or favor suffer me to fall.
>
> With forbidden pleasures would this vain world charm,
> Or its sordid treasures spread to work me harm,
> Bring to my remembrance sad Gethsemane,
> Or, in darker semblance, cross-crowned Calvary.
>
> Should Thy mercy send me sorrow, toil and woe,
> Or should pain attend me on my path below,
> Grant that I may never fail Thy hand to see;
> Grant that I may ever cast my care on Thee.
>
> When my last hour comes, filled with strife and pain,
> When my dust returns to the dust again,
> On Thy truth relying, through that mortal strife,
> Jesus, take me, dying, to eternal life.

Look at Your Savior, Not Your Sin

Satan delights when our sin replaces Christ in our thoughts. Therefore, don't be absorbed with your sins, how guilty you feel, or the discipline which you deserve. Concentrating on your deplorable sinful state keeps you focused inward on yourself instead of upward to Christ. The only reason to consider your daily sins is to recognize them as engraved in the body of Christ and judged by God. We won't forget our sinfulness when we remember our sin-covered Savior. Consider His covering of your sin, respond by confessing sins regularly, and move back into fellowship (1 John 1:9). When we confess our sin, we can experience the peace of His forgiveness and that pleases the Lord.

God Rules over Satan and the Sin Nature

Remember, by faith our new nature has power to defeat our sin nature. The power God has given us is reliable. *"For God has not given us a spirit of fear, but of power and of love and of a sound mind"* (2 Tim. 1:7). Our prayers should include the petition, *"that He would grant you, according to the riches of His glory, to be strengthened with might through His Spirit in the inner man"* (Eph. 3:16). Believing God rules over Satan, the world, and our sin nature is essential. Unfortunately, we often live as if sin still controls us.

In Satan's slave market of sin, we had no power to overcome sin, but in Christ, we are free from its dominance and have more power than Satan has. God's truth affirms, *"because greater is He* [God the Father, Christ, and the Holy Spirit] *who is in you than he who is in the world"* (1 John 4:4 NASB). The Lord also assures us, *"but you will receive power when the Holy Spirit has come upon you* [the moment of salvation]*"* (Acts 1:8 NASB). And Satan hates the verse, *"that through death He might destroy him who had the power of death, that is, the devil"* (Heb. 2:14).

The Lord is our power source, but our enemy, the devil, uses every trick and temptation to keep us from using divine power. Relying on God's power enables us to defeat temptation (1 Cor. 10:13; Gal. 5:16).

Christ leads us in the battle over sin, the battle against Satan who seeks to control our minds and disable us in the plan of God. *"Now thanks be to God who always leads us in triumph"* (2 Cor. 2:14). Christian soldiers tap into God's powerful ammunition—His Word of truth and

His promises. With our shield of faith, we believe Him when He commands: *"Do not be afraid nor dismayed because of this great multitude, for the battle is not yours, but God's...You will not need to fight in this battle. Position yourselves, stand still and see the salvation of the LORD, who is with you, O Judah and Jerusalem! 'Do not fear or be dismayed; tomorrow go out against them, for the LORD is with you'"* (2 Chron. 20:15, 17). Look to Jesus in every battle in the fight of faith.

> *By faith, Jesus Christ, our Commander-in-Chief, leads us to victory!*

The Mind of Christ Holds the Power

Scripture commands us to have a mind-set or viewpoint like Christ: *"Let this mind be in you which was also in Christ Jesus"* (Phil. 2:5) and *"Set your mind on things above, not on things on the earth"* (Col. 3:2). Think about the things of God, His promises and character instead of your circumstances. A mind occupied with Christ will have His peace. *"And the peace of God, which surpasses all understanding, will guard your hearts and minds through Christ Jesus"* (Phil. 4:7). Through His Word, our faithful Lord seeks to change our thinking to agree with the thinking of Christ. As He commands, *"that you may prove what is that good and acceptable and perfect will of God"* (Rom. 12:2). The Lord commands us to control our thoughts, which shape our emotions, viewpoint, beliefs, and behavior. For this reason, assign every thought to be obedient to Christ (2 Cor. 10:5b). Have the mind-set of Christ and be occupied with His promises and principles.

> *We are what we think* (Prov. 23:7).

The Mind of Christ Restores Us

Because Mark lost substantial sums of money in the stock market, he felt anxious, angry, and hopeless. After meditating on Scriptures, Mark felt comforted remembering God was in control. As Mark reset his priorities, he redirected his thoughts and trusted God to take care of him and his family. When he viewed life from God's perspective, the Lord replaced his fears with His peace.

Whether the trial is huge like the "charge of the elephant" or tiny like the "bite of the mosquito," God's solution is the same: trust Him. Am I going to align my thinking with the mind of Christ?

> *In the battle for our thinking, the mind of Christ is our weapon.*

"May the Mind of Christ, my Savior," a favorite hymn of mine, uses the principle of Philippians 2:5 and reflects the believer's desire to think like Christ. In prayer-like form the believer asks, "May the mind of Christ," the "Word of God," the "peace of God" (Col. 3:15), and the "love of Jesus" live in my heart throughout each day in "all I do and say." As you think about the words, you will find additional gems of encouragement.

www.hymntime.com

MAY THE MIND OF CHRIST, MY SAVIOR
"Let this mind be in you which was also in Christ Jesus" (Phil. 2:5).

May the mind of Christ, my Savior,
Live in me from day to day,
By His love and power controlling
All I do and say.

May the Word of God dwell richly
In my heart from hour to hour,
So that all may see I triumph
Only through His power.

May the peace of God my Father
Rule my life in everything,
That I may be calm to comfort
Sick and sorrowing.

May the love of Jesus fill me
As the waters fill the sea;
Him exalting, self-abasing—
This is victory.

May I run the race before me,
Strong and brave to face the foe,
Looking only unto Jesus
As I onward go.

May His beauty rest upon me,
As I seek the lost to win;
And may they forget the channel,
Seeing only Him.

~ Kate B. Wilkinson, 1859-1928 ~

Improving Your Quality of Life

How would you improve your life? Would you begin a diet, join a fitness center, or take a class? Have you ever considered diet, exercise, or continuing education for your mind? Our Lord details a healthy diet for our thoughts when He instructs us: *"Finally, brethren, whatever things are true, whatever things are noble, whatever things are just, whatever things are pure, whatever things are lovely, whatever things are of good report, if there is any virtue and if there is anything praiseworthy--meditate on these things"* (Phil. 4:8). Improve your thought life with a change of diet—remove harmful thoughts and replace them with the thinking of Christ.

Keep spiritually fit by exercising God's promises daily. Meditating on His Word and memorizing Scripture verses are helpful exercises for gaining the mind of Christ. Instruction in God's Word offers the mind of Christ and having the mind of Christ leads to trusting Him.

> *Faith in the facts [of Scripture] alone*
> *gives the rest of reliance.* —Miles Stanford

Replacing Destructive Thinking

As the Lord instills the mind of Christ in you through faithful intake of His Word, you'll gain His viewpoint to replace your pessimistic thinking. You can choose to squash your sinful, negative attitudes by thinking God's way. God's Word of truth confronts the lies we too often believe. His thoughts are encouraging substitutions for your thoughts since there is power in His Word.

You Say vs. God Says

You say, "It's impossible."
God says, "All things are possible" (Luke 18:27).

You say, "I'm too tired."
God says, "I will give you rest" (Matt. 11:28-30).

You say, "I can't."
God says, "I can" (2 Cor. 9:8).

You say, "I can't continue."
God says, "My grace is sufficient" (2 Cor. 12:9; Ps. 91:15).

You say, "Nobody loves me."
God says, "I love you" (John 17:23b; John 3:16).

You say, "I can't figure things out."
God says, "I will direct your steps" (Prov. 3:5-6).

You say, "I can't forgive myself."
God says, "I forgive you" (1 John 1:9; Rom. 8:1).

You say, "I can't do it."
God says, "You can do all things" (Phil. 4:13).

You say, "It's not worth it."
God says, "It will be for your good" (Rom. 8:28).

You say, "I'm afraid."
God says, "I have not given you a spirit of fear" (2 Tim. 1:7).

You say, "I can't manage."
God says, "I will supply all your needs" (Phil. 4:19).

You say, "I'm not smart enough."
God says, "I will give you wisdom" (James 1:5).

You say, "I don't have enough faith."
God says, "I have given everyone a measure of faith" (Rom. 12:3b).

You say, "I feel alone."
God says, "I will never leave you or forsake you" (Heb. 13:5).

You say, "I'm always worried and frustrated."
God says, "Cast all your cares on Me" (1 Peter 5:7).

Prevent truth decay; brush up on Bible facts.

Continually thinking from God's viewpoint prepares us to be patient when waiting for an answer to prayer or the end to a trial. By believing His truths, we can expect fulfillment of His promises.

Replacing Previous Responses toward Grieving

When a lifequake strikes and your life is falling apart, you might think, how in the world can I continue? You may want to share your feelings, but you believe grieving over a loss suggests a lack of faith or is a sign of weakness. Contrary to popular belief, openly grieving reveals your courage to express your vulnerability.

Grieving a loss is a normal response. Job teaches us how to respond despite our grief. What was Job's response when he grieved his losses—children, wealth, health, and friends? Despite his grief he responded, *"And he said: 'The LORD gave, and the LORD has taken away; Blessed be the name of the LORD'"* (Job 1:21b). At first Job looked to the Lord, but as his lifequake progressed, he took his eyes off the Lord, looked at his circumstances, despaired, and slid into self-pity. Afterward, however, he resumed his dependent faith in God.

During our suffering, we may drift away from the Lord and linger on our circumstances. How long before we return to dependency on the Lord. We always have a choice to replace our negative, sinful thinking with the truths of God's Word.

Does God Help Those Who Help Themselves?

Some common clichés are misconceptions that need replacing with truth. Not a single verse in the Bible says or implies "God helps those who help themselves." The phrase "help themselves" includes trusting yourself, others, or using substances for solutions instead of God. On the contrary, you don't have to help yourself before God will help you because God helps those whose hearts are His, those who trust Him. *"For the eyes of the LORD move to and fro throughout the earth that He may strongly support those whose heart is completely His"* (2 Chron. 16:9 NASB). God is the helper of those who trust as the psalmist recognized, *"The LORD is my strength and my shield; My heart trusts in Him, and I am helped"* (Ps. 28:7a NASB). Use His promises to replace faulty thinking. God helps us because of His character, not because of our effort to help ourselves.

The Lord helps those who trust Him!

Lifequake—Thrown to the Lions

Daniel, an Old Testament believer, is an excellent example of God helping someone who trusted in Him. God's Word describes Daniel's response during one of his lifequakes. In 605 B.C., the Babylonians captured a young man named Daniel. In time, King Nebuchadnezzar gave Daniel a place of prominence in his kingdom (Dan. 2). Of greater significance, Daniel was a prophet of the true God.

Men under Daniel's authority became jealous of him. They deceived King Darius into approving a decree to prohibit praying to any god or man other than the king—a law that carried the death penalty. The evil plotters thought their scheme would doom Daniel to death. Threat of death for praying to his God was a test of Daniel's convictions. King Darius cared about Daniel and was unaware his trusted servant was the target of this treacherous plot.

How Did Daniel Respond to His Lifequake?

Daniel didn't behave with toughness or argue that the decree was unfair. Instead, Daniel faithfully worshipped and prayed to Jehovah God. Seeing Daniel disobey the law, his enemies hastened to remind the king of his ruling. When King Darius learned Daniel disobeyed the law, he was distraught and for the rest of the day tried to save Daniel. However, Daniel's rival subordinates demanded that the king keep his word to kill anyone who disobeyed the king's decree. Having no other choice, the king ordered Daniel to be thrown into the lion's den—a certain death.

Morning brought a surprising revelation to the evil schemers and the king. As the evil men removed the stone from the lion's den, they were shocked to see Daniel alive and well. Daniel testified that His God had indeed protected him because he was innocent in God's sight. King Darius commanded his men to remove Daniel from the den. Then he ordered the evil men, with their wives and children, cast into the den of lions. The king also decreed that his entire kingdom should fear and tremble before the God of Daniel.

> *The Lord gets his best soldiers out of the highlands of affliction.*
> —Charles Spurgeon

Trusting Him Day by Day

When I seek His strength as a replacement for my weaknesses and inadequacies, I remember the encouraging hymn "Day by Day." Carolina Berg wrote this wonderful hymn after she had suffered a lifequake. Here is a brief biography of Berg and the story behind the hymn.

Psalm 46 declares, *"God is our refuge and strength, A very present help in trouble."* There was once a young Swedish woman who, like the Psalmist, learned early on to trust in the Lord's strength each day to help her overcome her troubles and trials. Her name was Carolina Sandell Berg, and she was born October 3, 1832. She grew up to become Sweden's most celebrated author of gospel hymns, and wrote so many that she is often called, "the Fanny Crosby of Sweden."

Like many Christians, she learned when pain and tragedy strike, God may use that experience to deepen our faith. When she was 26, Carolina—or Lina (pronounced Lie-nah) as she liked to be called—experienced a tragedy, which profoundly affected the course of her life. She was with her father, a Lutheran pastor, crossing a Swedish lake. Suddenly the ship lurched, and before her eyes, her father was washed overboard and drowned. Lina had written hymns before, but now she poured out her broken heart in an endless stream of beautiful songs. Her hymns mightily influenced the revival that swept across Scandinavia after 1850.

The words of Lina Berg's hymns were popular because of the simple, beautiful melodies written for them, especially those of Oscar Ahnfelt who played his guitar and sang her hymns throughout Scandinavia. Lina Berg once said Ahnfeld sang her songs "into the hearts of the people."

Even Jenny Lind, the world-famous concert vocalist, visited factories and sang Lina's beautiful hymns. In Matthew 12:34, Jesus said, *"Out of the abundance of the heart the mouth speaks."* Lina Sandell Berg's voice spoke more than 650 hymns from a heart filled abundantly with love for her Savior. Carolina S. Berg, 1832-1903 wrote the first three stanzas. *(christianhistorytimeline.com)*

Verse Added to Day by Day Hymn

As Paul battled cancer he wrote:

The words of the precious old hymn, "Day by Day"—"and with each passing moment," have ministered to my heart of late. In addition, I've been challenged by the knowledge that many don't know the "peace and rest," the "special mercy" or "faith's sweet consolation"—truths that anchor and sustain my family and me during this tumultuous time. At the risk of "tampering" with this iconic hymn, I penned a fourth verse.

The hymn "Day by Day" encourages us to think about God's strength and His loving care when we are suffering a trial. Paul Humphreys' new fourth stanza includes a heart-felt prayer asking God to prepare us with the right words for sharing the gospel of Jesus Christ with the unsaved.

Dear reader, be encouraged by the last two lines of stanza two: "As thy days, thy strength shall be in measure, This the pledge to me He made."

DAY BY DAY

"As your days, so shall your strength be" (Deut. 33:25).

Day by day and with each passing moment,
    Strength I find to meet my trials here;
Trusting in my Father's wise bestowment,
    I've no cause for worry or for fear.
He whose heart is kind beyond all measure
    Gives unto each day what He deems best–
Lovingly, it's part of pain and pleasure,
    Mingling toil with peace and rest.

Every day the Lord Himself is near me
    With a special mercy for each hour;
All my cares He fain would bear, and cheer me,
    He whose name is Counselor and Power.
The protection of His child and treasure
    Is a charge that on Himself He laid;
"As thy days, thy strength shall be in measure,"
    This the pledge to me He made.

Help me then in every tribulation
    So to trust Thy promises, O Lord,
That I lose not faith's sweet consolation
    Offered me within Thy holy Word.
Help me, Lord, when toil and trouble meeting,
    Ever to take, as from a father's hand,
One by one, the days, the moments fleeting,
    Till I reach the promised land.

Day by day and with each passing moment
    Souls abound that know not of God's grace.
Theirs is cause for worry and for torment
    Without Christ, his judgment they will face.
Help me Lord, when asked about life's meaning
    E'er to speak your Word so clear and plain.
To make known the Cross on which I'm leaning
    All my hope for blest eternal gain.

Replace Your Spiritual Liabilities with His Assets

Do you behave believing you need no one except yourself to help you through a trial? Perhaps your self-reliance is so subtle you don't recognize it—you think you are trusting the Lord. After a trial, most people can heal emotionally and reorganize their life without God's help. However, the Lord isn't looking for a superman Christian—tough skinned, and self-sufficient.

God won't rescue a prideful, self-sufficient person who thinks he doesn't need God. Self-confidence in our ability is one of our greatest spiritual liabilities. However, one of our greatest spiritual assets is Christ-confidence. Remember, God's servants in the Bible had to be broken spiritually to advance their faith and so do we.

Our Savior allows trials to "burn off" our rubbish of confident independence. The apostle Paul understood the Lord's words to him, *"My grace is sufficient for you, for My strength is made perfect in weakness." Therefore most gladly I will rather boast in my infirmities, that the power of Christ may rest upon me"* (2 Cor. 12:9). Only when we are aware of our weakness can His power uphold us. When we trust Him to help us, we will experience His power.

God won't rescue the prideful who have no need of Him; however, He can't resist us when we admit how desperately we need Him. *"Therefore humble yourselves under the mighty hand of God, that He may exalt you in due time"* (1 Peter 5:6; also Prov. 29:23). Our humility draws the Lord Jesus to supply our needs.

> *A prideful heart causes shame, but a humble heart is a wise heart* (Prov. 11:2).

A Forfeited Faith Adventure

Living by faith isn't only used for trials since God seeks daily dependence on Him in every circumstance. Several years ago, a friend and I presented a seminar. We didn't rely on the Lord; instead, we planned and presented the seminar from our own abilities. Despite our striving, we failed miserably and participants asked for a refund. The center's director told us not to return to complete the seminar—an embarrassing and humbling experience. Failing by self-reliance is a difficult way to learn to trust Christ.

Although self-reliant individuals, including believers, receive praise for their successful efforts, this doesn't please the Lord. He wants to display His power through us so we praise Him for the magnificent God He is.

> *Don't miss a faith adventure by relying on yourself.*

A Faith Adventure
Inadequacies Replaced by His Sufficiency

In contrast, the writing of *LifeQuakes* was a FAITH adventure—a Fantastic Adventure In Trusting Him. My first draft of *LifeQuakes* was fifteen pages when my thoughts dried up. I was confident if God wanted me to write this book, He would supply everything and He did.

Sometimes when I had difficulties with the manuscript, computer problems, setbacks, and other obstacles, I felt frustrated and helpless. When I finally realized I wasn't relying on the Lord, I laughed at myself in amusement. I was right where God wanted me to be—helpless and weak, but didn't realize it. Then I became excited because now the Lord could take over and I was eager to see where He would lead. I had to admit my weakness before the Lord could display His strength and His sufficiency in and through me. Looking to Jesus, I had renewed hope or assurance because I was in the right spiritual position for Him to move the project forward. Each time I yielded to Him in faith, He enabled me and guided me forward. Remembering that this project was a faith journey with the Lord encouraged me.

Despite occasional weariness, I was convinced the Lord wanted me to write *LifeQuakes* because I felt Him gently nudging me onward. When I kept my thoughts in the present moment and allowed my Shepherd to lead me one step at a time, I could avoid becoming overwhelmed.

When I couldn't see the next step, I believed my Shepherd knew and would guide me. Without my Lord Jesus upholding me, I couldn't have finished this book.

The timing of *LifeQuakes* was on the Lord's schedule. In retrospect, I see the Lord's plan for permitting obstacles to delay this book from completion on my schedule. During an interlude of several years between the first round of writing and this current one, the Lord helped me grow spiritually through His Word and of course, through lifequakes and tremors. Had I rushed this manuscript through on my timetable, I would have halted the Lord's activity behind the scenes coordinating and arranging details.

In addition, my sovereign Shepherd provided more than I had asked or imagined just as He promises. *"Now to Him who is able to do exceedingly abundantly above all that we ask or think, according to the power that works in us, to Him be glory in the church by Christ Jesus to all generations, forever and ever"* (Eph. 3:20-21). Best of all, not only did my Savior *"hold my hand"* through this faith adventure, He drew me closer to Himself—the sweetest part of this writing journey.

> *Replacing self-reliance with Christ-centered dependency is great gain.*

Does God Give Us More than We Can Handle?

Have you ever *felt* overwhelmed during a lifequake, a personal dilemma, or a work related challenge? Do you ever consider your trial to be more than you can bear? Perhaps you have heard the cliché, "God never gives you more than you can handle." God's Word does tell us that *temptation to sin* is never more than we can handle when we trust Him. God will never permit us to be tempted beyond what we can overcome *through His power* (1 Cor. 10:13). Scripture must be interpreted within the context and the context of 1 Cor. 10: 6-13 speaks of temptation to sin. Trusting the principle that Christ freed us from the power of sin, we can choose to follow His will (Rom. 6:6; Gal. 2:20; 5:1; 6:14) and overcome the temptation. Our temptations to sin may result from a failure to trust during lifequakes.

At times, our trials may seem to be more than we can endure. An example of a believer with devastating trials was Job—a wealthy married man with seven sons and three daughters. In one day, raiders stole Job's cattle and killed his servants (many were probably good friends) thus destroying his wealth. While a messenger was still reporting the news to Job, another brought news that a windstorm (tornado) had collapsed the house where his ten children were gathered. All his children perished. If that wasn't enough, he lost his health—painful boils covered his body. Job's lifequakes were further plagued when he lost the support of his wife and friends.

However, Job was not an "average" believer. *"There was a man in the land of Uz, whose name was Job; and that man was blameless and upright, and one who feared God and shunned evil"* (Job 1:1). How many of us could handle the heartrending deaths of our children and the murder of our employees in one day? In addition, how many of us could still praise the Lord if we lost all of our possessions that same day and had no property insurance? When the Lord was speaking with Satan, He knew all about Job's lifequakes—the beginning from the end. Job endured extraordinary trials showing he was not an ordinary believer. Initially his focus was on the Lord, though he did stumble toward the end. God gives us this account for our learning (Rom. 15:4).

How do you bear your trials? Believers can persevere in trials in their own strength and as a result learn nothing from it but self-reliance. Even unsaved people are able to rise above the challenge of trials. Often we will only look to Him and His promises when we feel helpless, when our prideful self-reliance fails us. Our wise Lord allows the exact pain intensity to bring us to the end of ourselves, to break our self-reliance (2 Cor. 3:5). God often encourages our trust through increments or progressive stages of trials; otherwise, trials would be too overwhelming.

Your loving Father's objective is your reliance in Him, never to cause you to have a nervous breakdown. He is with you in the trial to preserve you through it. *"When you pass through the waters, I will be with you; And through the rivers, they shall not overflow you. When you walk through the fire, you shall not be burned, Nor shall the flame scorch you"* (Isa. 43:2). We can choose to trust the Lord to carry us through trials, or we can yield to temptation and fail the test.

When you do fail a trial, when your faith falters during a trial, remember all believers fail from time to time (Mark 14:66-72). However, our faithful God offers restoration (Mark 16:7; John 21:1-23; 1 John 1:8-9). Our Lord Jesus is faithful even when we are faithless (2 Tim. 2:13).

You may fail to trust because your trial seems overwhelming and you become discouraged. Although it may seem to be more than you can bear, the Lord knows how much you can endure. Each one of us has a different endurance threshold; the all-knowing Lord Jesus adjusts the intensity accordingly. Then why do we feel overwhelmed?

When we feel overwhelmed and think we can't go on anymore, we are reacting to our circumstances. We aren't depending on the Lord, believing His promises. How often we perceive our trials from our viewpoint instead of seeing them from God's perspective. When we experience the feeling of helplessness, we can either stumble in our trial or trust the Lord and His promises. Feeling overwhelmed is good if it causes you to realize your need to depend on the Lord, if you allow Him to give you His strength to endure. Replace your thinking with *"My grace is sufficient for you, for My strength is made perfect in weakness." Therefore most gladly I will rather boast in my infirmities, that the power of Christ may rest upon me"* (2 Cor. 12:9; also Rom. 8:18). When you are weak, He is strong. When you see your weaknesses and infirmities, then you can see your need for the Lord.

When life's troubles are daunting and seem to be too many to handle, substitute your thinking with Scripture verses such as: *"Be strong and of good courage, do not fear nor be afraid of them; for the LORD your God, He is the One who goes with you. He will not leave you nor forsake you"* (Deut. 31:6). You can trust this promise because He cannot lie (Heb. 6:18). The Lord Jesus will never leave you because He loves you dearly.

> *If we feel able to handle our trials,*
> *we won't need to depend on the Lord.*

His Faithful Replacements

The Lord wants to substitute His strength for our human weakness. For example, look at the biblical account of David and Goliath. David, the shepherd boy, considered God greater than his problems. By human estimates, the youthful David, with his small slingshot, was no match for the nine-foot Philistine giant. God's power, displayed through the weakling David, defeated the giant (1 Sam. 17:1-54) and God received the glory.

The apostle Paul believed in a replacement (gain), *"For when I am weak, then I am strong"* (2 Cor. 12:10b). He also encourages, *"Finally, my brethren, be strong in the Lord and in the power of His might"* (Eph. 6:10). Our Lord Jesus Christ gives power to those who rely on Him (Isa. 40:29) and replaces their weakness with His strength (Isa. 40:31).

The heartaches of life may cause great emotional pain. The shuddering sufferings of any lifequake can cause us to be ineffective in God's plan unless we admit our weakness to gain His strength. When I tremble with heartaches or lifequake turbulence, one promise I rely on is from Isaiah. *"He gives power to the weak, And to those who have no might He increases strength...But those who wait on the* LORD *Shall renew their strength; They shall mount up with wings like eagles, They shall run and not be weary, They shall walk and not faint"* (Isa. 40:29, 31). Those who wait shall have the strength of the Lord.

To "wait" means to cling to, or to hold onto. When we cling to the Lord, He renews our strength (provides endurance) and we become confident in Christ. We "mount up" over obstacles with the power of eagle's wings. We "run" and aren't worried or hindered by the tremors and lifequakes. We "walk" and don't feel overwhelmed. We feel confident in our Shepherd. Every time we cling to the Lord He will renew our strength.

When my human frailties overtake me and I become too weary to continue, I pray the principles from the verses of Isaiah chapter 40. My prayer is like this,

> In Christ's name and in His power, I pray to you Father. You know everything, so You know I am weary and need energy to

complete my responsibilities. I can't go on unless You revitalize me. You promised if I trust You, you will renew my strength. You never fail me. I will run and not be weary and I will walk and not faint when I place my confidence in You. Father, You always renew my energy. I trust you now for renewed energy.

My faithful, loving Father supplies His strength and encouragement every time. Should we expect anything less?

> His replacement plan—His strength for your weakness.

Joseph Scriven suffered extraordinary lifequakes before he wrote "What a Friend We Have in Jesus." Reading Scriven's brief personal history below, we empathize with his grief and sorrow; we rejoice he found comfort in Jesus, his friend.

> Scriven graduated from Trinity College. His fiancée drowned the night before they were to marry, so in 1846 he moved to Canada. He taught in Woodstock and Brantford, Ontario and was a tutor for the Pengellys family near Bewdley, where he met and became engaged to Eliza Roche, a relative of the Pengellys. In what seems too amazing to be coincidence, Eliza died shortly before their wedding. Following the death of his second fiancée, Scriven joined the Plymouth Brethren, helping the aged members.
>
> Scriven wrote this hymn to comfort his mother, who was across the sea from him in Ireland. At first this hymn was published anonymously and Scriven did not receive full credit for almost 30 years.
>
> Cyber Hymnal, *www.hymntime.com*

WHAT A FRIEND WE HAVE IN JESUS

"You are My friends if you do whatever I command you" (John 15:14).

What a friend we have in Jesus,
All our sins and griefs to bear!
What a privilege to carry
Everything to God in prayer!
O, what peace we often forfeit,
O, what needless pain we bear
All because we do not carry
Everything to God in prayer.

Have we trails and temptations?
Is there trouble anywhere?
We should never be discouraged
Take it to the Lord in prayer!
Can we find a friend so faithful,
Who will all our sorrows share?
Jesus knows our every weakness
Take it to the Lord in prayer!

Are we weak and heavy laden?
Cumbered with a load of care?
Precious Savior, still our refuge.
Take it to the Lord in prayer!
Do thy friends despise, forsake thee?
Take it to the Lord in prayer!
In His arms He'll take and shield thee
Thou wilt find a solace there.

~ Joseph Scriven, 1819-1886 ~

Recognizing the Need for His Replacements

Discovering our misplaced confidence in ourselves usually takes time. We must recognize our helplessness before we can admit it to the Lord and experience His strength.

You can recognize your need for replacement
- when you are frustrated or worried.
- when you are overwhelmed and feel inadequate.
- when your self-reliance causes you to feel defeated.
- when you are depending on yourself.
- when you are hungry, tired, ill, or in pain.

When you realize your insufficiencies to handle the task with peace by faith, confess or admit this to your heavenly Father. *"Not that we are sufficient of ourselves to think of anything as being from ourselves, but our sufficiency is from God"* (2 Cor. 3:5). Admit your weaknesses and gain His power.

> *Jesus is attracted to our weakness.*

Only Jesus Christ can enable you to endure or continue in any circumstances (Phil. 4:13). Through faith, Christ will display His endurance through the believer. When you trust His promises, they become roots of energy in your soul.

In the next faith adventure, Mandy replaced her inadequacies with His sufficiency, which gives God the glory.

A Faith Adventure
The Lord is My Scheduler

When her workload became demanding, Mandy replaced her weaknesses with God's strength by relying on Him. She explains,

> As I prayed about my new responsibilities at work, I asked the Lord to help me with new leadership and management challenges. Work transitions included hiring a new draftsperson, changing engineers, taking on two disenchanted designers from another

division, plus moving our department to another part of the building. Another new challenge was training three people who knew nothing about our product line. Suddenly I had three new people reporting to me and looking to me for leadership.

Now I had additional responsibilities, but the Lord has been giving me great peace about it. He is directing me to take one day at a time and look to His leading one-step at a time—letting Him reveal to me the "next thing." Knowing I can trust Him to enable me each day in the leadership and management of co-workers has given me a new sense of confidence. I don't know many people who look to the Lord to help them schedule their work day, but how wonderfully that works! The Lord has given me these challenges so I learn that He will enable me to meet each day with Him walking beside me.

> *The task ahead of us is never as great as the Power behind us.*

Ponder the awe-inspiring comfort of the God of the universe who cares for you as He says: *"Fear not, for I am with you; Be not dismayed, for I am your God. I will strengthen you, Yes, I will help you, I will uphold you with My righteous right hand...For I, the LORD your God, will hold your right hand, Saying to you, 'Fear not, I will help you"* (Isa. 41:10, 13). He wishes to hold your hand, the hand of His humble, helpless child. The Lord Jesus promises He will support you, help you, and sustain you with His mighty hand.

> *Place your cares into His hands and He will put His peace into your heart.*

The next poem "Hands" asks us to consider the value of hands, which depends on whose hands they are.

> **HANDS**
> Author unknown
>
> A basketball in my hands is worth about $19.
> A basketball in Michael Jordan's hands is worth about $33 million.
> It depends whose hands it's in.
>
> A baseball in my hands is worth about $6.
> A baseball in Roger Clemens' hands is worth $4.75 million.
> It depends on whose hands it's in.
>
> A tennis racket is useless in my hands.
> A tennis racket in Andre Agassi's hand is worth millions.
> It depends whose hands it's in.
>
> A rod in my hands will keep away an angry dog.
> A rod in Moses' hands will part the mighty sea.
> It depends whose hands it's in.
>
> A slingshot in my hands is a kid's toy.
> A slingshot in David's hand is a mighty weapon.
> It depends whose hands it's in.
>
> So put your concerns, your worries, your fears, your hopes, your dreams, your families and your relationships in God's hands because...it does depend whose hands it's in.

Replacements Glorify Christ

Replacing our negative, sinful thinking with the mind of Christ honors Him and His viewpoint and rewards us with His peace. When we use our strength, we honor ourselves. To glorify the Lord we must replace our strength with His. Instead of feeling gloomy about our inadequacies, we should look to the capabilities of Christ and trust Him. Simply admit your inadequacy in prayer, tell the Lord you need His strength, and then trust Him to keep His promise to supply your need. Moreover, if your thinking is right, you will praise Him.

Reflection Questions

Support your answers with Scripture verses and, as always, with God's viewpoint.

1. Explain the battle for the mind.

2. What insights did you gain about sin?

3. How do we let the Lord fight the battle?

4. What insights have you gained about the power of the mind of Christ?

5. What is Satan's goal for the believer and how does he attempt to accomplish it?

6. How will you use God's replacement plan in your life of faith? Give specific examples.

7. What principles have you learned from this chapter to apply to your life?

CHAPTER 10 PREVIEW

 ↬ Characteristics of Anxiety
 ↬ What is Peace *with* God?
 ↬ Gaining the Peace *of* God
 ↬ How We Lose the Peace of God
 ↬ Overcoming Unbelief
 ↬ How to be a Blazing Torch for Christ

CHAPTER 10

Smoking Smudge Pot or Blazing Torch?

The Dark Room of Anxiety

Lisa has agoraphobia, an anxiety disorder. She has panic attacks often induced by the fear of being in an area with no easy means of escape. Lisa only feels comfortable in her house, which she rarely leaves. Her fears confine and control her life; consequently, she can't work outside her home. Although Lisa's fears are extreme, our anxieties can cripple anyone of us if we let them.

What are your anxieties? Do you worry about old age, loneliness, or death? Do you fear losing your job, your health, or your independence? Perhaps you worry what other people think. Fear is gloominess that engulfs us and if left unchecked it can lock us within ourselves.

> *Fear is the dark room where negatives are developed.*

What is Anxiety?

Where does anxiety come from? Anxiety can sometimes be the result of underlying physical causes. Check with your doctor to rule out medical disorders, nutritional deficiencies, food allergies, sensitivities to substances like medications, caffeine, or sugar that may cause or contribute to anxiety.

Although anxiety may have physical causes, it's often a spiritual problem. Simply stated, anxiety signals a failure to believe the Lord. What warning does God give us about anxiety? *"Anxiety in the heart of man causes depression, But a good word makes it glad"* (Prov. 12:25). Depression, despair, or sadness can result from any degree of uneasiness as listed below.

- *Anxiety* (consistent uneasiness) suggests *feelings* of fear. Fear of the future, expecting something unfavorable is apprehension.
- *Worry* is persistent doubt or fear.
- *Care* signals a mind burdened with heavy responsibilities.
- *Concern* is serious thoughts combined with emotion. At first, concern may not be worry; but later concern can become worry. For example, concern about dangers of terrorism to our country can easily become worry. Care and concern are normal feelings, but when uncontrolled, they become worry.

What Causes Anxiety?

Anxious people think too much about problems and themselves. Anxiety invades our feelings when we view lifequakes and tremors as too great for God. Unfortunately, from that perspective, we never consider trusting God to manage them. Uneasiness occurs when we think we must resolve something that is impossible to settle. However, God didn't equip us to solve problems beyond our control, problems that belong to Him.

We become anxious when we try to live in tomorrow by thinking about what may happen while we still live in today. Solution, live in the present—today, in the moment. Each day choose Christ as the center of your attentions, not your worries.

Anxiety stems from sinful self-importance, that is, our pride thinks we should control matters. In arrogance, we dislike thinking we can't solve our problems. Pride keeps us from confiding in fellow believers, asking for help when appropriate, turning problems over to God in prayer, and trusting the Lord. In contrast, humility is necessary for trusting the Lord, casting our cares on Him, and accepting God's comfort.

> *Anxiety does not empty tomorrow of its sorrows,*
> *but only empties today of its strength.* —Charles Spurgeon

Anxiety Linked to Depression

The anxiety of several consecutive trials caused Ellie's depression, but she learned Gods' truth to overcome her despair. She writes,

> I have learned we always have choices, even during trials. We either respond in faith to the Lord or react from our sin nature (flesh). Responding by faith is releasing the problem into God's hands and trusting Him to handle it because He is sovereign. When the sin nature is winning, we react with a display of anger, fear, worry, or other mental attitude sins.
>
> I learned about this respond/react principle through a series of distressing circumstances. At first, I responded with faith but as the number of trials increased, as did their intensity, I reacted with worry and fear. The pain of the trials and my focus on them hurled me into a deep depression. As a believer, I had never experienced depression in the past, sad at times but not depressed. Although I managed to perform at work and at home, I was despondent. At home, I couldn't stop the tears. In the middle of the night, I would awake and sob uncontrollably. I felt helpless to overcome my depression—the right place for the Lord to step in with His strength.
>
> Someone gave me a Bible tape message about trials presented by Pastor Dennis Rokser. In that message, God's Word revealed I was reacting in sin and not responding by faith. I learned about the principle of keeping God's Word in my soul to ward off sin. Psalm 119:11, *"Your word I have hidden in my heart, That I might not sin against You!"* This verse convicted me that I was sinning by failing to apply God's Word to my trials. When I confessed my sins of worry and fear (1 John 1:9), my depression lifted. I still fail by reacting; however, when I do react, I catch myself sooner, confess my sin, and resume my reliance on the Lord.
>
> To stabilize me during that time I claimed (believed) Scrip-

ture verses. I clung to Psalm 27:13-14 *"I would have despaired unless I had believed that I would see the goodness of the LORD In the land of the living. Wait for the LORD; Be strong and let your heart take courage; Yes, wait for the LORD"* (NASB). According to His character, the Lord faithfully strengthened me so I could thrive, not just survive the trials. Only when I relied on Him did I find His peace and strength.

I am so thankful to the Lord for revealing to me how I mess up my life when I lean on myself. In these trials, my Lord Jesus taught me that I can always depend on Him (Prov. 3:5-6).

> *Christ-centered dependency is the antidote for anxiety and depression.*

Does Worry Strangle You?

The history of the word "worry" explains the power of worry to place us in a stranglehold.

> Worrying may shorten one's life, but not as quickly as it once did. The ancestor of our word, Old English *wyrgan*, meant "to strangle." Its Middle English descendant, *worien*, kept this sense and developed the new sense "to grasp by the throat with the teeth and lacerate" or "to kill or injure by biting and shaking." For example, wolves or dogs might attack sheep in this manner. In the 16th century, *worry* took on the sense "to harass, as by rough treatment or attack," or "to assault verbally." In the 17th century, the word took on the sense "to bother, distress, or persecute." Next came a small step from this sense to the main modern senses "to cause to feel anxious or distressed" and "to feel troubled or uneasy," first recorded in the 19th century.
>
> Source: The American Heritage® Dictionary of the English Language, Fourth Edition, Houghton Mifflin Company, 2004.

A worrywart (also called a pessimist or fussbudget) is a person who thinks habitually and needlessly about unfortunate matters that might happen, but often never do. In addition, a worrywart annoys others by talking constantly about nearly everything that worries him. Worry is a sin common to young or old.

As a child I worried and my sixth grade teacher warned my parents about my worrying. He predicted if I didn't change, I would have a nervous breakdown. Thank the Lord, I never did. Eventually, through His Word, I learned how to avoid worry since believers have no cause to worry.

While believers have no reason to worry, the unsaved person has good reason to worry since he is without help. Who will carry the burdens of the unsaved? Unlike the unbeliever who must carry his own burdens, Christ can carry the believer's burdens. Yet, believers behave as if they have no Savior to carry their troubles. During lifequakes or tremors, the believer often chooses the chokehold of worry instead of the sturdy burden-bearing shoulders of the Lord Jesus.

Unfortunately, we often allow worry to strangle our spiritual life. The strangling sin of worry viciously attacks our fellowship with the Lord because it shreds our confidence in Him, harasses us with doubts about God, and kills God's peace in our souls.

Worry always results in suffering. We easily choose the misery of worry—that persistent mental uneasiness and mental anguish—over God's peace by faith. Not only do we suffer spiritually, but the sin of worry also injures us physically, mentally, and emotionally. Therefore, the Lord commands us not to worry, *"Do not fret—it only causes harm"* (Ps. 37:8). Because our loving Lord doesn't want us to hurt, He doesn't want us to sin.

Are You a Smoking Smudge Pot of Worry?

What is a smudge pot? From the 1950s until the 1970s, fruit growers used smudge pots or orchard heaters to protect their crops from a possible killing frost on cloudless, cold nights. A smudge pot was a portable oil-burning heater that produced a thick, heavy smoke. A smudge pot has a large round base with a chimney coming from the middle of the base. Fruit growers placed several of these between the trees in the evening to prevent the crop from freezing at night.

Smudge Pot
www.answers.com/topic/smudge-pot

Smudge pots don't produce sufficient warmth to heat up the orchard. However, the thick smoke cloud acts to reflect infrared radiation (heat radiation) from the orchard, thus "trapping" heat between the cloud and the ground. By reducing radiation to the night sky, the orchard cools more slowly and keeps it above the freezing point throughout the night. A smudge pot was an effective method to keep the orchard fruits alive and flourishing.

We can associate the *smoke* of the smudge pot to sins such as worry. When we worry, we throw smoke on the darkness of the trials, thus making the darkness darker. Our worry creates confusion in others who wonder why we Christians are so distressed, why we aren't depending on the Lord. When we scurry from person to person with our worry bug spilling our problems on them, we fan the *smoke* of disbelief and distrust in God.

The smoke of worry smothers trust.

In my series of trials, I worried myself sick and my doctor prescribed an antidepressant. Unfortunately, he didn't have the prescription for my soul—admit your sin of worry and resume trusting God's promises. In His grace, my great Physician used these trials to teach me about depending on Him as the means of overcoming worry and receiving His peace.

Worry Work Is Exhausting

Although Amber was a believer in Jesus Christ, she had not matured in her spiritual life. She was a smoking smudge pot who worried about her husband's drinking and made deals with him to stop. When that didn't work, she prayed to God for help. Repeatedly, Amber gave her problem to the Lord only to take it back. Her focus was on her husband, his drinking problem and on her next scheme to manipulate him to stop drinking. Amber thought if beer was available at home, he would drink fewer, so one day she bought enough twelve packs to fill the trunk of their car. She thought she could entice him to drink at home where he was less likely to drink too much, but her plan failed. Amber didn't understand they both had spiritual problems. He sinned by using excessive alcohol to fill the void in his soul that only a relationship with Jesus Christ could fill. She was trying to control an external problem because she couldn't alter her husband's internal spiritual deficiencies. She was sinning by worrying and "playing God" by using schemes to control her husband's drinking. When Amber stopped trying to solve her husband's problem and trusted the Lord with all problems, she had the peace of God even though the circumstances didn't change.

> *Worrying is like a rocking chair; it gives you something to do but gets you nowhere.*

Is worry work wearing you out? Do you keep trying to change someone or some difficulty? Perhaps you could pray the Serenity Prayer whose source dates back centuries and authorship is controversial. I have modified the second verse to align it with Scripture.

> **SERENITY PRAYER**
> Adapted
>
> God, grant me the serenity
> To accept the things I cannot change;
> Courage to change the things I can;
> And the wisdom to know the difference,
> Through Jesus Christ, our Lord.
>
> Living one day at a time;
> Enjoying one moment at a time;
> Accepting hardships as the pathway to growth;
> Taking, as He did, this sinful world
> As it is, not as I would have it;
> Trusting that He works all things together
> In His time, for His plan and for my good;
> That I may be content in Christ in this life
> And supremely happy with Him
> Forever in the next.

Discovering My Spiritual Bridegroom

During some troubling times, my marriage circumstances seemed hopeless. I worried and thought divorce was unavoidable. Because I looked at the circumstances, I wasn't in fellowship with the Lord.

One afternoon I locked myself in my darkened bedroom to be alone with God. In despair, I cried and sobbed as I unburdened my soul to the Lord reminding Him that He doesn't like divorce and neither did I. In prayer, I admitted I was helpless and unless He intervened to save my marriage, it wouldn't survive. God caused me to remember how He tested Abraham's obedience about the command to sacrifice Isaac.

Abraham had a dilemma. He could disobey God and not sacrifice Isaac or obey God and lose his son and the promises associated with him. Abraham's faith reasoned he must obey God who could resurrect Isaac to keep His promises.

Reflecting on Abraham's trial helped me remember God can resolve my problems and I became confident the Lord would work it out. Having admitted my helplessness, I was in position for the Lord to change me. I shifted my expectations to the Lord Jesus, my spiritual Bridegroom. The Lord was now in control and I accepted Christ's management.

I have fond memories of that afternoon with Christ, an encounter that changed my life. Christ drew me closer and I felt complete and secure in Him. Christ, my spiritual Bridegroom became real to me. From that afternoon on, I became preoccupied (like being in love) with Him; He filled my thoughts and became the center of my life. As time passed, I grew increasingly confident in Jesus Christ who never disappoints me and satisfies my every need.

Perhaps you haven't discovered your spiritual Bridegroom, Jesus Christ. If you are alone because you lost a spouse or your children left home, you may find little meaning or purpose in life. You may look to your children or another person to satisfy your emotional needs; therefore, you may expect too much time and attention from them. When others can't meet your high expectations, you may become angry, feel sorry for yourself, and you may send your children on a guilt trip. Instead of looking to others, look to Jesus and express your feelings and needs in prayer. Then believe Christ will meet your needs, fill the emptiness in your soul, and provide purpose for living.

> *Our Father can calm the quakes around*
> *us and the quakes inside us.*

The next time you have quakes look to the Scripture-based hymn, "His Eye is on the Sparrow" written by Civilla D. Martin.

The song's theme was inspired by the words of Jesus in the Gospel of Matthew in the Bible, as referenced by Mrs. Doolittle in

Elmira, New York: *"Look at the birds of the air; they neither sow nor reap nor gather into barns, and yet your heavenly Father feeds them. Are you not of more value than they?"* (Matt. 6:26) and *"Are not two sparrows sold for a farthing? And one of them shall not fall on the ground without your Father knowing. But the hairs of your head are numbered. Fear ye not therefore, ye are of more value than many sparrows"* (Matt. 10:29-31).

http://en.wikipedia.org/wiki/His_Eye_Is_on_the_Sparrow

Early in the spring of 1905, my husband and I were visiting in Elmira, New York. We contracted a deep friendship for a couple named Mr. and Mrs. Doolittle—true saints of God. Mrs. Doolittle had been bedridden for nearly twenty years. Her husband was an incurable cripple who had to propel himself to and from his business in a wheel chair. Despite their afflictions, they lived happy Christian lives, bringing inspiration and comfort to those who knew them. One day while we were visiting with the Doolittles, my husband commented on their bright hopefulness and asked them for the secret of it. Mrs. Doolittle's reply was simple: "His eye is on the sparrow, and I know He watches me." The beauty of this simple expression of boundless faith gripped the hearts and fired the imagination of Dr. Martin and me. The hymn "His Eye Is on the Sparrow" was the result of that experience.—Civilla Martin (1866–1948)

www.hymntime.com

HIS EYE IS ON THE SPARROW

Why should I feel discouraged,
Why should the shadows come,
Why should my heart be lonely,
And long for Heav'n and home,
When Jesus is my portion?
My constant friend is He:
His eye is on the sparrow,
And I know He watches me;
His eye is on the sparrow,
And I know He watches me.

REFRAIN: I sing because I'm happy,
I sing because I'm free,
For His eye is on the sparrow,
And I know He watches me.

"Let not your heart be troubled,
"His tender word I hear,
And resting on His goodness,
I lose my doubts and fears;
Tho' by the path He leads
But one step I may see:
His eye is on the sparrow,
And I know He watches me;
His eye is on the sparrow,
And I know He watches me.

Whenever I am tempted,
Whenever clouds arise,
When songs give place to sighing,
When hope within me dies,
I draw the closer to Him,
From care He sets me free;
His eye is on the sparrow,
And I know He watches me;
His eye is on the sparrow,
And I know He watches me.

~ Civilla D. Martin, 1905 ~

Weeding Out Worry

In circumstances we often have predetermined anxious thoughts about the ending without considering that what we fear may never happen. Ask yourself, can worry change matters or make them better?

Our Lord Jesus manages and directs every part of our lives. As our sovereign Lord, He sees the big picture and He knows best how He must work matters together according to His plan. So why worry? God has the universe and everything in it under control; therefore, you can trust His management of your life. Since the Lord has everything under control, He never worries.

In eternity, beyond the trillions of years of His existence, God has never once worried. God can't worry or fear because He is God. Since God manages, directs, and supervises everything, what a waste of time to worry. How absurd to worry about our problems when the sovereign God has our problems, even minor ones, under His perfect supervision. Besides, God commands us to become followers, imitators of Him (Eph. 5:1). We can't worry and follow God!

> *If we worry, all that changes is our stress level—*
> *it increases. The more we trust Him, the less we worry.*

The Transition from Worry Sins

When I began trusting more and worrying less, I felt peace. Because worry had been habitual, feeling calm felt abnormal, and I needed time to adjust to serenity. Just as it takes times for a recovering alcoholic to feel comfortable without drinking, it may take time for a believer to feel comfortable when he isn't worrying.

So familiar was the control of my sin nature that, when I chose not to worry, the calmness was unfamiliar. Was I still caring, I wondered. Confusing worry with caring shows how my sin nature dominated and confused my thinking. Often caring means stepping aside and letting God handle His business of managing and directing. In time, I experienced the comfort of His promise: *"Come to Me, all you who labor and are heavy laden, and I will give you rest. Take My yoke upon you and learn from Me, for I am gentle and lowly in heart, and you will find rest for your souls. For My yoke is easy and My burden is light."* (Matt. 11:28-30). Now when I let Him carry my burdens, I feel the load of sin, including worry, lifted from my shoulders and I have rest.

> *Before you go to bed, give your troubles to your Father, He will be up all night anyway.*

What Is Peace *with* God?

The Bible speaks of two forms of peace—the peace *with* God and the peace *of* God. As an unsaved person you had no peace *with* God since you were at war with Him spiritually and were under His wrath; His judgment for your sin was on you (Rom. 1:18).

The warfare between you and God ended when you became His child through faith in Christ; then you gained peace with God (Rom. 5:1). Peace with God means nothing—no sin, no guilt, no condemnation—separates us from God.

What Is the Peace *of* God?

The Greek word for the peace of God is *eirēnē* from the verb *eiro*, which means "to join together." The peace of God binds, joins what is broken or separated, and sets the divided parts together again. To "make peace" means to join those separated. This Greek word for peace means wholeness, completeness, or peacefulness in the soul that is unaffected by outward circumstances or pressures. *Eirēnē* strongly suggests order instead of chaos. Therefore, the peace of God isn't a result of changing circumstances; instead, the peace of God is His calmness, stability, and unwavering strength amid trials. *"For He Himself is our peace"* (Eph. 2:14). The peace of God comes in a person—Jesus Christ. We are joined with Christ and His peace.

The peace *of* God is incomprehensible as Paul described it as beyond our understanding (Phil. 4:7). We gain the peace of God repeatedly whenever we trust Him. God is the giver of genuine, lasting peace. Jesus told us, *"Peace I leave with you, My peace I give to you; not as the world gives do I give to you. Let not your heart be troubled, neither let it be afraid"* (John 14:27). How is His peace different from the world's peace?

What peace does the world offer? Where do people go for peace? Some think that changes in circumstances will bring peace. At times, we would like to change our circumstances, but we can't. Some believe, if I marry I'll be happy because I will have peace from the anxiety of being single. Others want more money and think that will make them happy. Maybe if I had opportunities for career advancement, maybe if I were thinner, if I looked better, if I was single then I would have contentment. Some use moving or a vacation as strategies for contentment. However, since we carry our sin nature with us, changing circumstances or lifestyles won't supply true peace.

Anxious people (including Christians) party in Satan's enticement park (the world) using distractions (sin) as an escape from problems or as a cover up for emotional pain. Distractions such as alcohol or drug abuse, excessive eating, sexual immorality (including pornography), or gambling only cause more misery. People who play in the world have anxiety because relief can't be found amid the rubbish of Satan's world.

How We Lose the Peace of God

The peace of God provides us with wholeness and unity with Him. However, living in a state of unconfessed sin disconnects us from God. Our fellowship with the Lord is broken, which results in the loss of the peace of God. Do you know what triggers your failure to rely on the Lord? Our failure to depend on the Lord invites worry, fear, and other sins. We find that God's viewpoint defeats worry in Matthew 6:31-34 where we read.*"Therefore do not worry, saying, 'What shall we eat?' or 'What shall we drink?' or 'What shall we wear?' For after all these things the Gentiles seek. For your heavenly Father knows that you need all these things. But seek first the kingdom of God and His righteousness, and all these things shall be added to you.*

Therefore do not worry about tomorrow, for tomorrow will worry about its own things. Sufficient for the day is its own trouble." What sets you up for spiritual failure? What causes us to lose the peace of God?

We lose the peace of God:
1. when we are out of fellowship because of unconfessed sin. If you are unaware of sin, ask God to show you.
2. when we worry and project tomorrow's cares into today. We may think, what will happen if...? How will I be able to...? Today's trouble is enough (Matt. 6:31, 34b).
3. when we permit our focus to drift from dependency on the Lord to our problems (Matt. 6:32-33).

An Emotional Roller Coaster

Christine keeps losing God's peace and describes her life as a roller coaster between His peace and her anger. She writes,

> When my anger flares, I lose faith in God's sufficiency. In my anger about my husband's chronic pain, I questioned why God had allowed so much suffering in our marriage. Why did God allow my husband to be a victim of several car accidents and suffer a stroke? Seeing him suffer in chronic pain is too much for me to bear. This suffering is a drain on my marriage and on me. I have too much responsibility. I am the breadwinner, do the household chores, the yard work, care for our child, and help him with his homework. I never dreamed marriage would be like this. When daily tasks overwhelmed me, I got angry and took my frustration out on my husband. Afterwards I felt guilty about my lack of compassion and I confessed my sins of anger and self-centeredness. The Lord melted my anger and I felt His peace for a while, but then the cycle repeated itself.
>
> I finally realized this cycle is a daily struggle between my sin nature and my new nature in Christ. When my sin nature is win-

ning, I focus on my problems and my feelings, and I lose the peace of God. Recently I learned that my desire to have my way—a need to control—triggers my anger. I know I can't overcome sin by my striving; instead, I must claim His promises and trust Him to change me. I am learning that my anger and worry are signals of my failure to trust Him. When I depend on the Lord, I am in fellowship and gain His blessings, especially His peace.

Avoid the emotional roller coaster; take a faith ride.

Are You Waiting on the Lord?

Waiting is the most difficult when we feel our need is the greatest, like during a trial. Faith rest suggests waiting on the Lord, not just waiting. He commands, *"Wait for the LORD; Be strong and let your heart take courage; Yes, wait for the LORD"* (Ps. 27:14 NASB). Often, waiting isn't a case of waiting for His help but waiting for His perfect timing since He alone recognizes the unknowns involved.

Besides waiting for God's timing, waiting on the Lord means to rest, that is, to stop fretting or worrying. We strive to resolve difficulties when we believe that God is *not* in control or that He can't resolve problems. We are waiting on Him when we "let go" the need to struggle to resolve the problem and instead, roll our worry on the Lord. Because our heavenly Father always does what is best, expect His perfect will on our behalf. *"My soul, wait silently for God alone, For my expectation is from Him"* (Ps. 62:5). Waiting during the trial isn't the same as inactivity. Tasks such as praying, diligently reading, and hearing His Word, plus believing His promises are God-pleasing activities as we patiently wait on Him.

Waiting is letting go and letting God.

Waiting on the Lord is not a matter of uncomplaining endurance, but it is expectant faith—quiet, restful, confident dependence on a faithful God. When you are trusting, you may discover that the Lord Jesus doesn't remove the pressures until you are able to take it quietly. In this waiting you learn His grace first, and then His mercy.

"All Your Anxiety" is another favorite hymn of mine because it expresses the confidence we have in Christ who cares so greatly for us.

ALL YOUR ANXIETY
"Casting all your care upon Him, for He cares for you" (1 Peter 5:7).

Is there a heart o'er-bound by sorrow?
Is there a life weighed down by care?
Come to the cross—each burden bearing,
All your anxiety—leave it there.

REFRAIN: All your anxiety, all your care,
Bring to the mercy seat—leave it there;
Never a burden He cannot bear,
Never a friend like Jesus!

No other friend so keen to help you,
No other friend so quick to hear;
No other place to leave your burden,
No other one to hear your prayer.

Come then at once—delay no longer!
Heed His entreaty kind and sweet;
You need not fear a disappointment;
You shall find peace at the mercy seat.

~ Edward H. Joy 1871-1949 ~

God's Faithful Patience Despite Worry

In Genesis 14, we read that Abraham had just experienced great victories. Earlier Abraham had a great military victory, yet he had remained humble, didn't boast, and thus his God-centered focus triumphed over pride. He didn't take the spoils of war because he trusted God who had provided and would continue supplying his needs. In contrast to a smoking smudge pot of worry, Abraham was a blazing torch of trust.

However, in chapters 15 and 16 Abraham smothered his blazing torch of trust with unbelief, thus fanning a smoking smudge pot that emitted worries, doubts, and fears. He worried because years had passed and still he didn't have the promised son. Abraham wasn't trusting God.

Abraham kept thinking about how old he and Sarah were—she was beyond childbearing age. Because Abraham failed to trust and wait for God's perfect timing, he remained in panic palace. Abraham had a choice to believe, but instead he *chose* to worry. Although he didn't lose his salvation, his flame of faith for daily living had turned into smoke. Although he was victorious in the past, now he was a smoking smudge pot of worry.

> *Never rely on your past spiritual victories to sustain you in future trials because your help is from the Lord alone.*

The Lord God encouraged Abraham through the trial. God came to Abraham in a vision and commanded him not to fear because fear is worry. We find the same thought in Isaiah 41:10 *"Fear not, for I am with you; Be not dismayed, for I am your God. I will strengthen you, Yes, I will help you, I will uphold you with My righteous right hand."* Fear not and do not have regrets for the Lord God is beside you. Perhaps Abraham regretted having turned down the spoils of war and feared poverty, so the Lord gave him a promise. *"Do not be afraid, Abram. I am your shield, your exceedingly great reward"*(Gen. 15:1). In other words, God was in essence asking Abraham, "Are you afraid that in your old age you are going to starve and wear rags? Stop right there, Abraham! You refused tremendous wealth, but I am your reward. My wealth is inexhaustible; all eternity won't exhaust My limitless wealth." Our patient God further reassured Abraham that no matter what trials and pressures he would have, He (God) would supply his needs.

What did Abraham do? Did he think, okay I am going to trust God's promises. No, he continued to worry. *"Lord GOD, what will You give me, seeing I go childless"* (Gen. 15:2). Not having the promised son was a crisis to him and God understood Abraham's anxiety. Therefore, in His gracious patience, God repeated the promise of a son for Abraham in his old age. Again, Abraham had a choice—he could believe God's Word or he could look at life from human viewpoint and worry.

God gave Abraham one promise with two parts. The Lord gave us over seven thousand promises—promises which we can apply to our circumstances. Why is it so difficult to believe Him?

When we worry, we don't trust. When we trust we don't worry.

Since God keeps His Word and never changes—He is the same as He was in Abraham's time. Will you believe He will always provide for you? Take time to meditate on the next Scripture verse and hymn.

O GOD, OUR HELP IN AGES PAST

"LORD, *You have been our dwelling place in all generations*" (Psalm 90:1).

O God, our help in ages past,
Our hope for years to come,
Our shelter from the stormy blast,
And our eternal home.
O God our help in ages past,
Our hope for years to come,
Be Thou our guide while life shall last,
And our eternal home.

~ Isaac Watt ~

More Reassurance from a Patient God

God directed Abraham to gaze at the billions of stars. In His patient love, God helped Abraham realize that his all-powerful God holds the universe together. If He keeps billions of stars in orbit, couldn't He provide a son? In addition, God reminded Abraham that just as the stars are too numerous to count, so his descendants would be countless. Just as God made the stars and keeps them in the sky, He can do anything.

This next illustration connects God's work with the stars with Gods' work in Abraham's salvation (Over twenty-two years earlier, God saved Abraham). In essence, the Lord God told Abraham, look at the stars—how they hang in the sky, I DO ALL THE WORK in maintaining them. In salvation, I DO ALL THE WORK (Rom. 8:32; Col. 1:17). God wanted

Abraham to understand that His God solved his greatest problem—salvation; consequently, He could solve the rest of his problems.

> *We rest in the One upon whom the universe rests.*
> —Miles Stanford

Abraham had sinned in many ways since his salvation, yet God remained faithful to him. Abraham confessed his sins of fear and worry and regained his right relationship with his Lord. Taking God at His Word was Abraham's cure for worry. When Abraham resumed trusting, God faithfully provided peace.

For lifequakes and daily circumstances, the Lord repeats, I DO ALL THE WORK (Phil. 2:13; Heb. 13:20-21). God controls and has a solution for every problem or crisis.

God Holds the Future so Why Worry

Relying on God's promises for the future is an antidote for worry. If Abraham had believed the promises, he would not have worried. We can trust God's promises for the future like the promise of an incorruptible resurrection body (Phil. 3:21). He is preparing a mansion for you in heaven, a heavenly home where our faithful Lord will wipe away every sorrow and tear (Rev. 21:4). God gives magnificent promises for eternity; therefore, we have no reason to worry.

> *When we trust in God who holds the future, we can relax.*

Maintaining His Unwavering Peace

First, trusting Christ is the means to gaining the peace of God. Routinely relying on the Lord in stress-free times trains us to continue the habit of trusting when lifequakes and tremors strike.

Second, develop a deeper attachment to the Lord Jesus by reading His Word and hearing sound Bible teaching. Through His Word, the Lord conforms your thinking to the mind-set of Christ. Thinking like Christ is necessary for gaining the peace of God.

Third, His peace comes from believing and applying His promises. He directs us, *"And let the peace of God rule in your hearts, to which also you were called in one body; and be thankful"* (Col. 3:15). Do you have difficulty believing in God's peace? Perhaps you think about a Bible verse but can't feel the peace of God, so you doubt His peace. If our compassionate Savior didn't want us to have His peace, He wouldn't have told us how to gain it. He tells us in Isaiah 23:6, *"You will keep him in perfect peace, Whose mind is stayed on You, Because he trusts in You."* The last phrase *"because he trusts in you,"* is the key to receiving God's peace. You must believe the promise to gain the peace of God. The choice is either you believe God's Word to be true or you don't. Therefore, take Him at His word, *"and the peace of God, which surpasses all understanding, will guard your hearts and minds through Christ Jesus"* (Phil. 4:7). He promises to protect (guard) your heart and mind with His peace when you keep His promises circulating in your soul.

Fourth, gain His peace by talking to God in prayer. If we don't throw our problems on the Lord, we continue to fixate on them. The longer we concentrate on problems the worse they appear since anxiety grows as we nurture it. Clinging to our problems, leads us to sins like worry, anxiety, fear, or anger. The Lord doesn't want us to hurt because of our sin and tells us, *"Be anxious for nothing, but in everything by prayer and supplication, with thanksgiving, let your requests be made known to God"* (Phil. 4:6). Worry, fear, or other sins are too heavy for us and weigh us down. Therefore, the only place to drop off this load of sin is on the Lord. As God's Word directs us, *"cast all your anxiety upon Him, for He cares for you"* (1 Peter 5:7 NIV). If we cast our cares on the Lord, sins like worry and fear won't dominate and strangle our thinking. Whenever you start to worry, stop, and pray.

Our Savior was our sin-bearer on the cross and He remains our sin-bearer. His victory at the cross enables us to release our sin burdens and afflictions, which He never intended for us to carry. Our reassuring Savior invites us to throw our burdens on Him through prayer and eagerly waits to remove our stress (Matt. 11:28-30).

Anxiety weighs us down but confidence in God uplifts us.

Rescued from Worry by Grace

Making Christ the focus of your life and living by faith prepares you for trials. As the pattern of Christ-centered dependency becomes your standard, shifting your thoughts back to Christ and His promises will be easier.

Keep in mind you are always in the presence of the living Lord Jesus who promised He would carry your burdens and provide rest—the absence of fretting. True, you may feel stunned, heartbroken, and fearful when a trial knocks you off your feet, but God's rescue plan for regaining your spiritual balance is always available.

With tear-filled eyes of gratitude, I praise my Savior for His grace to rescue me from living daily in the bondage of worry. Having suffered daily in the *smoke* of worry, I rejoice in the freedom of living by faith in the bright *light* of His grace.

Look to Christ for worry-free living.

Reflection Questions

Support your answers with Scripture verses when possible.

1. List three cause of anxiety, which underlie a lack of trust.
    1.
    2.
    3.

2. Why doesn't God want you to worry?

3. Give examples of behaving like the smoke of a smudge pot.

4. List several things you lose when you fail to trust because of anxiety.

5. List the four principles for gaining the peace of God.
    1.
    2.
    3.
    4.

We noted how the sin of anxiety is harmful to our fellowship with Christ. The remainder of this chapter will concentrate on overcoming unbelief, the sin underlying anxiety, and living as a blazing torch for Christ.

A Missed Faith Adventure
An Unbelieving Believer

Zack was a smoking smudge pot of worry and doubt. He had experienced his share of trials—job losses, financial struggles, and relationship problems. Because Zack had an abusive father, he viewed God as unloving and uncaring. Zack professed his trust in the Lord in past trials, but he couldn't give this one over to God. His wife needed gallbladder surgery and he feared something would go wrong—that she might die. Zack was distraught and overcome with anxiety explaining that he wanted assurance that his wife would not die.

Friends encouraged him to trust the Lord who was in control. They confronted him about his sins of worry, fear, and pride (all signs of unbelief). Believers urged him to name these sins as often as they occurred so he could resume fellowship with the Lord. Often, they told him of God's love and compassion and reminded him that God would reveal His love to him through this trial. Zack knew Bible verses and principles, but he chose not to believe; therefore, he couldn't gain the peace of God. Zack lived in unbelieving rebellion against God.

In time, Zack admitted he was fighting God for months insisting God guarantee that his wife would survive the surgery. Finally, Zack came to the end of his own strength—too weak to keep fighting God. Zack confessed his pride of wanting to have his way and trusted God in this trial. Our faithful Lord restored Zack to fellowship and he once again experienced the peace of God.

A doubting believer looks at the circumstances and leaves God out.

God Warns Us about Unbelief

We use our free will to believe God or to resist Him by doubting. The Lord alerts us about the sin of unbelief, also called "hardening of the heart." Hebrews 3:7-15 warns against unbelief citing the example of the Israelites who became hard-hearted and disobeyed God's command to conquer Canaan. Unbelief is stubborn rebellion against God and our sinful nature will always seek to deter us from trusting Him.

To sidetrack us from trusting the Lord, our sin nature tempts us with pride, unbelief, and indifference. Our pride demands we have our way, convincing us we can handle our own problems. Unbelief may result from a believer not knowing God and His powers; however, often unbelief is just sin. A believer may show indifference or unresponsiveness to the Lord and His grace, turning his back on the Lord. The sin of unbelief is pride blinding us from trusting the Lord and seeing the need to ask Him for forgiveness. Although our sin nature predisposes us to sins of pride, unbelief, rebellion, or indifference toward God, we choose whether to sin or to trust.

> *The Lord resists a proud spirit but delights in humble faith.*

What Hinders Your Belief?

Examine the reasons you may not trust God, which will take honesty to admit.

- Am I angry with God for allowing the trial?
- Am I blaming God or others? (Blame is a part of anger.)
- Am I angry God hasn't resolved my problem?
- Am I reluctant to let go and let God handle the problem?
- Do I see my problems as enormous and bigger than God?
- Am I worrying how the trial will turn out?
- Is my attitude demanding my way?
- Am I bargaining with God for the resolutions I want?

- Am I striving to resolve the problems my way?
- Am I convinced God doesn't care?
- Am I indulging in self-pity?
- Am I worried or fearful?
- Am I grumbling and complaining?

Have you noticed the statements focus on you, on your feelings, your attitude, and on what you want? Ask yourself, what is in it for me? Do I enjoy the feelings self-pity causes? What am I gaining from feeling sorry for myself? Does clinging to negative feelings toward your trials give you satisfaction? What do you gain by hanging on to your feelings or problems? Are you enjoying the attention you receive from complaining about your problems? The sin nature's pride always seeks to please itself and make itself the object of attention.

A self-absorbed viewpoint reveals a need for control—an underlying prideful attitude. A controlling manner doubts God's care and power. Seeking to control suggests an attitude of knowing better than God knows. Amid suffering or lifequakes, our sins of unbelief hinder fellowship between God and us.

A believer out of fellowship can't cooperate with the Lord Jesus. What cooperation does the Lord seek? He looks for an attitude of quiet surrender to Him—the all-powerful, sovereign, and all-wise God. Instead of trying to control by fretting or demanding that God remove the trial, the faith-dependent believer cheerfully honors the Lord in all circumstances. Furthermore, unbelief is the greatest obstacle to the Holy Spirit's work, especially His work of conforming us into the likeness of Christ. What do we gain from doubting if we lose God's best?

We have much to lose when we fail to believe God can do more than we think or ask (Eph. 3:20). The more we concentrate on ourselves, the more we restrain the use of our faith. Why not trust the Lord, receive His best, and avoid the misery of angry unbelief?

Trust Christ and the fog of doubt will disperse in the glow of His truth.

Challenging Your Belief

Another key to defeating unbelief is asking questions that challenge your belief. Do I believe God is working all things together for my spiritual good? Am I trusting God to take care of my child and working all things together for his good? Do I believe God loves my friend and is taking care of him? Am I confident my spouse is in the palm of God's hand and not in a "free fall"? Can I honestly say I believe I am not in a "free fall," but in His grip of grace? Answering "yes" to these questions coupled with faith is the key to peace, not just knowing God's truths. No one can have the peace of God unless he believes God's truths.

God challenged my faith often during my husband's long stretches of unemployment in the economic recession of the 1970s. Whenever my faith flickered, the worry bug crawled out. (The sin nature is always ready to cause worry and offer human solutions when the new nature fails to trust.) When I had difficulty believing, I asked the Lord to help me overcome my unbelief (Mark 9:24).

Only by taking God at His Word could I regain peace; only believing God's truths offered peace. God promises to take care of birds and flowers; surely, He would take care of me whom He values more (Matt. 6).

Sometimes during a crisis, meditating on a verse or principle didn't bring peace until I discovered the missing link—belief. I specifically asked myself if I believe this. When I decided to believe God could handle everything, He supplied His peace.

> *Believing God's truths is the Christian's daily choice.*

Entrusting Our Children to God's Care

Karen raised her kids in the Christian faith, but they had abandoned God's ways to "do their own thing." The rebellion of her children caused Karen to worry and grieve. Karen admitted she knew Bible promises, but couldn't find peace. "I repeat them, but the worry and anxiety remain," she admitted. Karen had difficulty believing God's promises. She needed to ask herself if she honestly believed God was watching over her kids, that He loved them and seeks to draw them closer. Consider the example of Moses' parents who entrusted the life of their infant son to God's care (Ex. 2). As a parent, do you trust God enough to take care of your children?

> *Don't let your worries get the best of you;*
> *remember, Moses started out as a basket case.*

As parents we have fears about the future of our children. If our children are believers walking with the Lord, we relax. However, if they are unsaved, we may uselessly worry. Instead of fretting, pray for the salvation of your children and believe the Lord will save those who accept Christ's payment for sin (Luke 19:10; 1 Tim. 2:3-5).

How should we respond when our saved children have turned away from God's principles? Since God has a plan for each life, we pray for our children asking the Lord to prepare them to be receptive to His directives. When our children resist their Savior, we ask God to convict them of their sin. We ask God to motivate them to hear, read, and believe His Word. The Lord is watching over our children, His children whom He pursues so He can restore them to fellowship with Him. If He pursues sinners to save them, do you think He will forget His beloved children?

The Lord Jesus delights when we believe our kids aren't in a free fall but have God's everlasting arms under them. The Lord is the one who holds your child's hand in His hand.

> *The steps of a good man are ordered by the* LORD, *And He delights in his way. Though he fall, he shall not be utterly cast down; For the* LORD *upholds him with His hand* (Ps. 37:23-24).

Defeating Unbelief

Faulty thinking is the source of our unbelief. The more we think about our doubts the greater they seem until they swallow our faith, our strength, and our joy. When our thinking doesn't reflect God's viewpoint, our feelings and mental attitude sins engulf us in distrust; we believe lies. A key to defeating unbelief is refusing to believe the lies of Satan, the world, and our sin nature. Rise above doubt by refusing to pay attention to it. Treat disbelief as any other sin by confessing it and choosing to resume dependence on the Lord.

Believing God's Word is the spiritual weapon that overcomes doubt. Refuse to doubt God's qualities of grace, love, faithfulness, wisdom, and the countless others. For example, when you doubt God loves you, replace that thought with the truth of God's love for you. Look to the cross for God's supreme demonstration of His love. Say (even write it down) "God does love me and the love of God in Christ displayed at Calvary confirms His love for me" (John 3:16; Rom. 5:8; 1 John 4:19). When you pray, ask your Father to restore your belief in Him and then trust Him to do it. Remind yourself that His promises are trustworthy and your feelings are not. Shift from your doubts to Jesus Christ, the Truth (John 14:6), and the clouds of doubts will blow away.

The Most Offensive Sin

People regard sins in degrees such as stealing is worse than lying, committing adultery is worse than gossiping, committing serial killings is worse than a onetime murderer. A sin is a sin in God's eyes, although He does regard one sin to be repulsive. God considers unbelief the most appalling, the most contemptible sin.

God judges a sinner's failure to trust Christ for salvation as the most offensive sin. The sinner's failure to believe in Christ's work alone is the only sin that condemns the sinner to hell. Similarly, the believer's most offensive sin is his failure to depend on Christ in all matters— through lifequakes, the tremors, the disappointments, and throughout trial-free times. A believer out of fellowship is not trusting and this is offensive to the Savior.

God commands us in Colossians 2:6 that as we have received Christ by faith we are to live by faith. A believer who fails to trust in daily living is a deserter from the cause of Christ; he acts and looks like an unsaved person. Unbelief in a believer is an insult to the Savior and cancels the believer's profession of faith. Therefore, prideful unbelief is the most destructive sin of the unsaved or the out of fellowship (carnal) believer.

In our pride, we rebel and refuse to trust God, thus we disconnect ourselves from Him and His blessings. A believer who isn't living by faith is a short-circuited Christian who prefers to unplug himself from his power source—the Holy Spirit. The most disgraceful, ineffective Christian is the one who doesn't trust the Lord. Our failure to live by faith suggests to others that God can't deliver us into His peace.

> *Smoking smudge pots of unbelief smother the display of faith.*

A Blazing Torch Magnifies the Lord

In contrast, God wants us to use His rescue plan of faith to thrive in our trials, proving to others what a great God we have. We give glory to Christ and magnify Him when we endure our trial with faith. People watch us when we are doing well, but when trouble strikes they watch us more closely to see how we respond. Will we react as a smoking smudge pot of anger, worry, despair, fear, or unbelief, which draws attention to our circumstance and to us? If so, we smother our testimony or expression of faith. Or will we respond as a blazing torch of faith that shows the greatness of Christ, our help in time of need?

> *Living by faith is the best testimony to the sufficiency of Christ.*

Reflection Questions

Wherever possible support your answers with Scripture verses.

1. What hinders Christians from believing?

2. What sins suggest a desire to control?

3. What sin does God consider most offensive? Why?

4. How will you challenge and defeat your unbelief?

5. Specifically explain how to be a blazing torch for Christ.

CHAPTER 11 PREVIEW

◌ Your Perception and Perspectives

◌ Does Faith Heal?

◌ The Principle of A fortiori

◌ How Big is Your God?

CHAPTER 11

What Determines Your Faith?

Perceptions and Perspectives

Perceiving is awareness that occurs through our senses, especially sight or hearing but also refers to understanding. For example, during his water walk, Peter saw a large wave and sensed he might drown; he perceived danger and his emotions followed his perception.

Like perceptions, our perspectives determine our feelings and our actions. Perspectives include our beliefs, our attitude, or our frame of reference. For example, when some of Jesus' followers abandoned Him, Jesus asked the twelve if they also wanted to leave Him. Simon Peter answered Jesus, *"Lord, to whom shall we go? You have the words of eternal life. Also we have come to believe and know that You are the Christ, the Son of the living God"* (John 6:68-69). Peter, speaking for the disciples, said that their belief was in Christ, the God-Man—their Savior; therefore, they wanted to remain with Him.

Truth Must Precede Faith

Although our perceptions and perspectives may deceive us, God's truth is real, factual, accurate, reliable, and consistent. God's character portrays the truth and everything about our Lord is honest, perfect, and indisputable (Deut. 32:4; John 1:14; 14:6). God is truth and His word is truth (John 1:17); therefore, we can take Him at His Word. On his water walk, Peter believed the truth about Christ's power to save him from drowning. Jesus' disciples and the apostle Paul believed Jesus Christ was the Messiah; their perspective aligned with God's truth.

Our heavenly Father wants our viewpoint on life's circumstances to match His truth about them. Believing His truths about life's difficulties frees us from attitude sins such as anxiety, worry, fear, and unbelief. So when we bypass God's truth, the Lord will often set up roadblocks or obstacles to reroute our attention and faith back on Him. For example, our caring Lord may set up roadblocks to halt our plans when we fail to trust Him, or He may frustrate our project with obstacles because we display self-sufficiency. God regularly placed obstacles or roadblocks in Israel's path to redirect them to Him, to the truth that He is the only true God. When we align our perspective with His truth, He blesses us with serenity.

> *God's perspective promotes peace.*

Misplaced Trust from Faulty Perspective

Molly had a fascination with angels; she had a collection of angel figurines and filled her pastime reading about them. She believed angels had special powers and could help her during trials. Unfortunately, Molly had some false beliefs about angels because she didn't know what the Bible teaches about them. She looked to angels for answers to her problems, thus she placed her faith in the wrong object.

Our Sovereign Lord Jesus Christ reigns supreme over the angels that He created (John 1:3; Col. 1:15-6); therefore, angels are subordinate to God. God commands angels to worship Jesus Christ (Heb. 1:6). John the apostle stated that angels worship God (Rev. 7:11). Angels themselves commanded the apostle John to worship God, not them (Rev. 19:10; 22:9). We always worship and trust God, the Creator, never His creation (John 5:23). Relying on angels is idolatry—a misplacement of the trust and admiration God requires of us. The psalmist testifies he didn't believe in others or things but in the Lord God (Ps. 20:7).

> *We ought all to rely with confidence on the promises of our dear Redeemer, and give Him our hearts.*
> —President Andrew Jackson, Sept. 11, 1834

Other misperceptions of faith include trusting in self, in others, in dead people to intercede for us, or even fate. Some people trust in faith itself or faith and prayer, instead of God alone.

What the Bible Says about Faith Healers

Besides unbiblical beliefs in angels, some people place their faith and hope in people such as faith healers. Desperation drives some Christians, like Elliot, who has been in a wheelchair the last ten years, to seek faith healers. While Elliot watched a Christian TV channel, he heard about a faith healer coming to his area. Excited Elliot believed the faith healer could heal him. He placed his faith in a faith healer instead leaving the decision to the Lord.

Do "faith healers" today have power from God? Is faith healing a valid gift of the Holy Spirit today? God gave the "gift of healings" to the early church (1 Cor. 12:9). What was the purpose of this gift? If the main purpose of this sign gift was to heal, then why were some people healed while others were not? The purpose of the gift of healing (a sign gift) was not healing but revelation; sign gifts (miracles) signaled or pointed people to Christ.

God used these sign gifts, including the "gift of healing" to confirm His new disclosure of truth. Healings revealed and confirmed the truth about Jesus Christ. Christ sometimes used His supernatural works (miracles) as signs or proof that He was indeed the long awaited Messiah (John 4:48; 5:36; 6:30). The apostles also used miracles (signs) to support their message about the identity of Jesus Christ, the Messiah and His truths.

As the New Testament neared completion, the use of sign gifts decreased (1 Cor. 13:8-10). One example is Paul who wrote in his last letter that he left Trophimus sick in Miletus (2 Tim. 4:20). Therefore, if Paul still had the gift of healing, he would have healed Trophimus.

How does modern so-called "faith healing" differ from the biblical healings of Christ and the apostles? Biblical healings had specific characteristics such as being immediate, complete, obvious, always successful, undeniable, and never for money. Furthermore, biblical healings brought glory exclusively to God, never to man (Acts 3:1-13; 4:13-16; 14:8-18). Notice the difference between biblical healing and today's faith healings—long, drawn-out, uncertain, partial, often failures, in other words fake healings. (Modern day "faith healers" may be instruments of Satan that he uses to deceive and to distract Christians from Christ.) Today's wealthy faith healers always solicit money, drive expensive cars, wear diamond rings, and bring glory to themselves. They are fake healers, not faith healers.

Does Faith Heal?

The statement, "You weren't healed, because you didn't have enough faith," deceives many people, even believers. Lindy in the next story believed her faith would heal her.

Life was pleasant and normal for Lindy, her husband, and their twelve-year-old son until her doctor diagnosed her with cancer. When we visited with Lindy, she repeatedly told us God would heal her because she believed He would. Confusion occurred because the doctors told her and her family that she was in the final stages of cancer, yet she repeatedly told us she would survive. Lindy clung to her faith believing it would save her since she didn't know God's healing doesn't depend on a person's faith. Healing is God's choice since His will is perfect (Isa. 55:8-9).

Only a reliable object of faith saves or delivers you, not your faith. For example, you trust a chair (the object) to hold you when you sit on it. You trust a firefighter (the object) will catch you in his net when you jump from a second floor window. Imagine you are on the tenth floor of a burning building; you see some people below waving their arms and assume they have a net to catch you so you jump. As you free-fall towards the third story, you see no net, just some panicky people waving and shouting; you placed your faith in an unreliable object.

The object of faith delivers not faith itself.

What Must be the Object of Your Faith?

If faith doesn't heal, then what must be the object of our faith? True healing power comes from the Lord, the object of deliverance, not our faith. On occasion Jesus did recognize someone's faith such as the woman He healed (Matt. 9:18-22). However, her "faith" wasn't the object of her healing, Jesus Christ was. When Jesus commented about someone's faith, His remarks encouraged the person to continue trusting Him. A lame man, healed by Jesus, showed no faith when his friends brought him to Jesus (Mark 2:1-12). The man born blind exercised no faith when Jesus healed him (John 9). Through Peter, God healed the lame man who asked for alms, not healing. The crippled man exercised no faith since he was unaware of what God could do (Acts 3). Dead Lazarus had no faith when Jesus raised him from the grave (John 11).

Although the Lord may recognize a person's faith, He does the healing; faith doesn't heal. God, the great Physician, may use medicine, natural medicine and sometimes no human means—the unexplained healings or modern day miracles. Since the Lord has the power to heal and raise the dead, will you believe He can take care of all your problems?

Our healing Savior prescribes the course of sickness and healing for His purposes in trials. Since our heavenly Father loves His children, He allows trials—bitter medicine for diseased souls needing healing.

> *God's promises are like medicine and only restore when believed.*

Lessons from Peter's Water Walk

One of my favorite biblical accounts is Peter walking on the water on the stormy Sea of Galilee. Peter walked on the water because he placed his confidence in Jesus; he trusted Jesus word, *"Come."* Peter's confidence (reliance) on the Lord brought courage towards his circumstance—the stormy sea. However, when Peter shifted his stare away from Jesus he noticed the boisterous winds increasing the waves. Seeing the waves, he became afraid of drowning; he forgot Jesus word of empowerment. Peter's faith sunk, and he began to sink into the sea. However, in dependency, Peter looked to the Lord and shouted, *"Lord save me!"* (Matt. 14:30). He chose to resume his trust in the Lord and of course, Jesus extended His hand to rescue him.

When we shift our focus to the circumstances, which may not only confuse and overwhelm us, they distract us from Christ, who alone can rescue us.

> *We don't need to have great faith; the Lord only asks us to rely on His faithfulness.*

The Power and Faithfulness of God

Satan or our sin nature will tempt us to look at our faith. If our faith is weak, we may become discouraged, if our faith is strong, we may become proud. Either way, looking at our faith weakens us by distracting us from the Lord. Remember, the power in our life doesn't come from our faith but from our Savior and His promises.

Our Father's faithfulness to keep His promises doesn't depend on us, or on our faith or lack of it. Since God is perfect, it is impossible for Him not to keep His promises (Deut. 32:4; Matt. 5:48). God's promises are as strong as His character and as reliable as the sun rising tomorrow. His Word is as powerful now as the day He commanded the light, sun, stars, water, plants, and the rest of creation into existence. His power keeps the heavenly bodies in perfect movement without collisions.Compared to controlling the universe and coordinating the events of the world, our problems are tiny. Your life isn't too complex for God to understand or preserve.

> *Nothing is too difficult for Him!*

Many hymn writers wrote about the object of our faith, Jesus Christ. One such hymn is "My Faith Has Found a Resting Place" written by Eliza Edmunds Hewitt.

The Philadelphia born author of this hymn text, Eliza (Lidie) Edmunds Hewitt was an invalid for much of her life. A reckless student striking her with a piece of slate caused her spinal injury. Out of this experience, she developed an intimate relationship with God, a love for the Scriptures, and a desire to share her feelings with others through writing. She became a prolific author of children's poetry and Sunday school literature. Various gospel musicians soon became aware of her many fine poems and set them to suitable music. In later years Eliza's physical condition improved, and she increased her activity in Christian ministries. She was a close friend of Fanny Crosby and often met with her for fellowship and discussion of new hymns they had written. One of her best-known hymns, "More About Jesus" was first published in 1887. Miss Hewitt's prayer, *Spirit of God, my teacher be, showing the things of Christ to me*, was beautifully answered in her many hymns with heart-felt words of faith.

Scripture and Music, *www.scriptureandmusic.com*

Had Eliza never been bed-ridden, she might not have written so many hymns. In the following hymn, observe the many biblical thoughts on which to anchor your faith.

> **MY FAITH HAS FOUND A RESTING PLACE**
> *"Therefore, having been justified by faith, we have peace with God through our Lord Jesus Christ"* (Rom. 5:1).
>
> My faith has found a resting place,
> Not in device or creed;
> I trust the ever living One,
> His wounds for me shall plead.
>
> REFRAIN: I need no other argument,
> I need no other plea,
> It is enough that Jesus died,
> And that He died for me.
>
> Enough for me that Jesus saves,
> This ends my fear and doubt;
> A sinful soul I come to Him,
> He'll never cast me out.
>
> My heart is leaning on the Word,
> The living Word of God,
> Salvation by my Savior's Name,
> Salvation through His blood.
>
> My great Physician heals the sick,
> The lost He came to save;
> For me His precious blood He shed,
> For me His life He gave.
>
> ~ Eliza Edmunds Hewitt, 1851- 1920 ~

Perspectives for Christ-centered Living

Do you recognize the moment-by-moment presence of God enough to trust Him with all matters, even everyday trivial happenings? I remember how the Lord encouraged me through school exams. He gave me poise, confidence, and clarity of thought for public speaking. When I felt overwhelmed, He supplied what I needed to teach a class. My all-knowing Lord showed me where I had misplaced my keys. Jesus, my best Friend provided a nearby parking space when I was late for an appointment. Many times my great Physician healed me from sickness or halted the ambush of a cold. The Lord Jesus, my faithful Provider, often supplies a friend to encourage me. My Deliverer saved me from injury or death by maneuvering an unexpected fast moving semi-truck to swerve onto the shoulder of the road to avoid plowing into me.

My Lord Jesus reminds me of His presence when He comforts me with His promises. He enables me to endure with confidence through regular dependency on Him. Are you aware of God's presence and workings in everyday matters in your daily routine? Is your view of your Savior one of consistent companionship?

How to Get Closer to Christ

We become emotionally close to those with whom we share conversation, spend time with, or support during tough times. Do you share more about your life with a friend than you do with your best Friend, the Lord Jesus? How do you think your friendship with the Lord would change if you shared your problems in prayer? Could trusting God's promises cause you to feel closer to Him? How often do you seek the Lord in prayer to praise Him?

> *A Christ-centered perspective is the driving force of a life of faith.*

Choosing God's Viewpoint

Remember Vince, who suffered a paralyzing injury when he fell from a tree while deer hunting? As he lay helpless on the ground, his focus was on the Lord. Later as he grieved his losses in a hospital bed, he sincerely confessed, *"the LORD gave, and the LORD has taken away; Blessed be the name of the LORD"* (Job 1:21b). The often-omitted words, *"Blessed be the name of the LORD,"* not only praise the Lord but also imply submission to God's perfect will. Because God had another plan for Vince, He changed his life and Vince accepted that.

Perspectives on Comparing Trials?

When I told others about Vince's accident and his faith perspective, they thanked me and said it helped them put their problems into perspective. Are there benefits for comparing our trials with the troubles of others? How long might we feel better if our trial isn't as severe as the other person's? Suppose you don't have other people's problems to compare with yours to help you feel better. Will you continue to wallow in self-pity and worry about your problems? Will you continue in human viewpoint?

Instead of comparing your suffering with the trials of another, consider the following comparisons. What would your life be like if Jesus wasn't your best friend but your worst enemy? You wouldn't have peace, comfort, joy, security or the other blessings the Christian life offers. If Jesus hadn't suffered the penalty of your sin, what would happen to you? Without your position in Christ, you couldn't go to heaven; you would be on your way to hell—eternal separation from God. Instead of comparing your earthly trials with those of others, compare your trial to being alone without Christ now and forever. Comparing our trials doesn't offer lasting comfort, but reflecting on our life with Christ gives us comfort and the peace of God.

Do You Need a Perspective Adjustment?

Do you usually react or respond during a difficulty or trial? The next story describes three responses to difficult times. Which response describes you most of the time?

Carrots, Eggs, or Coffee?
Author unknown

Analise, a young woman filled with anxiety and fears, went to her mother and whined about her difficult life. Analise complained she didn't know how she was going to make it through her troubles. Exhausted from struggling, she wanted to give up.

Her mother took her to the kitchen, filled three pots with water, and placed each on high temperature. Soon the pots came to boil; she dropped carrots in the first pot, she placed eggs in the second, and she dumped ground coffee beans in the last. Without saying a word, she let them sit and boil.

In about twenty minutes, she turned off the burners. She fished the carrots out and placed them in a bowl, scooped out the eggs and set them in another bowl, and then ladled some coffee and poured it into a third bowl. Turning to her daughter, she asked, "Tell me what you see." "Carrots, eggs, and coffee," Analise replied.

Her mother brought her closer and asked her to feel the carrots. Analise touched them and noted they were soft. Her mother asked her daughter to take an egg and peel it; Analise noted the hard-boiled egg. Finally, her mother asked the daughter to sip the coffee and Analise smiled, as she tasted its rich flavor.

Her mother explained that each of these objects had faced the same adversity—boiling water. Each reacted differently. The carrots went in strong, hard, and unrelenting, but after sitting in the boiling water, they softened and became weak. The egg had been fragile; its liquid interior protected by its shell, but after soaking in boiling water, its inside became hardened. The ground coffee beans were unique—they had changed the water. "Which are you?" Mom asked Analise.

Dear believer, when troubles shake you up, how do you respond? Are you the carrot, strong at first, but with difficulties, you wilt and become soft and weak?

Are you the egg that starts with a malleable heart but changes with the heat? Did you start with a fluid spirit and after the loss of a loved one, a disappointment, or a financial hardship did you become hardened? Does your shell look the same, but are you bitter and tough on the inside? Do you have an inflexible spirit and hardened heart?

On the other hand, are you like the coffee bean which changes the hot water—the same circumstance that brings the pain? When the water gets hot, the coffee bean releases the aroma and flavor. If you are like the coffee bean, you choose to depend on the Lord when circumstances become difficult. The dependent believer identifies with the words of the apostle Paul: *"We are hard pressed on every side, yet not crushed; we are perplexed, but not in despair; persecuted, but not forsaken; struck down, but not destroyed"* (2 Cor. 4:8-9). Leaning on Christ prevents discouragement. A Christian who lives by faith in the boiling pot of trials is a sweet-smelling aroma to Christ.

> *God controls what we go through. We decide how we go through it.*

How Big Is Your God?
Someone shared this with me; the author is unknown.

Consider the faith of two believers. Abraham trusted when God commanded him to sacrifice his only son (Gen. 22:1-4) and David relied on the Lord when he fought Goliath (1 Sam. 17). Their view of God aligned with the truth about Him, which gave them confidence in Him. They believed God had control over their circumstances. What is your view of God? Now take time to meditate on the magnificent character of our Lord Jesus Christ.

- God is good and He is good all the time. As you focus on His goodness, remember His greatness.
- He is unparalleled and unprecedented.
- He is the centerpiece of civilization.
- He is the greatest of all excellence.
- He is the source of divine grace.
- His name is the only One able to save.
- His life sacrificed as payment for sin is the only power able to cleanse.
- His ear is open to the sinner's call.
- His hand is quick to lift the fallen soul.
- He is the eternal lover of us all.

Jesus is God and you can trust Him!
- He is the essence of human greatness.
- He sympathizes with the wounded and broken.
- His mercies are new every morning to comfort the suffering soul.
- He helps the tempted and the tried.
- He strengthens the weak and weary.

- He guards and He guides the wanderer.
- He heals the sick and cleanses the leper.
- He delivers the captives and defends the helpless.
- He binds up the heartbroken.
- He is for you.

You can trust Jesus!
- He knows all your fears and needs.
- He is all-powerful and can take care of your problems.
- His power is sufficient to transform you into the likeness of Jesus Christ.
- He is for you. "If God is for us, who can be against us?"
- Jesus is the key to all knowledge, the fountain of all wisdom.
- He is the doorway of deliverance.
- He is the pathway of peace.
- He is the roadway of righteousness.
- He is the highway to heaven.
- Jesus is the gateway to glory.

Yes, you can trust Him!
- Jesus is enough; He is sufficient.
- He is King, King of heaven, King of Glory and LORD of lords.
- Rejoice that He is your sovereign King.
- No gauge can measure His limitless love.
- No barriers block His overflowing blessings.
- He is enduringly strong.
- He is supreme.
- He is eternally steadfast.
- He is regally powerful.
- He is impartially merciful.

Jesus is God and you can trust Him!
- Christ is incomprehensible.
- He is invisible.
- He is irresistible.
- You cannot live without Him.
- Death could not conquer Him and the grave could not hold Him.
- He is the First and the Last—the Alpha and the Omega.
- He is the God of the future and the God of the past.

What Determines Your Faith?

With all those glorious traits, how can you not trust Him? Faith is only as reliable as the character of the person you are trusting. Faith in God expects Him to answer. Faith says, "God, You are true to Your character and Your Word." Have you been perceiving your problems as "big" and your God as "small"?

> *Reliance on God's greatness makes faith effective.*

The hymn "Trusting Jesus" depicts the faith reliance of a believer during challenges to his faith. When your faith seems small, lacking courage or persistency, shift your focus to Jesus Christ—the mighty object of your faith.

The history of the hymn:

> The author, Edgar Page Stites, was for many years an obscure but active lay-worker in the Methodist Church of Cape May, New Jersey. One of his ancestors was John Howland who came to America on the Mayflower. Mr. Stites served in the Civil War and later for a time was a riverboat pilot. He also worked for a time as a Methodist home missionary in the Dakotas.
>
> The composer, Ira D. Sankey, is well known to Christians. He has been called the "Father of Gospel Music" because of his many contributions to gospel hymnody [hymn collections] during the latter quarter of the 19th century. Mr. Sankey has contributed the music to such favorites as "A Shelter in the Time of Storm," and "Hiding in Thee." Ira D. Sankey, the composer, relates the following incident regarding the birth of this hymn:
>
> The words of this hymn were handed to Mr. Moody in Chicago, in 1876, as a newspaper clipping. He gave it to me and asked me to write a tune for them. I agreed if he would vouch for the doctrine and he said he would. The hymn was first published in Sankey Gospel Hymns No. 2, published in 1876. The hymn was widely used in the great Moody and Sankey evangelistic meetings in the following year. This simple text and musical expression of childlike trust in Jesus has met the daily spiritual needs of many of God's people in the present time.
>
> Bible Study Charts, *www.biblestudycharts.com*

> **TRUSTING JESUS**
> *"The righteous...his heart is steadfast, trusting in the Lord"* (Ps. 112:7).
>
> Simply trusting every day,
> Trusting through a stormy way;
> Even when my faith is small,
> Trusting Jesus, that is all.
>
> REFRAIN: Trusting as the moments fly,
> Trusting as the days go by;
> Trusting Him whate'er befall,
> Trusting Jesus, that is all.
>
> Brightly does His Spirit shine
> Into this poor heart of mine;
> While He leads I cannot fall;
> Trusting Jesus, that is all.
>
> Singing if my way is clear,
> Praying if the path be drear;
> If in danger for Him call;
> Trusting Jesus, that is all.
>
> Trusting Him while life shall last,
> Trusting Him till earth be past;
> Till within the jasper wall,
> Trusting Jesus, that is all.
>
> ~ Edgar P. Stites, 1836-1921 ~

Perspectives on Overcoming

Have you heard the statement, just accept Jesus as your Savior and your life will be better? You know that isn't true if you have suffered for the faith. Have you ever been in a crisis where there is nothing you can do or say; you are so stunned by the lifequake that you couldn't pray?

God will often bring a believer to the end of his own strength so he must look to Christ. Yet Jesus cheers us on with encouragement: *"These things* [Bible principles] *I have spoken to you, so that in Me you may have peace. In the world you have tribulation, but take courage* [have confidence]; *I have overcome the world"* (John 16:33 NASB). Do you believe Christ has overcome the world? What does He mean "overcome the world"? At the cross, Christ conquered everything that opposes Him (the world, Satan, and the sin nature).

Jesus Christ is the conqueror over sin, Satan and the world, and as a believer in Christ, you are also an overcomer (Rom. 8:37; 1 John 5:4-5). The believer can conquer opposition through dependence on Christ. In other words, faith that depends on Christ's character, His work, and His promises can overcome sin, Satan, and the world.

The Perspective of a *Fortiori*

Many years ago, I learned an encouraging principle to apply to my trials. The principle comes from the Latin word a *fortiori* (ah fohr-ti-oh-ree) which means for a still greater reason, even more, for similar but more convincing reasons. A fortiori reasons that if one can accomplish the greater task, he can complete the lesser one. If I can walk a marathon, I can walk around the block. If I can drive my car across the country, I can drive to the grocery store.

Applying a *Fortiori* to Our Trials

We can apply the "a fortiori" principle to our trials. For example, which is the greater problem: suffering the penalty of your sins or your current lifequake? Since Christ did the most for you at Calvary when He gave his life for you, it follows He will take care of the rest of your smaller problems.

When we recognize the enormous suffering of Christ at the cross, we can adjust our poor attitude towards our miniature-like suffering. Since God spares us from what we deserve, will we accept minimal (by comparison) suffering in trials?

> *Reflecting on Christ's cross work*
> *is a key to regaining your perspective.*

First the Cross, then the Glory

We will gain a God-pleasing perspective when we accept suffering as part of identification with Christ. He is our example for enduring suffering. *"Therefore, since Christ has suffered in the flesh, arm yourselves also with the same mind, for he who has suffered in the flesh has ceased from sin"* (1 Peter 4:1). Only at the cross of Christ can we learn to accept our trials because the Lord allows them as part of sharing in His suffering. Since we share in His suffering, we will share in His glory as Paul wrote. *"Beloved, do not think it strange concerning the fiery trial which is to try you, as though some strange thing happened to you; but rejoice to the extent that you partake of Christ's sufferings, that when His glory is revealed, you may also be glad with exceeding joy"* (1 Peter 4:12-13; also, 2 Cor. 1:5, 7). First comes the cross of suffering and then comes the glories of heaven. Christ willingly suffered in your place to please His Father. Will you choose to accept trials as the will of your heavenly Father?

Faith dependency during trials will shine glory on the Lord. In the darkness of a lifequake, look to Jesus Christ for guidance on trial journeys. *"When I sit in darkness, the LORD will be a light to me"* (Micah 7:8c). A Christ-centered view of trials assures you His peace (John 14:27; 16:33) regardless of your lifequake.

> *"The LORD is my light and my salvation; Whom shall I fear? The LORD is the strength of my life; Of whom shall I afraid?"* (Ps. 27:1).

Reflection Questions

Wherever possible support your answers with Scripture verses.

1. How does your perception of God determine your faith?

2. What did you learn about the "object" of faith?

3. God's promises are as strong as His character. Give examples of how this truth will affect your faith life in the future.

4. How is the believer an overcomer?

5. Describe how your dependency on Christ has changed so far.

CHAPTER 12 PREVIEW

~ What is Faith?

~ The Faith-Rest Life

~ Applications for Using Faith-Rest

~ Pictures of Faith in Action

~ Guarding the Faith-Rest Life

CHAPTER 12

The Spiritual First Aid Kit—Faith-Rest

The Essence of Faith

Faith is a decision. We make up our mind about something. In addition, faith is a confident belief in the truth, value, or reliability of a person, idea, or item and doesn't always rely on proof or material evidence. (Of course, dishonest people may deceive us into believing lies, but we are discussing scriptural truths here.) Belief, a synonym for faith and trust, is the mental act, condition, or habit of placing trust or confidence in another.

Faith that accompanies prayer refers to the confidence we have in God to answer our prayers according to His will (1 John 5:14-15). In addition, faith gives substance to the unseen things spoken of in Scriptures (Heb. 11:1-3).

The real meaning of biblical faith is a deliberate decision to believe what God has revealed in the Bible. Saving faith is a person's trust in the finished work of Christ apart from any work of his own (Rom. 4:5, 23-25; 5:1; Eph. 2:8-9). At your faith decision, God the Holy Spirit "locked" you into eternal life (John 10:27-30; Rom. 8:35-39). Again by faith, you believe that since God saved you, no one and nothing can cause you to lose your salvation (Rom. 8:38-39). God saves you forever, and Christ holds your eternal destiny securely in His hand (John 10:28-30).

As you know, after salvation from the penalty of sin, God wants the same faith applied to overcome the power of sin. Just as faith in Christ was the focus at salvation, now after salvation, faith, not works, is the way to live (Col. 2:6). Furthermore, just as the Holy Spirit provided your salvation, He now works to produce the life of Christ (the fruit of the Spirit*) though you.

> *Faith is a decision to trust Christ for salvation and then for daily living.*

---

*The fruit of the Spirit (Gal. 5:22-23) is the character traits of Christ, which the Spirit works through the believer who is in fellowship.

What Does Faith Mean?

In Matthew 18:3-4, Jesus instructs His listeners to *"become as little children,"* in other words "to have a childlike faith," which is necessary for salvation. The faith of a child is simple, uncomplicated and means "to take another at his word." A child will believe what mommy and daddy tell him, i.e., this is a red ball, God created all things. In humbleness, a child believes what his parents tell him. Similarly, God looks for a humble spirit to accept whatever He tells us. Simply stated, either we take Him at His Word or we call God a liar. Faith is a choice, not a feeling; therefore, faith is a matter of our will. We must draw on that same childlike faith to live dependent on Christ.

Synonyms for faith are hope, confidence, trust, and belief. In Scripture, "hope" confirms God working behind the scenes. *"Now faith is the assurance of things hoped for, the conviction of things not seen"* (Heb. 11:1 NASB). In English, when we use the word "hope" we refer to the desire for something, usually with confidence in the *possibility* of its fulfillment. In English, hope suggests the idea that although something hasn't happened yet, we anticipate its coming. In biblical language, the word "hope" depicts certainty; hope is an old word for trust or for confidence. Hope is confident anticipation of the future because of what God has told us as we read in Hebrews 11:1, *"Now faith is the substance of things hoped for, the evidence of things not seen."* Replace "hope" with "confidently trust" in Romans 8:25, *"But if we hope for what we do not see, we eagerly wait for it with perseverance."* In this verse, "hope," suggests confident expectation in His promise to provide endurance during trials.

Faith-Rest: The Spiritual First Aid

The Principles of Faith Rest

1. Faith is a system of thinking; it believes without seeing.
2. The faith-rest method applies God's promises and principles to circumstances and thereby stabilizes thinking.

3. Faith rest believes in the power of God's character and His Word.
4. The faith-rest approach to circumstances offers inner peace and freedom from mental attitude sins.
5. Faith rest is not an end in itself; instead, it sets the stage for thinking God's viewpoint.
6. Faith rest revolves around a relationship with Jesus Christ.
7. Faith rest is effective when the believer is in fellowship with God—filled with the Spirit.

The Faith-Rest Formula

Have you discovered that human solutions don't eliminate your stressful feelings? When there seem to be no solutions, do you notice that you lack peace? Our loving Father yearns to give you His peace, but you may not understand how to have His peace. The Lord has given you His Word—promises and principles as part of His faith-rest plan. He wants you to *know* the promise and principles, to *believe* them, and then *apply* them to your problems. Before you can *believe* promises, you must *know* them. A method for learning Scripture is through verse cards. Carry God's promises with you on 3"x 5" index cards to meditate on and memorize throughout the day. Memorizing Bible verses during sunny days will cloak you with their comfort on stormy days.

Faith rest is dependent on believing the facts of the Word of God; it is mixing faith with His promises (Heb. 4:2). You can have perfect peace whenever you apply this formula:

Know God's promises + Believe God's promises = Enjoy God's Rest

Procedure for Faith-Rest Application:

1. Recall a promise or principle from God's Word.
2. Meditate on what it means—think of its underlying biblical principle.
3. Believe the promise and believe that Jesus Christ is in control of the situation. He understands the problem from beginning to end.

Believe that from God's viewpoint, the problem or circumstance isn't hopeless.
4. Relax and enjoy His rest.

> *Remember, you can't break God's promises by leaning on them!*

How Can We Gain Consistent Faith?

Christ's finished work on the cross must be the source of our spiritual growth (John 15:5). Without this fundamental belief, our faith can't grow or be consistent. If you have trusted Jesus Christ for *your greatest need*—salvation from sin's penalty (Eph. 2:8-9), it follows you can trust Him for minor necessities such as your daily needs (Matt. 6:25-35; 7:7-11; Rom. 8:31-32). God promises "rest" to His children. For the background of faith rest, please read Hebrews 4. This chapter describes Israel who disobeyed through unbelief and therefore failed to enter God's rest (Heb. 4:5-6). Faith simply rests and rejoices in God's work.

For salvation from the penalty of sin, we rested from our work to save ourselves and instead we relied on the finished work of Christ. So also in living, we rest from working or trying to resolve unsolvable circumstances, we stop striving; instead, we rely on Christ.

> *But how to get faith strengthened? Not by striving after faith, but by resting on the Faithful One.* —Hudson Taylor

"How Firm a Foundation" is a favorite hymn of many Christians. The American love and preference for this remarkable hymn was strikingly illustrated on Christmas Eve, 1898, when an entire corps of the United States Army, Northern and Southern (encamped on the Quemados hills, near Havana, Cuba) took up the sacred tune and words.

Cyber Hymnal, *www.hymntime.com*

This powerful hymn demonstrates the courage gained from leaning on the sufficiency of the Lord.

> How Firm a Foundation
> *"The firm foundation of God stands"* (2 Tim. 2:19 NASB).
>
> How firm a foundation, you saints of the Lord,
>   Is laid for your faith in His excellent Word!
> What more can He say than to you He hath said,
>   To you who for refuge to Jesus have fled?
>
> "Fear not, I am with you; O be not dismayed,
>   For I am your God, I will still give thee aid;
> I'll strengthen you, help you, and cause you to stand,
>   Upheld by My righteous, omnipotent hand."
>
> "When through fiery trials your pathway shall lie,
>   My grace, all sufficient, shall be your supply:
> The flame shall not hurt you; I only design
>   Your dross to consume and your gold to refine."
>
> ~ John Rippon, 1877 ~

The "Rest" of Faith

The "rest" in Hebrews chapter four isn't the same rest as described in Leviticus 19:3, 30. This rest is not the Sabbath or seventh day of rest and neither is it a sabbatical year (Lev. 25:2, 4). The "rest" described in the Old Testament refers to physical rest (cessation from work) or the rest for the soil (no planting). Since Christ won the victory at the cross, we are no longer under the Law or under the Sabbath (day of rest) to keep these times of rest. Instead, we are under grace and Jesus Christ is our rest. His rest is not once a week rest but a moment-by-moment rest. We trust the Lord to handle difficult circumstances and to carry us through them. We rest in Him to provide our spiritual needs. Just as we don't work (verse 4) to earn salvation we must stop striving to gain His rest for daily living.

> *Faith is always the absence of work; faith is resting not striving.*

Pictures of Faith in Action

Hebrews eleven illustrates the faith responses in the lives of believers in the Bible. By faith (total confidence, hope), David was certain that God was greater than Goliath, the nine-foot Philistine giant. David was convinced that God had already provided the victory. (Read David's declaration of faith in 1 Sam. 17:37, 46-47.)

By faith, Abraham obeyed God's instruction to offer his only son Isaac as a sacrifice. Although Abraham wondered why God commanded this sacrifice, he didn't question God's authority and sovereignty. What thoughts must have entered Abraham's mind? God wants me to kill Isaac, my long expected, promised son. What about God's promises linked to this son—promises of many descendants and land for them? If Jehovah God detests human sacrifice, a practice used by surrounding heathen nations, how could He command me to murder my son on an altar? Abraham didn't run away from God's command as Jonah did nor did Abraham throw a "pity party." Instead, Abraham chose to obey God believing that He could resurrect Isaac afterward. Abraham told his servants, *"we will come back to you"* (Gen. 22:5b). Isaac had questions, too. He saw the fire and the wood and asked, *"where is the lamb for a burnt offering?"* (Gen. 22:7). Without wavering Abraham answered, *"My son, God will provide for Himself the lamb for a burnt offering"* (Gen. 22:8). By faith, Abraham modeled his conviction that God would provide a lamb substitute for his son, Isaac. His faith confirmed what he couldn't see. If you are afraid to trust the Lord with your prized possession, your dream, or a loved one, what can you learn from Abraham's display of faith?

We have just considered the faith model of two believers, David and Abraham, who had complete confidence in God; a belief that God was in control of their circumstances. The Bible records examples of believers who lived by faith, which is listed in the "Heroes Hall of Faith" (Heb. 11). Our Lord recorded the faith of these believers to strengthen us, to guide us, and encourage us to trust consistently in Him who keeps His promises. *"Let us hold fast the confession of our hope without wavering, for He who promised is faithful"* (Heb. 10:23; also Deut. 7:9a; 1 Thess. 5:24; 1 Peter 4:19). Faith includes the confidence in a mighty Lord God, who can accomplish more than we could ever imagine (Eph. 3:20).

> *Faith brings the power of God into the life of the believer.*
> —J. Hampton Keathley III, ABCs for Christian GROWTH

Faith Rest, the Remedy for Stress

Are you stressed and longing for serenity? Have you become unemployed? Have the stock market plunges caused you to lose half of your retirement funds? Are you grieving a loss? Perhaps you have a significant health problem, which causes distress. Are you worried about the future of the country? What is causing you stress? As you have heard, stress adversely changes your health. The longer you stay stressed, the more likely your body will succumb to pain or disease.

The Scriptures reveal the many trials of David and his responses or reactions to them. At one point, enemies captured his family. David's grief overpowered him and he lost his strength. In addition, David's men were so angry with him that they talked of stoning him—a reason for further distress. However, David regained his faith in the Lord his God (1 Sam. 30:6) and by faith he followed the Lord's guidance. The Lord enabled him and his men to rescue their families and their belongings. Afterward, David rejoiced in the Lord recognizing God who protected them in a battle with the enemy.

Are you striving or thriving in your trials? Consider the next two responses to stress. Ted hurried through life striving to take care of himself and his family. He believed that Jesus is his Savior, but he didn't have dependent faith for everyday living. Ted wished to be like his believer friend, Nick, who also had work pressures and family responsibilities, but he was relaxed and calm. Nick trusted Christ, first for eternal salvation, and then he practiced living by faith, which gave Him God's peace.

How are you handling your stressful circumstances? Perhaps you have slipped back into old habits of leaning on yourself or an addictive behavior to help you cope. Has your spiritual health declined because you are using your own remedies to cope with life's circumstances? Have you forgotten that the Lord gave us His grace prescription for spiritual wellness?

> **The Grace Remedy for STRESS**
> **S**earch the Scriptures
> **T**rust the truths of God's Word
> **R**est on His Promises
> **E**ffectively Pray
> **S**ing His Praises
> **S**eek the Sovereign Savior

Faith resting is the means for inner peace and power amid minor difficulties or devastating lifequakes. God desires that every believer would trust Him consistently; yet, many believers never use this grace provision of faith rest. Perhaps you don't know where to begin. Start faith resting by naming your sins and then your troubles to the Lord in prayer (Phil. 4:6). Many people have a faith that seeks, but not a faith that rests in the Christ. *"Rest in the LORD, and wait patiently for Him"* (Ps. 37:7) is a command to let go of your burdens and rest (stop worrying). The rest of faith is the absence of fretting. Choose to place your confidence in His ability to see you thrive in the difficulties. Faith rest is a mind-set of trust and submission to God's will as He commands: *"Come to Me, all you who labor and are heavy laden, and I will give you rest"* (Matt. 11:28). Stop trying to control circumstances and people in an effort to find peace; instead, throw your cares on the Lord.

> *Spiritual rest is the absence of effort.*

When we use the faith application not just for difficult circumstances but also in every area of life, then we will have contentment. The more often you seek Christ Jesus in your lifequakes, in your sorrows and during stress-free times, the more you attach yourself to Him. As we trust more, our relationship with Christ grows. The more we live for Him, the more distractions, diversions, and anxieties of the world fade away.

> *Rest is God's deliverance into His peace,*
> *not the rescue from our problems.*

Faith Rest and His Service

We need time for relaxation, rest, and renewal in today's hectic lifestyle. Often believers who experience burnout while serving God fail to take time to relax and fail to faith rest. The next story depicts a believer who lost his focus. As you read, consider what comes before faith resting.

A Missed Faith Adventure
What Must Come before Serving the Lord?

Take time to reflect on: *"For he who has entered His rest has himself also ceased from his works as God did from His. Let us therefore be diligent to enter that rest, lest anyone fall according to the same example of disobedience"* (Heb. 4:10-11). Bill pondered that verse and wrote,

> Fresh out of college and encouraged by what I had been learning within my local church, I was ready to do "great things for God." I failed to realize the Lord wanted me to learn to rest in Him before doing works. Witnessing for Christ whenever an opportunity arose was a tendency of mine. I do encourage evangelism; however, if not put in its proper place, it can become a yoke of bondage. At times, my witnessing was uneasy and fearful and absent of the Spirit of God, but I didn't care because the gospel was going out to the lost!
>
> Even though I would never admit it, I was subtly seeking to witness my way into God's graces instead of allowing God to work in and through me. So I wasn't enjoying His rest along the way. The Lord began to show me the error in my thinking on

one occasion when I gave the gospel to a co-worker. She was a twenty-something teller who lived life on her terms and didn't want any religion to get in her way—especially coming from me, her year-younger superior. She became a thorn in my flesh whenever I tried to speak to her or anyone around her about spiritual matters.

This experience taught me to bring my petitions to the Lord, find His grace sufficient instead of looking for the positive response from my evangelism efforts. When I couldn't see my works in action, I began to realize what I was trusting in all along—my works! I began to see more need to connect with the Lord moment by moment instead of adding up my evangelism encounters. My relationship with the Lord must come first, then my service to Him.

Although I still fail, I am encouraged to know the Lord offers His rest when I mix faith with His promises. The Lord uses us when we are trusting since only by faith can we experience Him and the inner peace He offers.

> *Don't miss the joy of the Lord because of your service to Him.*

Has service become your life more than the Lord Jesus has? Take time now for this spiritual inventory about your service and your relationship with Christ.

1. Have you lost God's peace as you hurry in service for Him?
2. Has service for the Lord become a work from your own strength, not from faith?
3. Has your *goal of service* for Christ taken the limelight and set Christ Himself in the shadows?
4. Are you so engrossed with serving the Lord that your service overshadows your devotional time with the Lord?
5. Has His Word become a mine out of which you dig spiritual "gems" to use in your service, thus Christ becomes lost in your digging for knowledge?

6. Does your serving the Lord interfere with resting in Him by faith?
7. Does your service overshadow your relationship with the Lord?
8. Have you lost your joy in the Lord because you feel driven by service to Him?
9. Are you in or out of fellowship with the Lord when you serve Him?

When Bill placed Christ Jesus above his service, he found rest. When he learned to give up his works and let the Lord work through him, he learned a truth about living by faith. Think about the meaning of the following verse. *"Therefore, since a promise remains of entering His rest, let us fear lest any of you seem to have come short of it. For indeed the gospel was preached to us as well as to them; but the word which they heard did not profit them, not being mixed with faith in those who heard it. For we who have believed do enter that rest, as He has said: "So I swore in My wrath, 'They shall not enter My rest'"* (Heb. 4:1-3a). How does this verse apply to your own life and service?

Readiness for His Service

As Bill shared with us, a right relationship of fellowship with the Lord comes before service to the Lord. Without fellowship, we serve in our energy, which indicates our lack of dependent faith to do His work. Our service to the Lord must stem from our faith, not work from our flesh (Heb. 4:10). When we rely on the Spirit of the Lord to produce works in and through us, our service pleases Him (Heb. 11:6).

Since service to the Lord begins with our relationship with Christ, we will want to spend time learning from Him. Therefore, preparation from God's Word comes before we offer ourselves into His service (2 Tim. 2:15). When we remain in His Word, He will prepare us for specific service. Unless we trust Him to prepare and guide us, we hinder His work in us and we will pursue, in the flesh, that which He hasn't called us to do. Instead of launching into service, yield to the Spirit's prompting to serve and allow Him to funnel His work through you. Make fellowship with the Lord your priority, and He will give you rest in the service He designs for you. If you begin with your service for the Lord, you will not truly seek Him in His Word. However, if you make your relationship with Him your priority, you will please Him with your service.

Failing to Faith Rest

Unless we use the faith rest approach to circumstances, the weight of our worries, fears, anger, and other sins will burden us. When we try to change what we can't, or if we worry, we fail to live by faith. Faith rest requires fellowship with the Lord, and without fellowship, our problems will distract us, and we will miss Him and His rest. The next story pictures how believers miss the blessings of living by faith.

A Missed Faith Adventure
Why We Do Not Receive God's Best

As you read, consider reasons Rex, a believer, didn't experience God's best. Rex reports:

> God didn't provide a thing when I lost my business, my house, and my cars. My wife had to take $10 per hour jobs, and we had to move into a cramped apartment. We had to sell most of our belongings at garage sales and to pawn shops. We couldn't get a bank account and had to learn to use only cash, which was tough. We had to buy a $400 car.
>
> God didn't provide any of this; we earned it all. It has been five years, and we still have no health insurance and no savings. God doesn't care about us.
>
> I was an avid church member before this happened. No person on this planet has any idea who God is or how God thinks or acts. No one knows! God has never spoken to anyone on this planet and has never spoken to you or me. Don't kid yourself and especially don't be fooled into giving your hard earned money to a church.

Failure to trust can happen to any believer who is not in fellowship. Meditate on the following Bible verses, review the Lord's viewpoint, and then answer the questions that follow.

"*God resists the proud, But gives grace to the humble*" (James 4:6).

"*You ask and do not receive, because you ask with wrong motives, so that you may spend it on your pleasures*" (James 4:3 NASB).

"*But without faith it is impossible to please Him, for he who comes to God must believe that He is, and that He is a rewarder of those who seek Him*" (Heb. 11:6 NASB).

Reflection Questions

1. What principles does God give the believer in these verses?

2. What have you learned or reviewed here that you can apply to your life of faith?

Confidence in Christ Produces Courage

Sally was a young, unmarried, Christian woman, who yielded to temptation and became pregnant. Although she confessed her sin and the Lord forgave her, she knew there would be lifelong consequences; she knew that her sin affected many people. People she knew urged her to have an abortion, to think about herself, to consider her future. However, Sally believed life begins at conception; therefore, she didn't have an abortion and kept her baby. Sally relied on the Lord Jesus to work it out for His good purpose for her life (Rom. 8:28). She took refuge in her Savior, who promises to help in times of trouble. Confidence in the Lord gave Sally courage towards her circumstances.

> *The greatest place to be is in the position to trust God only—then you are ready to see His faithfulness.*

The Lord is faithful to carry you in your tremors and quakes as His Word encourages, *"For the LORD will be your confidence"* (Prov. 3:26). Believing the promise, not just reciting the verse, is the key to receiving courage from God to do His will. By faith, we grasp the principles of God's Word, and we gain the courage to continue; we don't lose heart or become distraught.

David took shelter in the tabernacle (the house of the Lord). *"For in the day of trouble He will conceal me in His tabernacle; In the secret place of His tent He will hide me; He will lift me up on a rock"* (Ps. 27:5 NASB). Perhaps David used the word temple to mean "the presence of the Lord."

Since we have the same unchanging God, finding refuge in troubled times is easy when we look to Him. When life gets difficult, we can seek comfort in the presence of the Lord. We can hide behind His promises and we can feel secure leaning on His character. Like standing in safety on a rock over raging waters, the Lord holds us up when lifequakes shake around us.

> *The promises of the Lord are His words of empowerment.*

The next hymn, "A Shelter in the Time of Storm," based on a Scripture verse from the book of Isaiah, was found in "The Postman," a small London paper. People said it was a favorite song of the fishermen on the north coast of England. People on shore often heard the fishermen singing it as they approached their harbors in the time of storms.

A SHELTER IN THE TIME OF STORM

"For You have been a strength to the poor, A strength to the needy in his distress, A refuge from the storm, A shade from the heat; For the blast of the terrible ones is as a storm against the wall" (Isa. 25:4).

The Lord's our Rock, in Him we hide,
A Shelter in the time of storm;
Secure whatever ill betide,
A Shelter in the time of storm.

REFRAIN: Oh, Jesus is a Rock in a weary land,
A weary land, a weary land;
Oh, Jesus is a Rock in a weary land,
A Shelter in the time of storm.

A shade by day, defense by night,
A Shelter in the time of storm;
No fears alarm, no foes to fear,
A Shelter in the time of storm.

The raging storms may round us beat,
A Shelter in the time of storm
We'll never leave our safe retreat,
A Shelter in the time of storm.

O Rock divine, O Refuge dear,
A Shelter in the time of storm;
Be Thou our Helper ever near,
A Shelter in the time of storm.

~ Vernon Charlesworth, 1839-1915 ~

A Faith Adventure
His Grace Carried Us

Two years ago without warning, Lisle's husband, Ben, lost his job. Since it was a great job, this was a doubly painful experience. For six years, Ben enjoyed working in a major distribution company of healthcare products. Cutbacks in the company caused his dismissal.

Lisle decided to tell her two small children, Troy (6) and Maggie (4) with carefully chosen words. "Kids, we have to take better care of our things and not waste our money because Daddy doesn't have a job anymore." The children understood and bluntly blurted out, "Daddy was fired!"

Losing a job is always painful, even if it comes with severance pay. Although Lisle was thankful for continued income, she remained anxious; she wondered how long their family would survive on the severance pay. Lisle wavered between worry and confidence in the Lord.

The first few months offered hope since Ben got an average of two job leads per week with invitations to come for interviews. As the months stretched into a year and then longer, the leads and interviews became fewer. As Ben led the family devotion, he reminded his family that this was a test from God—a test to challenge their faith in the Lord. He encouraged his family to keep trusting the Lord no matter what happened.

During the almost two years of her husband's joblessness, Lisle was going through her own anxiety. As a mother to two growing schoolchildren, she saw their savings dwindling. As an emergency measure, she left her part time job of eight years to accept a full time position.

Besides the concerns of their dwindling savings, she was also worried about Ben's self-esteem.* He was trying to find work, but job opportunities for middle-aged men with his background and experience were scarce. Ben accepted two jobs, but they didn't last either because of personality conflicts and a clash of styles. He couldn't see himself working at either one long term, so Ben quit each one. Ben realized that he needed the Lord's help and direction finding a suitable job, so he prayed and prayed.

---

* Our feelings of self-worth must not come from what we do. Rather, our significance should come from who we are in Christ. We are so important to Him that He gave His life for us. Christ's work on our behalf, not our work is the blueprint for fulfillment. Furthermore, *"If anyone will not work, neither shall he eat"* (2 Thess. 3:10b) refers to laziness (choosing not to work) not unemployment.

Their marriage started to suffer too, because now Lisle was earning the income for the family. "Will my husband's ego take this for long?" she wondered. As each month passed, her anxiety about Ben grew, and she took her fears to the Lord in prayer.

As the months rolled on Lisle began questioning God, "Lord, I don't understand, what are you trying to teach us? How should we pray? What else should we pray for?" That was when Lisle realized their prayers had to be specific. Therefore, she gathered her two kids around her and said, "Let's pray for Daddy, that he would find a suitable job with a good boss—someone like his first boss in his former company." That became the family's specific prayer.

One day, about a year later, Lisle came home from work and saw the kids and her husband in a huddle. "What's all this about?" she asked. She heard her kids whisper excitedly, "Show it to her now!" Ben handed her a brown envelope, which Lisle thought was something from the kids' school, but it wasn't. As she slowly pulled out the paper from the envelope, she read the name of a company, next her husband's job title, and then his salary. At these, she merely nodded in satisfaction, but when she got to the end of the paper, she was shocked when she read the signature of Ben's favorite boss!

In confusion, the kids stared at mommy because she began to cry and laugh at the same time. She could hardly believe it! To the kids' amusement, she jumped up and down with joy like a child, so they jumped and laughed with her. Troy asked his mother, "Mommy, why are you crying and laughing at the same time?"

Lisle explained, "I'm crying because I'm so happy, Troy. Kids, remember how we prayed for a good boss for Daddy? Look at this name," she pointed to the paper she was holding. "We were merely asking for a boss who would be like Daddy's old boss, but God gave your Daddy exactly the same boss! He answered 'yes' to our prayers! Besides that, the Lord provided more than we had asked for or imagined!" That was when Troy began to sob. "Why are you crying?" Lisle asked. "Because I'm so happy too," the little boy said, as the entire family embraced each other.

Later Ben assembled the family for Bible time and afterwards Ben told them he wanted to talk about what they had learned in the trial. Lisle admitted, "I learned that I should have trusted more and not worried because God had it all figured out from the beginning." Ben told his family, "My faith wasn't as steady or consistent as I thought. Through this two-year trial, I began to trust the Lord more than ever. God is good and knows what is best for us because that is part of His grace. Even when we were unfaithful by not trusting at times, God was always with us taking care of our needs. Let us thank Him." They thanked God again for His loving care the last two years, for this new job, for the same boss, and for growing closer to Him.

> *Self-reliance = stressed out! Christ-reliance = Graced out!*

Living the faith-rest life is confident reliance on Christ in daily living. The more we live by Christ-centered dependency, the more real Christ becomes, and then trusting Him with our cares becomes a habit. Additionally, the more we look to the Lord, the more we realize that He never fails to provide rest for our souls.

Living Close to the Lord

Although God desires that we live in His presence moment by moment, many believers don't even think about Him in their daily routine. When life is comfortable, our focus may drift from Christ, and we may not feel connected to Him. The Lord Jesus seems distant when we are busy with life, which takes our attention from Him. In good times, we may forget our need for His care; however, in trials we may question God's care. When trouble strikes, we look for Him, we go running back to Him. A personal awareness of Him, including Christ-centered dependency as we go about our daily routine, keeps us connected. Are you staying close to Christ by trusting Him and keeping Him in your thoughts?

> **MOMENTS IN THE LORD**
>
> If God brings you to it,
> He will bring you through it.
> Happy moments, praise God.
> Difficult moments, seek God.
> Quiet moments, worship God.
> Painful moments, trust God.
> Every moment, thank God.

Giving attention to Christ reminds me of the hymn, "Moment by Moment" written by Daniel Webster Whittle. Whittle, named after American politician Daniel Webster, reached the rank of major in the American Civil War, and was known as "Major" Whittle.

History of the hymn "Moment by Moment"

While I [Ira Stankey] was attending the World's Fair in Chicago, Illinois, Henry Varley, a lay preacher from London, said to Major Whittle, "I do not like the hymn "I Need Thee Every Hour" very well because I need Him every moment of the day. Soon after Major Whittle wrote this sweet hymn, "Moment by Moment" and brought the hymn to me in manuscript a little later. He said he would give me the copyright of both the words and music if I would print for him five hundred copies on fine paper, for distribution among his friends.

His daughter May Whittle, (who later became the wife of Will R. Moody—the son of 19th Century evangelist Dwight Moody) composed the music. I did as Mr. Whittle wished, and sent the hymn to England.

In England, the hymn became popular. The well-known Rev. Andrew Murray of South Africa, who was visiting London, adopted it as his favorite hymn. A year later Mr. Murray visited Northfield, Massachusetts, and while holding a meeting for men in the church he remarked, "If Sankey only knew a hymn which I found in London, and would sing it, he would find that it embraces my entire creed."

I was eager to know what hymn it was. When he recited it, I said to him, "Doctor, that hymn was written within five hundred yards of where we are standing."

For years, Dr. Murray had his wife sing this hymn in nearly all his meetings. It also became a great favorite in South Africa during the war.

Cyber Hymnal, *www.hymntime.com*

MOMENT BY MOMENT

Dying with Jesus, by death reckoned mine;
Living with Jesus, a new life divine;
Looking to Jesus till glory doth shine,
Moment by moment, O Lord, I am Thine.

REFRAIN: Moment by moment I'm kept in His love;
Moment by moment I've life from above;
Looking to Jesus till glory doth shine;
Moment by moment, O Lord, I am Thine.

Never a trial that He is not there,
Never a burden that He doth not bear,
Never a sorrow that He doth not share,
Moment by moment, I'm under His care.

Never a heartache, and never a groan,
Never a teardrop and never a moan;
Never a danger but there on the throne,
Moment by moment He thinks of His own.

Never a weakness that He doth not feel,
Never a sickness that He cannot heal;
Moment by moment, in woe or in weal,
Jesus my Savior, abides with me still.

~ Daniel Webster Whittle, 1840-1901 ~

Guarding Our Faith-Rest Life

Sometimes I fear that I may have a trial so intense that I will fail to live by faith. From experience, I know how miserable it is to go through a trial alone, without God. We must guard and protect our life of faith.

We protect our faith-rest life:

- by hearing and meditating on God's Word to gain the mind of Christ,
- by building a relationship with Christ by spending time with Him in His Word,
- through prayer and praise,
- by applying the principles and promises of the faith-rest life.

> *Trial-free times challenge the believer to keep his attention on the Lord.*

Stockpile His Word in Your Soul

We need to know and believe God's Word to apply it daily. Minimal amounts of God's Word in the bank account of our souls yield insignificant deposits to withdraw during difficult times. In other words, we can't apply Scripture verses we don't know or believe. Accumulating His Word in our souls allows the Lord to recharge and fortify us for the routines of daily life. Regular fellowship with the Lord through intake of His Word is fundamental for a victorious life of faith. *"This Book of the Law [God's Word] shall not depart from your mouth, but you shall meditate in it day and night, that you may observe to do according to all that is written in it. For then you will make your way prosperous, and then you will have good success"* (Josh. 1:8). God's Word is essential for godly living today just as it was for believers in ages past.

What Is Your Excuse for Neglecting God's Word?

How many times have you said, I can't understand this? I often lamented that I couldn't understand math. When algebra, geometry, or college math teachers tried to help me grasp math principles, not much changed. I never grew in my knowledge of math; there was no infusion of understanding. What subject is difficult for you to comprehend?

Perhaps you say, "I can't understand the Bible; it's too hard." Since God's intelligence is infinitely superior to ours, we can't understand the whole realm and depth of His revelation to us. Often I didn't understand what was taught or what I read in the Bible. However, when I looked back over many years of my positive response to God's Word, I realized something extraordinary had taken place. Despite my human limitations, the Spirit of God taught me. Although I didn't always understand what I read or heard, my faithful Lord infused His Word, His principles and promises into my soul, into my belief system. The more I heard the teaching of God's Word, the more I understood the Bible when I read it. For diligently seeking Him in His Word, God richly rewarded me with knowledge of Himself, a closer relationship with Him, and a more consistent living faith (Heb. 11:6).

No one will ever understand everything in the Scriptures. Not even Bible scholars understand the entire realm of God's Word. However, God is faithful to His Word; it will go out and not return void but will accomplish what He wills (Isa. 55:11). He desires that we get to know and trust Him; He will accomplish that purpose. For that to happen we must read, hear, learn, and believe His Word.

The Lord is greater than our lack of understanding.

God encourages regular meditation (reading slowly and thinking about what you are reading) which is beyond merely reading it. Let the Spirit of God train you so that His Word becomes part of your thinking, part of the fabric of your being. From Scripture meditation, we learn to think His viewpoint, consider how to serve Him, and how to respond to life's difficulties according to His will.

Bible meditation guidelines:

1. Since the Spirit enables a believer to understand God's Word, fellowship is essential. A believer in fellowship with the Lord is ready to learn.
2. As you read, keep in mind you are in God's presence. Bible meditation is more than sitting with a book, it is a meeting with a person, namely our Lord Jesus Christ—the revealed Word. As we read His Word, the Holy Spirit reveals Jesus Christ to us.
3. Give God time to speak through His Word. Allow God to reveal Himself to you by reading slowly and thinking about what you read. Listen to God through His Word and allow the Holy Spirit to reassure you of Christ's presence and power working within you.
4. Read one book of the Bible at a time because reading a book in its entirety will aid you in understanding God's message in that book. As you meditate on His Word, keep in mind the theme of the book, to whom it was written and the context. You may want to record the date of your reading, the book name, chapter and verses.
5. Include prayer in your Bible reading time by asking God for guidance. In prayer say something like, "Father, you know my life and what I need to learn. Show me Your will and Your promises." God is faithful to teach those who desire to learn and grow closer to Him.
6. Connect with God as you read. When you see something that you have learned or something that makes you think, "that's me," write God a note (written prayer) and tell Him what you learned. This forces you to think while reading and gives you a record of how God is working in your life.
7. Believe the truths and promises of God's Word. During the day and those that follow, think about what you learned or how God changed your thinking.

> *When faced with a busy day, save precious time by skipping your devotions.* —Satan

Even during times of suffering and pressure, we can have the same peace and joy in the Lord as we do in trial-free times. Call on and believe passages such as, *"He has granted to us His precious and magnificent promises"* (2 Peter 1:4a NASB). When we apply His promises, the power of God will encourage us (Heb. 4:11-14). In addition, hiding His Word in our hearts will prepare us for future trials.

> *God's Word, spiritual food, is nourishment for the soul, not just to ponder and study, but to eat and digest daily* (Jer. 15:16).

In summary, the spiritual first-aid kit—faith rest—is the remedy for stress or worry. We can thrive during difficulties when we keep our attention on our Savior, meditate on His Word, trust His truths, believe His promises, continue in prayer, and sing His praises.

Reflection Questions

Use Scripture verses to support your answers wherever possible.

1. What does "rest" mean in the context of "faith rest"?

2. Apply the faith-rest formula to a predicament or trial.

3. Who and what is the source of your spiritual growth?

4. How are biblical "hope" and "anticipation" related to the faith-rest life?

5. What significant principles about faith rest will you apply to your Christian life?

CHAPTER 13 PREVIEW
- The ABCs of Prayer
- Scriptural Meditation and Prayer Models
- Prayers that Delight God
- Praise Changes Things
- The Sacrifices of Praise
- How to be Grateful for and during Trials

CHAPTER 13

Soaring on Prayer Wings

Our relationship with Jesus Christ must be the focal point of our faith. As you know, healthy relationships include good communication between individuals.

> Prayer is the Christian's breath.
> We communicate to God in prayer
> and He communicates to us through His Word.
> Faith is our exhale response to Him and His Word.

A Perspective on Prayer

People have concerns about prayer. The men in the following story offer suggestions.

Three preachers sat discussing the best positions for prayer while a telephone repairman worked nearby. "Kneeling is without doubt the best," claimed one.

"No," another contended. "I get the best results standing with my hands outstretched to heaven."

"You're both wrong," the third insisted. "The most effective prayer position is lying prostrate, face down on the floor."

The repairman could contain himself no longer. "Hey, fella," he interrupted, "the best prayin' I ever did was hangin' upside down from a telephone pole."

Maybe you chuckled as I did at those responses to a prayer question. Often believers don't know how to pray, nor do they know which prayers please the Lord. In His desire for a relationship with us, God gives us much information about communicating with Him through prayer. We begin with a closer look at facets of effective prayer.

The Fundamentals of God-Pleasing Prayer

Unless we are in fellowship with the Lord we may just rant and rave about our problems and fail to remember Him as we pray.

The Lord hears us when we are in fellowship; therefore, naming our sins is necessary. Did you know that sin or a sinful habit blocks God's best to you? We read in Jeremiah 5:25b, *"And your sins have withheld good from you."* Admitting our sins should be the first part of our communication with the Lord.

The prayers of believers in fellowship with the Lord, have great benefits (James 5:16). God hears prayers offered in the name (authority) of Christ, not merely for the sake of Jesus, but because we belong to Him (our position in Christ as God's child).

According to His will and timing, our faithful God may change circumstances in answer to prayer. Often we don't receive because we don't ask the Lord, or we ask from wrong motivation (James 4:2b-3). When we ask for anything according to God's will, He will fulfill it in His perfect timing (1 John 5:14).

ABC's of Prayer

- God's speaks to us through His Word, and we talk to Him in prayer.
- Prayer should begin by admitting sin and follow with trust.
- Prayer, talking to God, needs to be personal in nature.
- Effective prayer rolls concerns and requests onto God.
- Prayer should be humble and submissive, not demanding.
- Prayer includes praising and thanking Him for who He is and what He does.

- Prayer should convey patient waiting for His response believing that He answers prayers.
- Prayer is a necessary part of the faith-rest life.

You may pray from a grace perspective by believing that Jesus died and lives again; that you are sealed or preserved with Jesus Christ for eternity; that you are in a real living union with Christ; and that you are identified with Him forever.

The Building Blocks of Effective Prayer

Prayers that delight and honor the Lord are those that admit sin and the need for forgiveness, seek to know Him better, desire His purposes, rehearse His character qualities, roll the problems onto Him, concentrate on Him and His ability to handle the problems, and give Him thanks and praise.

These building blocks of effective prayer not only bring honor and praise to our Lord, but they bring blessings to us. The Lord instructs us about proper praying, which includes blessings when we pray by faith. *"Be anxious for nothing, but in everything by prayer and supplication, with thanksgiving, let your requests be made known to God; and the peace of God, which surpasses all understanding, will guard your hearts and minds through Christ Jesus"* (Phil. 4:6-7).

Take a moment to remember the last time you prayed in faith and received God's supernatural peace. When you experienced His peace, did you give thanks?

Reasons that Encourage Prayer

As a believer in Christ, you have incentives to pray because:

1) ***you have an empathetic High Priest in Jesus Christ*** (Heb. 4:14-16). Jesus has empathy towards you. He identifies with and understands

your problems, feelings, and motives. Because Jesus is compassionate, He tells you to cast your cares on Him (1 Peter 5:7).

In the Old Testament, the high priest interceded for the people of Israel. Today, however, believers in Christ have direct access to their heavenly Father. He commands us to come boldly to Him in prayer. In Ephesians 3:12 we read, *"in whom we have boldness and access with confidence through faith in Him."* We can pray boldly (confidently) in faith because of Christ's cross work. Nothing stands between the Father and us; we can go fearlessly in prayer to the throne room of God anytime and anywhere.

2) *you have an exalted position in Jesus Christ* (John 14:12-14; 16:23-24). Our high-ranking position of union with Jesus Christ rewards us with a privilege—to pray "in Jesus name." What does that phrase mean? "In Jesus name" means you have a new position from which to pray. The Father sees you in the Son (identified with Him) and accepts you in the Son. You are just as loved by the Father as He loves Jesus (John 17:23) and you can pray on that basis. Just as the Father hears the prayers of Jesus, so the Father hears your prayers. Do you add "in Jesus name" at the end of your prayers? Have you ever thought of beginning your prayers in His name?

Knowing our Father hears us as if Jesus Christ was praying, we can have joy when we pray. *"And in that day you will ask Me nothing. Most assuredly, I say to you, whatever you ask the Father in My name He will give you. Until now you have asked nothing in My name. Ask, and you will receive, that your joy may be full"* (John 16:23-24). We have joy when we believe what the Father has told us about prayer.

3) *you have an amazing promise to claim since you are in Christ* (Eph. 3:20-21). By praying with faith, we claim the power of our Savior Jesus Christ who can do whatever He desires. If you ask for more from the Lord and that suits His plan, He will provide that and much more.

> *Seek the Lord first and He will cause all things to fall into place according to His plan for your good.*

How God Answers Prayers

In His perfect wisdom, our heavenly Father responds to prayer in several ways. He may answer with a "yes" or a "no" or He may give an unexpected response. He may delay or have us wait. Let us look at examples of each.

In His wisdom, God may answer "yes" immediately or in a short time.

- One March night I lay awake listening to the howling winds and their force battering against our house. I decided to pray asking God to stop the winds, but before I finished my prayer, God hushed the winds (Isa. 65:24). His answer to my prayer reminded me of His calming the winds on the Sea of Galilee thousands of years ago. Jesus Christ is the same yesterday, today, and forever. He helped believers of the past and He continues to come to our aid today. The Lord's display of wind control in His instant answer caused me to pray again—this time asking Him to calm my excitement in Him so I could sleep.

- Hezekiah, king of Israel, became fatally ill. The prophet Isaiah visited him with a message from the Lord that he was going to die. Hezekiah pleaded for his life and God healed him because He chose to heal him (2 Kings 20:1-11; Isa. 38).

In His wisdom, the Lord may encourage weak faith with speedy answers to prayers; but He may strengthen the stronger faith with delays.

In God's wisdom, delay or wait may be part of a "yes" answer. Even though you pray with the right motives, God does what is best for you according to His plan. Another reason God may delay His answer is unconfessed sin in our life. At other times, the Lord waits until the "last minute" to deliver money for a bill or to provide a job.

Sometimes when we feel hopeless the Lord moves to fulfill a need or a desire such as the gift of a baby. God may delay because we aren't ready or He has details to work out. At times, you will sense the Lord isn't delaying but has said, "no." Often we may continue to pray because we don't know whether His answer is a "no" or if He is delaying a "yes" answer.

- In their old age, Abraham and Sarah waited for the son God promised to them. When God's timing was right, God kept His promise and presented baby Isaac to them. God always keeps His promises in His perfect time.

- Rick has a similar account of waiting for the Lord's timing and shares his story:

    My wife and I know from experience something about Abraham and Sarah's prolonged trial of infertility. My wife and I married in the summer of 1987 and waited to start a family until we bought our first home in the spring of 1989. We thought it would only take months to conceive, but we were mistaken. The Lord had a different plan for our lives and we waited year after year for the Lord to bless us with a child.

    We worked with fertility doctors, but had no success. I reminded my disappointed wife that Jehovah Jireh (the Lord will provide) had provided Isaac for Abraham and Sarah and he could provide for us.

    After some time, we resolved that having a child wasn't in God's plan and we accepted the Lord's will for our lives. Then, after 16 years of marriage, Katie was pregnant and she gave birth to a beautiful baby boy we named…Isaac. Then Christian friends spoke openly telling us how they had been praying for us for years. God answers prayer in His way and timing.

- Mary and Martha sent word to Jesus to come quickly to heal their brother, Lazarus, but Jesus delayed (Luke 11). He had lingered and Lazarus died. According to Mary and Martha's schedule, He was late. However, our Lord Jesus Christ arrived on His perfect timetable. Both Mary and Martha grew in faith after witnessing the power of Jesus to raise Lazarus from the dead. The delay followed by an unexpected answer to prayer further convinced them that He was their Messiah. In addition, because this sign miracle pointed to Christ, the Messiah, many Jews accepted Him as their personal Savior.

A delayed answer is not only part of the trial of faith; it is an opportunity to honor the Lord with consistent faith.

In His wisdom, the Lord may give an unexpected answer. He may answer differently from what you specifically asked. He may answer "yes" to the underlying desire of the prayer.

- The previous narrative of the delayed answer to Mary and Martha's prayer included an unexpected answer—Jesus raised Lazarus from the dead!

- We read in Genesis 18–19 that Abraham prayed for the preservation of the cities of Sodom and Gomorrah. The reason for his prayer was the preservation of his nephew, Lot, and his family. Although God destroyed the evil cities, He answered the loving motivation of Abraham's prayer when He spared Abraham's relatives. As always, God's answer was the best.

In His wisdom, God may deny the request. The "no" answer may not come immediately or be apparent from the beginning.

- The apostle Paul prayed for God to remove his affliction, but God denied Paul's request. God advised Paul that His grace was sufficient, which Paul accepted (2 Cor. 12:1-10).

- In the Garden of Gethsemane, Jesus prayed for the removal of His impending suffering. In His wisdom and grace towards us, God the Father denied Christ's request.

Do Your Responses Reflect God's Character?

When God answers "yes" to a prayer I often hear someone say, "God answered my prayer" or "God is good!" This implies that He is good because He did it their way. Is He not still a good God if He answers "No?" Do you believe, *"For the LORD is good; His mercy is everlasting"* (Ps. 100:5)? Do you believe that *"good and upright is the LORD"* (Ps. 25:8)? A better response would be "Praise God" or "I thank the Lord for His grace to me."

When our Lord answers, "no" or "wait" I rarely hear believers say, "God is good." When God says "no" or keeps us waiting, a God-pleasing response would be, "God loves me. He is in control of the situation. He knows best and I will trust Him." Do your responses to God's answers to your prayers show that God is wise and good no matter what answer He gives?

> Our responses to God's answers must truthfully reflect Him.

Tap God's Grace Reservoir through Effective Prayer

Prayer is the outflow of a believer's life. The more a believer appreciates Christ's cross work, the more he grows in his relationship with the Lord, and the more his prayer life expands. As the believer's appreciation for God's grace grows, so does the believer's prayer life.

The grace of God is an inexhaustible reservoir that is accessible to every believer in Jesus Christ. The faith of a believer is the means for tapping into His grace. While faith itself has no power, God responds to the genuine prayer of a believer. *"The effective, fervent prayer of a righteous man can accomplish much"* (James 5:16 NASB). The Lord views effective prayers as those offered by the believer in fellowship with Him.

Effective prayer trusts in the Lord who can accomplish anything He pleases. If we think that our prayers motivate, prompt, or persuade God to act on our behalf, we exhibit the sin of pride. When we tap into God's grace reservoir by faith through prayer, the Lord takes action according to His perfect plan for our lives.

James 5:17-18 records the effectiveness of the faithful prayer of Elijah, an Old Testament believer. God held back the rain for three and a half years when Elijah prayed and God didn't send more rain until Elijah prayed again (1 Kings 17:1; 18:41-45). Elijah didn't control the weather through prayer. He was a just a man who trusted God to cause a drought and later on to produce rain.

The Evidence of Faith in the Prayer Life of George Mueller

George Mueller (1805-1898) was living proof that we can personally know the Lord as a faithful, compassionate God. Through Mueller we see evidence that the effective fervent prayer of the believer may yield miraculous results. Mueller is best known for his work establishing orphanages in Bristol, England. When God prompted the heart of George Mueller to build these orphanages, he had only two shillings (fifty cents) in his pocket. Without making his wants known to anyone, Mueller prayed to God for money for the orphanages. Over the course of many years, the Lord motivated believers to donate the English equivalent of 7,200,000 dollars to him for the building and maintaining of these orphanages. Access to God's inexhaustible resources comes by faith through prayer.

> *Faith only looks at God and leaves out circumstances.*

Prayer Tips from Mueller

One of Mueller's prayer policies was "never ask anyone for help" no matter how great the need might be. Ask God directly and believe His promises to care for His servants and to hear their prayers. By praying this way, God receives the glory for answered prayer. Mueller never prayed for something just because he wanted it or because he thought it was necessary to God's work. He waited to be sure it was God's will.

When George Mueller felt burdened to pray for anything, he would search the Scriptures to discover if there was some promise that addressed that situation. He would open his Bible, find (not at random) a promise, place his finger on it, plead that promise and he received what he asked. Mueller discovered that after meditating on Scripture he experienced better prayer time. He testified that he knew of at least fifty thousand specific answers to his prayers.

The secret to George Mueller's prayer life was his discovery of the connection between scriptural meditation and prayer. Mueller's testimony to our faithful God is an encouragement to us.

> *Prayer is not overcoming God's reluctance;*
> *it is laying hold of His willingness.* —George Mueller

Prayer Thoughts from the Psalms

Is consistent, persistent prayer missing in your life? Are you stuck in self-pity or anger because of troubles? Are worries obstructing the path of trust that leads to the peace God promises? Perhaps you are forgetting that prayer is a part of faith rest.

The Lord gave us many psalms, which serve as prayer models. We can identify with the psalms because they express many of our thoughts and feelings. In Psalm 3, King David told God how he felt about his circumstances when he was fleeing for his life from his rebellious son, Absalom, and his followers. When the odds are against us, we may be tempted to think God is against us; however, not David. Within four verses, King David realized that God's presence, power, and strength made the odds seem small. *"But You, O LORD, are a shield for me, My glory and the One who lifts up my head. I cried to the LORD with my voice, And He heard me from His holy hill...I lay down and slept; I awoke, for the LORD sustained me. I will not be afraid of ten thousands of people Who have set themselves against me all around"* (Ps. 3:3-6). Many of the psalms reflect our feelings of helplessness. However, as we consider God's abilities, we gain hope and confidence in God's sufficiency.

Benefits of Reflecting on God's Character

Prayers that review God's character qualities honor Him. Concentrating on God, His character, and His work helps us refocus our direction upward away from our problems. When psalm writers felt abandoned by God, they vented their thoughts and feelings to God. When the psalmists were impatient and disagreed with God's time schedule, they let Him know about His alleged "tardiness" in answering their prayers. In humility, they recognized the distinct difference between themselves and a holy, perfect God. They honestly expressed their human weaknesses and sins to the Creator.

Some psalms begin by expressing feelings and problems and close by expressing confidence or trust in God once again. One example of this pattern is Psalm 55. The psalmist begins by releasing his problems and feelings to God. He concludes by confirming his confidence in the Lord when he affirms, *"cast your burden on the LORD, And He shall sustain you; He shall never permit the righteous to be moved. But You, O God, shall bring them down to the pit of destruction; Bloodthirsty and deceitful men shall not live out half their days; But I will trust in You"* (Ps. 55:22-23).

As you read the psalms, notice that often the pattern begins with an expression of feelings and troubles and ends by confirming God's character. As you use this prayer model of honesty in prayers with praise, you will discover that your awareness and appreciation of the Lord will grow.

Prayers that Change Our Perspectives

When we praise God and concentrate on Him and His qualities, our focus begins to shift away from our problems. Naming God's character traits causes us to renew our belief that He is greater than our problems. The Lord delights in an attitude that credits Him and He rewards our faith with His peace.

Sometimes, we need only discuss our problems to put them into perspective. Who better to speak with than the Lord? Writing your prayers, even jotting notes, will help you to concentrate and focus on your thoughts. I have found that written prayers help me to cleanse my soul of burdens.

Examples of Praying God's Attributes

The Lord delights in prayers that acknowledge Him and His character. The following prayer examples show honor to God's character. The first prayer is a general one recognizing God's faithfulness in a difficult time.

> Heavenly Father, I praise You that You are a God that I can talk to when things seem hopeless or when nothing makes sense. Amid my fear, hurt, tears, chaos and confusion, I can come to You and You will give me peace. Your peace, Father, is beyond human understanding. The thought of your great love and power refreshes my soul. I praise You for Your unfailing love and promises. In this journey of faith, I pray to You, Father, trusting in Your unconditional love and faithfulness. Your management and supervision of everything, including my problems, reassure me. I trust You to see me through this difficult time. I praise You in the power of my Savior, Jesus. Amen

In the next prayer example, notice the increased anxiety, the honest expression of feelings and problems. The prayer shifts direction from self to God's character.

> Lord God Heavenly Father, I am so distressed. I do not know what to do. I do not know how I can continue. I feel so hopeless and helpless because my world has collapsed. My husband told me he no longer loved me and left me. My unemployment compensation is running out. How will I have enough money to live? My family criticizes me and offers no support. My car is old and needs many repairs. The tires need replacement, the banging noise under the hood is louder; this car may not run much longer. Why, Father, are you letting this happen to me? How long, Lord, must I live like this?
>
> Help me, Lord. I confess my sins of unbelief and despair. I name my sin of worry. Lord, you alone can help me. You are my refuge and strength, my helper in time of trouble. Help me to

believe. I am helpless—right where you want me to be—so You can demonstrate Your power through my weakness. I give up trying to solve my problems. I surrender to Your will and plan. I trust You will work all things together for my good, especially my spiritual growth. Lord, You are all knowing and You know what I need. You know the perfect answer and have the perfect time to provide it. You love me with an unconditional love that endures forever. Underneath me are Your everlasting arms so I am not in a free-fall.

You took care of my greatest problem at the cross when I was Your enemy. Therefore since I am Your child, You will take care of the rest of my problems. Oh, Lord, just to think of what Your love did for me at Calvary comforts me. You know how everything will turn out, so why should I worry? You aren't worried so why should I? You have everything under control from the stars and planets down to my little problems. You can handle everything so I roll my problems onto You, Lord. Help me to lean on You each step of the way. Help me to have consistent faith in Your power to work everything out for good. Give me eager anticipation that You will resolve these problems. I trust You to draw me closer to You in these trials.

Lord, cause me to focus on You and Your promises. Father, bring to my mind the Scripture verses to claim in these difficult times. Ah, you brought one to mind, *"Peace I leave with you, My peace I give to you; not as the world gives do I give to you. Let not your heart be troubled, neither let it be afraid."* You promised me peace and I am beginning to feel Your peace. Father, I praise You for the unchanging God You are, for always keeping Your promises, and for always being with me. Thank You for Your Word, Your promises and especially for my Savior in whose power I pray. Amen

Remember, our viewpoint only changes when we believe in His Word and character. By praying and trusting, God will give us the endurance to praise Him and think about Him instead of ourselves.

Does Praise Change Things?

Do you sometimes feel so overwhelmed with your trial that you ask, "How long, Lord?" as David cried out in Psalm 13. David probably wrote this psalm during the fifteen years he was running from King Saul. David pleaded his cause and ended with praise to God. Yes, he praised God during his trials. In your prayers do you praise Him? Are you able to praise Him during a trial? The Lord tells us to keep praying. We should be praising Him continually as well. The Lord desires our prayers and our praises because that is a major part of our relationship with Him.

You may have heard the expression "prayer changes things." Strictly speaking, prayer changes nothing since only God can change circumstances. When we pray and praise, our thoughts focus on Him and away from our circumstances. Similarly, the mere deed of praising God doesn't change things. Praise isn't spiritual magic used to bring change. In addition, we shouldn't make praise a work, that is, praise for the sake of praise. God looks for a genuine attitude of praise.

We can compare our prayers to a pigeon with one prayer wing and one praise wing. Our prayer pigeon can soar when both wings are functional. Someone said that the secret to spiritual victory is praise with prayer. What happens when a pigeon's wing is clipped or broken? He can't fly. The pigeon can't do what he is designed to do—fly. What breaks our prayer pigeon and causes prayer or praise to be ineffective? A clipped prayer wing hinders effectiveness. One clipped wing can be the result of unconfessed sin, complaining, or feeling sorry for yourself thinking, "How can I be thankful?" A clipped wing may also suggest that praise is missing. But, you ask, "How can I praise or thank God when I am hurting?"

When we are suffering, thanksgiving can be a sacrifice or offering to Him. A sacrifice to the Lord occurs when we praise and thank Him when don't feel like it, when we hurt, when we are depressed, or when we are in a trial. God desires our sacrifices of praise when we are suffering just as He wants our frequent praises during trial-free times.

What are some types of praise?
We praise the Lord when we talk to others about His character traits and His faithful deeds. The Lord loves to hear us name His works and traits in prayer. A great form of praise is our dependency on our Savior since He continually seeks our trust.

What are some results of praising the Lord?
Praising the Lord can change our perspective from distress to comfort, from insecurity to assurance, from anxiety to peace, and from discontent to joy. If we keep praising the Lord, we can keep our focus on the Lord.

When we sincerely praise the Lord amid a trial, we are proving our trust in the Lord. Our praise shows that we believe He can manage the difficulty and thus we honor Him. We reflect His glory and we magnify Him when we praise Him.

Praise as trust and obedience results in God's deliverance into rest. We find an encouraging example of trusting praise in the Old Testament story of King Jehoshaphat (2 Chron. 20:1-30). Take time now to read that encouraging chapter about the approaching danger of enemy forces against Judah. Notice King Jehoshaphat expressed his response of trust in the Lord through praises.

Benefits of Praise Hymns

The hymns based on Scripture texts make great prayers and provide much comfort to us. The following is one of many comforting hymns. Notice the many references to God's character.

SING PRAISE TO GOD

"I will praise the LORD according to His righteousness, And will sing praise to the name of the LORD Most High" (Ps. 7:17).

Sing praise to God Who reigns above,
The God of all creation,
The God of power, the God of love,
The God of our salvation.
With healing balm my soul is filled
And every faithless murmur stilled:
To God all praise and glory.

What God's almighty power hath made
His gracious mercy keepeth,
By morning glow or evening shade
His watchful eye ne'er sleepeth;
Within the kingdom of His might, Lo!
All is just and all is right:
To God all praise and glory.

Thus, all my toilsome way along,
I sing aloud Thy praises,
That earth may hear the grateful song
My voice unwearied raises.
Be joyful in the Lord, my heart,
Both soul and body bear your part:
To God all praise and glory.

Let all who name Christ's holy Name
Give God all praise and glory;
Let all who own His power proclaim
Aloud the wondrous story!
Cast each false idol from its throne,
For Christ is Lord, and Christ alone:
To God all praise and glory.

~ Johann J. Schultz, 1640-1690 ~
The Cyber Hymnal: *www.hymntime.com*

Using Scripture Verses to Praise God

Sometimes a word catches my attention and I start thinking of God's character or biblical principles. Consider the following verse, *"in the multitude of my anxieties within me, Your comforts delight my soul"* (Ps. 94:19). Each letter of the word *"comforts"* depicts a divine attribute followed by a Scripture verse and a short prayer thought that reflect His attributes. Notice these prayers have no requests, just praises for the Lord.

God's C O M F O R T S

Changeless Love   *"The LORD has appeared of old to me, saying: "Yes, I have loved you with an everlasting love; Therefore with lovingkindness I have drawn you"* (Jer. 31:3). Dear loving Father, Your faithful love holds me close, especially when I am weak. You desire my dependency so You can reveal Your changeless loyal love to comfort me.

Omnipresent   *"God is our refuge and strength, A very present help in trouble"* (Ps. 46:1). Father, You are always with me, both in trials and in good times. When I meditate on Your Word, I sense Your comforting presence.

Mercy   *"Through the LORD's mercies we are not consumed, Because His compassions fail not. They are new every morning; Great is Your faithfulness"* (Lam. 3:22-23). Father God, in my sinful state I don't deserve Your leniency; yet everyday You provide the comfort of Your mercy to me.

Faithfulness   *"Therefore know that the lord your God, He is God, the faithful God who keeps covenant and mercy for a thousand generations with those who love Him and keep His commandments"* (Deut. 7:9a NASB). Dear Lord Jesus, Your trustworthiness comforts me. I can always count on You to be faithful to Your Word.

Omniscience   *"Casting all your anxiety on Him, because He cares for you"* (1 Peter 5:7 NASB). Lord, You know everything about me. You know my thoughts, my anxious fears and You tell me to give them over to You. How comforting to know that You care so much for me and will carry my burdens.

<u>R</u>ighteousness — *"For the LORD is righteous, He loves righteousness; The upright will behold His face"* (Ps. 11:7 NASB). Father, You are a righteous God who does all things right and never makes a mistake. You allow what is best for me. I am comforted believing that You work all circumstances together for my spiritual good (Rom. 8:28).

<u>T</u>ruth — *"The entirety of Your word is truth"* (Ps. 119:160a). Lord God, You are the source of all truth. Your Word is truth so your promises are true. Your promises comfort me because they dissolve my anxious thoughts. When I believe your promises, You comfort me.

<u>S</u>overeignty — *"For the Lord God Omnipotent reigns!"* (Rev. 19:6b). My Lord and King, You have power over the universe; therefore, You are greater than my little problems and my lifequakes. I praise You for being a supreme and sufficient God. Knowing You, Lord Jesus, is a treasured delight!

Praising the Lord is a prescription for a healthy soul.

We conclude this chapter with the topic of praising the Lord through thanksgiving. *"In everything give thanks; for this is the will of God in Christ Jesus for you"* (1 Thess. 5:18).

Thanksgiving during a Trial

Are you aware of the lessons or blessings that resulted from your last adversity? Have you thanked the Lord for sending you the "thorns" to draw you closer to Him? Perhaps you are unable to be grateful in all matters, even trials. If so, now is a good time to consider some hindrances to gratitude.

Reasons for Inability to Thank God in a Lifequake

1. If our souls are starved from a failure to learn and believe the Word of God, we won't be able to give thanks to the Lord. An empty or malnourished soul can't thank God.
2. If we don't know the Lord, we can't thank Him properly. The more we trust God's character and His promises the more grateful we will be.
3. When we are angry with God, resentful or bitter, we can't be grateful.
4. When we are in a state of unconfessed sin, or lacking trust, we can't thank the Lord for any trial.
5. If we are prideful (sin), and we are fighting with God in our trial by demanding our way, we won't be able to thank God during or for the trial.
6. When we are self-centered and looking at our circumstances, we won't thank the Lord.

Trusting God Leads to Thanksgiving

Hudson Taylor made the choice to follow the Lord to the mission field. Even after the break up with the young woman who would not follow him into the mission field, he testified, "And though He does not deprive me of feeling in my trial, He enables me to sing, 'Yet will I rejoice in the Lord, I will joy in the God of my salvation.' I can thank Him for all, even the most painful experiences of the past, and trust Him without fear for all that is to come" (*Hudson Taylor's Spiritual Secret*, p. 29).

Thankfulness keeps us positive by replacing negative thoughts. Appreciation lightens our burdens by directing our focus to things to be grateful for taking it and off our troubles.

God never commands us to like the trial. It may take time to be grateful during a crisis. Instead of complaining about what we don't have, let's give thanks for the many things we do have, including the knowledge that He works *all* things together for good.

Thank the Lord Jesus for salvation. The most important gift to be grateful for is God's grace gift of salvation—His rescue plan. Give thanks that Christ Jesus remained on the cross until God's judgment on Him for trillions of sins was "finished" (John 19:30). Christ's victory secures a place in the family of God for us. Therefore, our position in Christ is another reason to give thanks.

Give thanks for God's undeserved mercy. God's mercy spares us from much deserved suffering. He displayed His mercy towards us—no mercy towards Christ at Calvary. Christ didn't deserve to suffer; we deserve only suffering. We can thank God for not giving us what we deserve—we will never have to suffer judgment for our sins. Thanks to Christ who willingly suffered what He didn't deserve so we would escape what we do deserve.

Be thankful for physical blessings. We can thank Him for many physical blessings, family, friends, and our daily needs. The Lord is our Shepherd who supplies all our needs.

Give thanks for many spiritual blessings. Thank the Lord for our relationship with Christ, our Savior and Friend. Give thanks for His Word, which comforts and guides us; give thanks for the faith-rest rescue plan. Instead of complaining, grumbling, or throwing a pity party, take time to count your spiritual blessings.

Be thankful for God's character and His Word. Believing in the character qualities of God helps us to thank Him. Express gratitude to God for His sovereignty, for His loving-kindness and faithfulness, and for all His unique qualities. Thank the Lord for the trial, which drew you closer to Him. Thank Him because He revealed His character to you, that you learned something greater about Him. For His seven thousand promises that He keeps because of His character, show your gratitude by believing them.

Give thanks for the privilege of sharing in His suffering. As we share in His sufferings, we also share in the benefits of Christ's divine nature (1 Peter 4:13-14; 2 Peter 1:3-4). Thank Him that because of His sufferings we always have His grace benefits.

Express gratitude to God for sending the suitable trial. Thank God for caring enough to send the best trial. Express your gratitude for customized trials, which God uses to mold us to the likeness of Christ—for our spiritual good (Rom. 8:28). When trials draw us closer to Christ, we find reasons to give thanks. The Lord knows the good that He will accomplish through the lifequake. Therefore, thank your heavenly Father for His wisdom in designing your lifequakes and tremors. With the right perspective, you can thank Him for any trial.

Give thanks for benefits from trials. We can be thankful for the trial if we desire to learn from it—learn to trust Him more consistently. When the trial pushes us to God's Word, we can indeed be grateful. *"It is good for me that I have been afflicted, That I may learn Your statutes"* (Ps. 119:71). God uses trials to work good for us or through us to benefit someone else. Remember God allowed trials into Joseph's life to bring about good for his family many years in the future. Paul's suffering helped the church and continues to help believers to this day.

Thank Him for His comfort, peace, and joy. Thank Him for His loving care and comfort during trials. Thank Him for faithfully providing His peace and joy through the exercise of faith resting.

> *Being thankful helps us think about what we have and not what we have lost.*

Our Savior's Love—Motivation for Thanksgiving

Lingering on our troubles is distressing, but considering the love of Christ is uplifting. How can we consider Christ's matchless love in suffering for us and then fail to thank Him? Every day Jesus displays maximum love for us by pleading for us at our Father's throne. How can we fail to thank Him often—even for our trials?

Have you been able to sing and praise God amid adversity? Although devastated by a lifequake, Luther Bridgers chose to concentrate on Jesus and not the pain of personal tragedy. The hymn "A Song of Faith" is his testimony to living by faith.

A Song of Faith

In 1910 Luther Bridges was a thirty-four year old husband and father of three sons. Being an evangelist required him to be on the road. While he was away conducting a revival, his wife took their boys to visit her parents in Harrodsburg, Kentucky. During the night, a neighbor saw the house was on fire and he rushed to warn the family. The parents were roused in time, but Luther's wife and boys could not be reached in the intense heat of the flames. Tragically, all four perished.

As soon as the news reached him, Bridgers returned to Harrodsburg and experienced indescribable grief. The question that flooded his heart and mind was how he could sing a song of faith with a broken heart. But he stood strong in what he had preached and turned to the Word of God. When he did, the process of healing began and "He Keeps me Singing" was born as an expression of Luther's bedrock faith.

Hymn commentary by J. D. Sherrow, *www.naznet.com*
Audio: The Cyber Hymnal, *www.hymntime.com*

HE KEEPS ME SINGING

"You shall have a song...and gladness of heart" (Isa. 30:29).

There's within my heart a melody;
Jesus whispers sweet and low,
"Fear not, I am with thee, peace, be still,
"In all of life's ebb and flow.

REFRAIN: Jesus, Jesus, Jesus,
Sweetest Name I know,
Fills my every longing,
Keeps me singing as I go.

All my life was wrecked by sin and strife,
Discord filled my heart with pain,
Jesus swept across the broken strings,
Stirred the slumbering chords again.

Feasting on the riches of His grace,
Resting 'neath His sheltering wing,
Always looking on His smiling face,
That is why I shout and sing.

Though sometimes He leads through waters deep,
Trials fall across the way,
Though sometimes the path seems rough and steep,
See His footprints all the way.

Soon He's coming back to welcome me,
Far beyond the starry sky;
I shall wing my flight to worlds unknown,
I shall reign with Him on high.

~ Luther Bridgers (1884-1948) ~

Reflection Questions

Support your answers with Scripture verses and God's perspective.

1. What insights can we learn from the prayer style of many of the psalms especially David's psalms?

2. What are the benefits of recalling God's character attributes in prayer?

3. List the benefits of praising God.

4. Name the things you can thank God for during trials.

5. What significant things did you learn about thanksgiving in trials?

CHAPTER 14 PREVIEW
- God's Grace in Faith Rest
- The Power of Faith Resting
- Experiencing God's Comfort

CHAPTER 14

The Comfort of His Grace

The faithfulness of God's grace will either rescue us from suffering or carry us through. The next faith adventure shows God's mercy, His grace in action.

A Faith Adventure
New Mercies

My doctor scheduled an MRI test to determine the cause of my neck pain. As you may know, an MRI requires confinement in a medical test machine. Most of us feel uncomfortable in a confined area. Although I am not claustrophobic, I was apprehensive about lying still in a coffin-like cylinder for thirty minutes.

I worried about sinus drainage and the need to clear my throat to avoid choking. My anxiety intensified when the technician told me I shouldn't swallow for periods of two to five minutes. "If I swallowed, the technician cautioned, the scan results would blur and I would have to repeat the test. Repeat it? I am having difficulty agreeing to this one," I thought.

With my anxiety level high, I was near the panic mark. I barely managed to keep my composure as anxious thoughts raced through my mind—tell the technician that I can't do this, maybe some other time. OK Lord, I have to do this and it's obvious I'll never get through this on my own. Help me, Lord! I silently prayed. The technician placed me in the cylinder bed and closed the lid of this metal open-ended chamber.

If I focused on the difficulties, I knew I would fall apart emotionally. I redirected my thoughts away from the moment and onto Christ. I could endure with His peace if I "rolled" it on the Lord—apply the faith-rest exercise. I realized I needed to put all my energies into concentrating on the Lord. Despite wearing earplugs, concentrating in this noisy oversized can was an Olympic challenge, but my Savior enabled me.

I thought about His promises and principles. I claimed Psalm 23:1, "The LORD is my Shepherd, I shall not want." I thought about the underlying principles to this verse. The Lord will supply all my needs; He is all I need to endure this. My Savior reminded me of another verse. *"My grace is sufficient for you, for My strength is made perfect in weakness. Therefore most gladly I will rather boast in my infirmities, that the power of Christ may rest upon me"* (2 Cor. 12:9). Again, I prayed the underlying principles of this passage—I am helpless to find peace unless You provide. In my thoughts I "sang" some of my favorite hymns. His grace enabled me to keep my faith focused on Him during the scanning.

At last the "endless" thirty minutes were over and the technician helped me out of the cylinder. Since anxiety causes fatigue, I expected to feel exhausted. Instead, I felt refreshed, rested, and invigorated. These unexpected emotions lifted me beyond any feeling of relief. Excited about my Savior's rescue, I thought about what He and I had been through together. I had a deeper understanding of *"through the LORD's mercies we are not consumed, Because His compassions fail not. They are new every morning; Great is Your faithfulness"* (Lam. 3:22-23). My heavenly Father used this unusual place to draw me closer. God revealed His mercies, His new compassion for this test of my faith—just for me! By using His faith-rest exercise for the test, He blessed me with refreshment and renewed energy. In this faith adventure Christ Jesus showed His love, faithfulness, and the meaning of new mercies.

> *When you reach to Christ in faith,*
> *He is waiting with His hand extended!*

Like many hymns, the next one is filled with grace messages. "Jesus, I am Resting, Resting" was written in 1876 by Jean Sophia Pigott. This hymn comforted Hudson Taylor, the missionary to China, in the terrible days of the Boxer uprising. As one report followed another of mission stations being destroyed and missionaries massacred, Taylor remained quietly at his desk, singing softly these words that he loved so dearly.

JESUS, I AM RESTING, RESTING

"Come to Me, all you who labor and are heavy laden, and I will give you rest" (Matt. 11:28).

Jesus! I am resting, resting
In the joy of what You are;
I am finding out the greatness
Of Your loving heart.
You have bid me gaze upon You,
And Your beauty fills my soul,
For, by Your transforming power,
You have made me whole.

Oh, how great Your loving kindness,
Vaster, broader than the sea!
Oh, how marvelous Your goodness,
Lavished all on me!
Yes, I rest in You, Beloved,
Know what wealth of grace is Yours;
Know Your certainty of promise,
And have made it mine.

Simply trusting You, Lord Jesus,
I behold You as You are,
And Your love, so pure, so changeless,
Satisfies my heart,
Satisfies its deepest longings,
Meets, supplies its every need,
Surrounding me with Your blessings,
Yours is love indeed!

Ever lift Your face upon me,
As I work and wait for You.
Resting 'neath Your smile, Lord Jesus,
Earth's dark shadows flee.
Brightness of my Father's glory,
Sunshine of my Father's face,
Keep me ever trusting, resting,
Fill me with Your grace.

~ Jean Sophia Pigott, 1845-1882 ~

Look for God's Grace

Have you lost hope? Has life lost its meaning? Is it difficult to think of moving forward? Thinking about God's grace can help you. Looking unto God's grace by trusting His promises will restore hope (confidence in God). *"Why are you cast down, O my soul? And why are you disquieted within me? Hope in God; For I shall yet praise Him, The help of my countenance and my God"* (Ps. 42:11).

What does God's grace mean to you? God's grace is all that God is willing to give you in blessing, apart from human merit or works because of Jesus Christ. In short, grace is God's undeserved favor.

Occasionally for a brief moment, I get discouraged about my health problems. However, when I choose to return to Christ-centered thinking, I experience the grace of His contentment. God's grace is everything He is free (justified) to do for me because of Christ's finished cross work. Stated another way, grace is God giving me what I don't deserve and, in His mercy, not giving me what I do deserve. He shows mercy (faithful love) to me today just as He did to believers of the past. Therefore, I can choose to rest in His unchanging grace!

> *Don't miss experiencing God's continual grace by only seeking Him during hardships.*

The Bible records many accounts of the God's grace despite the unfaithfulness of His people. The Bible book of Jeremiah portrays God's judgment on Israel for sinfulness and unfaithfulness. Besides the prophecy of judgments, our loving God showed His grace toward Israel because He desired that they would return to Him. The book of Lamentations, also written by Jeremiah, depicts Jeremiah's mourning as he anticipated the destruction of Jerusalem. The mood of both books is somber. The Lord commissioned Jeremiah to warn Israel to return to God or He would judge them. God's prediction of Jerusalem's destruction, especially the sin that would cause it, and the suffering that would result, overwhelmed Jeremiah. Yet in the middle of this gloom, Jeremiah proclaimed a beautiful expression of hope and trust. *"The LORD's lovingkindnesses indeed never cease, For His compassions never fail. They are new every morning; Great is Your faithfulness. The LORD is my portion"* (Lam. 3:22-24 NASB). Reading these heartbreaking books of Jeremiah and Lamentations we notice the love and grace of God shining through the gloom and doom. Look for God's mercy and you will experience it.

God's Grace Is Continuous

In review, God in His grace tells us about the types of salvation. For the unsaved, God's Word explains the rescue plan from the penalty of sin through faith in the work of Jesus Christ alone. Scripture also reveals God's rescue plan for believers from the power of sin by faith through the ministry of the Holy Spirit.

Perhaps you are thinking everything is going well. Thank God for that! Maybe you think you never have any problems that you can't handle. Eventually you may have a trial that you can't handle, and then where will you turn? If you live long enough, you will experience lifequakes because you belong to Christ; you are a friend of His (John 15:18-27).

In His grace, your Father gives you times of prosperity (absence of suffering) in which to prepare you for trials. Since His grace can deliver us in all circumstances, we only need to trust Him.

The hymn *"By Grace I'm Saved"* reminds us of our loving, faithful Lord's constant grace to us. Christian Scheidt celebrates God's unparalleled grace in the three stanzas that follow. (The first four stanzas are given in chapter one.) Take time now to meditate on these remaining stanzas.

BY GRACE I'M SAVED

"For by grace you have been saved through faith, and that not of yourselves; it is the gift of God, not of works, lest anyone should boast" (Eph. 2:8-9).

By grace! This ground of faith is certain;
As long as God is true, it stands.
What saints have penned by inspiration,
What in His Word our God commands,
Our faith in what our God has done
Depends on grace—grace through His Son.

By grace to timid hearts that tremble,
In tribulation's furnace tried,
By grace, in spite of fear and trouble,
The Father's heart is open wide.
Where could I help and strength secure
If grace were not my anchor sure?

By grace! On this I'll rest when dying;
In Jesus' promise I rejoice;
For though I know my heart's condition,
I also know my Savior's voice.
My heart is glad, all grief has flown
Since I am saved by grace alone.

~ Words: Christian L. Scheidt,1709-1761 Music: Kornelius H. Dretzel, 1731 ~
For audio visit: *hymntime.com* and search by title or lyricist.

Mercy is God's Grace in Action

When trials strike, you won't become distraught if you remember that God is at work in your life. Just because you can't see Him working doesn't mean He isn't involved orchestrating every event. Someone has said, "The next time your 'little hut' is burning to the ground, it just may be a smoke signal that summons the grace of God." In His grace, God is always working on your behalf, most often behind the scenes (Rom. 8:28).

God's mercy supplies His power to act on our behalf. The Bible offers many accounts of God's mercy that answered the prayer of believers. For example, because of His mercy, God rescued Lot and his family before He destroyed Sodom and Gomorrah. God's mercy protected the shepherd boy David from Goliath, the giant. The mercy of God protected Daniel in the lion's den in response to his faith. The Lord waits for our faith response of drawing on His inexhaustible grace reservoir.

> *Look for His grace in your trials.*

A Faith Adventure
Faith Resting Taps into God's Mercies

Cindy's husband has suffered from chronic severe neck pain for many years. In faith, she appealed to God's mercy. She writes:

> Two nights ago, my husband, Jonathan, said that he hates and dreads waking up in the morning because his pain medication is worn off by then. He wakes up in such terrible pain that it takes all the strength he can muster just to get up. The realization that each new day is a dreaded curse to him hit me hard. I suddenly felt so sad for him as I thought about how he starts each day.
>
> The Lord recalled to my mind the Scripture verse, *"His mercies are new each morning."* I remembered that Leah told me to believe the Scripture promises. I claimed that promise for my husband asking the Lord to show my husband His mercy each morning. So far, he has woken up two mornings in a row feeling good. I know that was an answer to prayer. His pain got bad again last night but the Lord showed His mercy by removing the intense pain two mornings in a row.
>
> I shared with Jonathan that I prayed a promise from Lamentations and the Lord answered "yes" by giving him two mornings with only slight pain. Sharing that with my husband encouraged him to remember the Lord is with him in his suffering.
>
> Although God has the power to remove my husband's pain, that isn't the Lord's will now. However, God clearly and mercifully gives my husband special times of pain relief. Sometimes the Lord gives relief in answer to prayer or for a special event. When we are at the end

of our rope and need encouragement, God reminds us that He *is* with us and He *is* for us.

God is merciful to us when we need it most and that encourages us to keep going. He is showing us that He is right there with us, holding us through the trial He has brought into our lives. Remembering that He ordains the trial for a reason—to exercise our dependent faith helps us cope. We won't know all of God's purposes in this trial until we get to heaven, but we are sure that it has passed through the Father's hands before it came into our lives.

> *When we call on God's power supply through faith, God's grace produces remarkable things.*

Faith Taps God's Grace Provisions

Since faith in Christ is a way of life, the faith-rest formula is for small and great problems. If this has been a normal week, you have had irritations, difficulties, frustrations, disappointments—maybe even heartbreaks or disasters. Perhaps you have been depressed or emotionally upset and have pushed the "panic button." When terrible things happen or when you experience everyday difficulties, you can choose to either doubt or believe God's word. Trials that are more difficult may catch us off guard and it may take us longer to switch our perspective. The secret for experiencing God's peace is following His rescue plan—faith rest.

A Faith Adventure
God's Grace during Unemployment

How many times have you planned and the Lord had other thoughts about your plans? This reminds me of the verse *"the mind of man plans his way, but the Lord directs his steps"* (Prov. 16:9). Though He changes our plans, His grace always provides as Clint tells us.

> I had my plans but God directed my steps. In 2008, things were going well for my family and me. My wife was pregnant with our third child and would deliver in two months. Because we needed the income, my wife worked until our child was born. One day it became heavy on my heart to do something. After praying to God about this, I realized

I must stock up on supplies. I bought three of everything that would not spoil. This meant deodorant, toothbrushes, Ziplock bags, trash bags, diapers, wet wipes, cleaning supplies, paper towels, toilet paper, etc. Over the next month we stocked up on everything. God blessed us with a home a few years before this and we had plenty of storage area.

Our baby was born in February and about one month later, I was fired from my job through no fault of mine. I realized this was a test from God. Believing this was a trial from God allowed me to relax in Him. I knew we had no source of income and still felt the peace of God.

Yes, I did panic for a while but my faithful Lord calmed me down. He helped me realize that He had positioned us to be able to make it financially without having to sell our home. We simply needed to have faith in God and trust Him 100%.

I filed for unemployment and received the maximum amount of pay. After about a month, I learned that I would not be getting unemployment. In His grace, the Lord provided a job working part time for a different company.

Our problems grew worse—we were down to less than $20 in our checking account and the credit card was full. Then the company I was working for part time surprised me by offering me a full time job as a drafter. There I made enough money over the next few months to pay our bills and start a savings account.

God knew every detail of my circumstance and worked it out in His time and for my good. He provided for my family and me. Thank you Lord!

> When you get to your wit's end, Jesus is waiting to meet your need!

Trusting in Jesus is so delightful, so sweet. Leaning on the Lord provides the Lord's "rest" which we so desperately need when lifequakes shake us. When hymn writer Louisa Stead experienced a lifequake, trusting in Jesus kept her attitude sweet. The Schafer family web site provides historical backgrounds to many traditional hymns including this one about Louisa Stead (1850-1917).

One day Louisa with her husband and four-year-old daughter went to enjoy the beach at Long Island, New York. While there, they heard a call for help from a young child in the water. Mr. Stead went to his rescue, but instead both he and the child were drowned. Louisa and her daughter were left to experience poverty. One day she found some food and money that had been left for her on her doorstep. The hymn "'Tis So Sweet to Trust in Jesus" was born from her struggles as a widowed, single parent. Later Louisa and her daughter left for South Africa where she found a new husband, and together they led a missionary life.

Commentary: *www.schaefer-family.com/hymns/sweet.htm*
Audio: Cyber Hymnal, *www.hymntime.com*

'TIS SO SWEET TO TRUST IN JESUS
*"And those who know Your name will put their trust in You;
For You, LORD, have not forsaken those who seek You"* (Ps. 9:10).

'Tis so sweet to trust in Jesus,
And to take Him at His Word;
Just to rest upon His promise,
And to know, "Thus says the Lord!"

Refrain: Jesus, Jesus, how I trust Him!
How I've proved Him o'er and o'er
Jesus, Jesus, precious Jesus!
O for grace to trust Him more!

O how sweet to trust in Jesus,
Just to trust His cleansing blood;
And in simple faith to plunge me
'Neath the healing, cleansing flood!

Yes, 'tis sweet to trust in Jesus,
Just from sin and self to cease;
Just from Jesus simply taking
Life and rest, and joy and peace.

I'm so glad I learned to trust Thee,
Precious Jesus, Savior, Friend;
And I know that Thou art with me,
Wilt be with me to the end.

~ Louisa M. R. Stead, 1850-1917 ~

He Gives Us More Grace

If you feel that you can't endure a trial then you have forgotten about God's grace. Once you settle in with God's grace through Christ, you will recognize His grace in all areas of your life. When the trial comes, expect to find Christ waiting there with His grace. The more we suffer the more grace He supplies. His grace is more than sufficient, yes, more than enough; His grace is abundant (2 Cor. 9:8). God has more grace—special grace for special needs.

Our heavenly Father supplies us with overflowing grace for every need—all the grace you need to be content. However, many believers don't experience the grace of God or don't remember to thank Him when things are going well. Dear believer, look for the grace of His comfort in your trials.

> *We shall experience His grace when we grieve—not that we have lost—but seeing how much we have been given.*

Comfort from His Grace

Some believers think the removal of the suffering is the means to relief. Do most believers find comfort only when the suffering subsides? If comfort or relief only comes with removal of the suffering, we are looking for a spiritual aspirin. How often do we merely pray to the Lord for pain relief? Don't you know or have you forgotten our Lord God is the God of all comfort? We would please our Father by accepting His comfort in our suffering instead of seeking the removal of our suffering.

> *God isn't a pharmacist who distributes pain relievers, but He will soothe us with His comfort as He prepares the remedy.*

The Source of True Comfort

Where do people look for help and comfort? Some look to a higher power, astrology, and positive thoughts. Often people try to comfort others with their religious beliefs, optimistic thoughts, or positive energy.

People often say "time heals all wounds," "keep thinking about the good times," or "keep busy." Have you noticed that clichés, positive thoughts or energy, and ideas from secular or religious beliefs offer no comfort? They are empty words that focus on weak ideas of man, fate, or lies.

True comfort comes from God, from His powerful character. Consider one of God's masterpiece verses about His comfort. *"Blessed be the God and Father of our Lord Jesus Christ, the Father of mercies and God of all comfort"* (2 Cor. 1:3). Let your loving Father comfort you.

> *Without trials we could not know Him as the Father of mercies and the God of all comfort.*

God's Comfort during Chronic Pain

Anyone with chronic pain knows the pain often intensifies at night. Experts recommend that we not concentrate on the pain; moaning is focusing on the pain. Thinking about the pain may increase its intensity, lengthen its duration, or cause us to tense up. Sometimes my pain strikes in the night as it did last night.

Instead of focusing on my pain, I prayed recalling God's character traits. I "sang" (in the quiet corners of my soul) several hymns. As I reflected on Him and the greatness of His character, my comforting Father supplied me with peace. In His mercy, He removed the pain and then He "tucked me in" to sleep.

> *"But if we are afflicted, it is for your comfort and salvation; or if we are comforted, it is for your comfort, which is effective in the patient enduring of the same sufferings which we also suffer"* (2 Cor. 1:6 NASB).

Let God Collect Your Tears

Opinions or expectations on how we should respond in difficult times vary between people. When my mother died, my tears flowed profusely because I felt so lost and so empty. As I sobbed beside her casket a relative scolded, "Pull yourself together, you have a husband and baby to consider." After that I stuffed my feelings. In time I developed chest pains and my husband rushed me to the hospital emergency room. Finding nothing physically wrong, the doctor asked, "Has anything traumatic happened recently?" Hearing that my mom died, he asked if I was expressing my feelings and crying openly. "No," was my husband's response, so the doctor urged the open expression of my feelings. Although I felt all alone, my Lord Jesus saw my tears.

Nineteen years later my brother died. Although I grieved deeply, I didn't have a void in my soul as I did when my mother died. By this time, I had grown closer to the Lord Jesus who filled the emptiness in my soul. When waves of grief washed over me, I earnestly prayed to the Lord to carry my grief. The Lord saw my tears and comforted me.

Grieving in a trial or disappointment is normal. Share your feelings. Let others see your sorrow, and above all, admit your feelings to your heavenly Father. Since God created us with emotions, expressing heartaches, even through tears, is a human response. Jesus understands our grief since He was a man of sorrows, stricken with grief. He expressed His grief when He wept (John 11:35). King David grieved often as his psalms describe. The apostle Paul didn't minimize his feelings of despair and helplessness in a trial (2 Cor. 8–11). Instead, he emphasized his weakness to show how powerless he and the Corinthian believers were apart from God.

Above all, roll your feelings onto the Lord in prayer. Amid the tears remember that your Savior and Friend understands your deepest sorrow. He knows how many tears you will need to release as part of the healing.

We read in Psalm 56:8, *"Put my tears into your bottle."* As J. Vernon McGee explained,

> My tears have been put into thy bottle. A note in The New Scofield Bible concerning this subject says, "Sometimes, in olden days in the East, mourners would catch their tears in bottles (water skins) and place them at the tombs of their loved ones" —

to show how much they had grieved. Let me add to that something John Bunyan, the tinker of Bedford said, "God preserves our tears in a bottle, so that He can wipe them away." When I read that, I wished I had cried more. We need to weep more. Matthew Henry said, "The tears of God's persecuted people are bottled up and sealed among God's treasures." —*Thru The Bible with J. Vernon McGee*

When you feel that no one understands, remember the Lord knows every detail of your life including every pain and every tear. The picture of the Lord collecting our tears means He sees our suffering; therefore, we can say with complete confidence that God is for us.

> *Unless we admit our pain and sorrow and look to the God of all comfort, we will not be comforted.*

Comforting One Another

When my brother died people tried to comfort me by expressing memories of my brother. Some thought that reminding me what a great personality my brother had would comfort me. Others just held my hand or gave me a hug; some didn't know what to say.

Have you ever been speechless when you had an opportunity to comfort someone? Can you remember a time when you were nervous or over-zealous and said too much to the grieving person? Perhaps you said the wrong thing when someone needed comforting. Notice how the boy in the next story comforted his neighbor.

> Author and lecturer Leo Buscaglia once talked about a contest he was asked to judge. The purpose of the contest was to find the most caring child. The winner was a four-year-old child, whose next-door neighbor was an elderly man who had recently lost his wife. The four year old knew just how to "be there" for his neighbor. Upon seeing the man cry, the little boy went into the older man's yard, climbed onto his lap, and just sat there. When his mother asked him what he had said to the neighbor, the little boy just said, "Nothing, I just helped him cry."

Maybe you remain quiet and let your presence speak of your caring concern. At first, our presence with someone who is grieving may be enough. Allow him to pass through the early moments or hours of shock without flooding him with excessive comments.

Pray for insights about the right words and best time to offer comfort. Quoting *"all things work together for good to those who love God"* might be the right words but at the wrong time. For example, when a child dies or when the diagnosis is terminal, give the person time to adjust to the news. We must discern when to reserve some Scripture verses for a time when the receiver can accept them.

Pray for guidance in choosing words of comfort. Consider great comfort verses such as *"Come unto Me, all you who labor and are heavy laden, and I will give you rest"* (Matt. 11:28) or *"Cast your burden upon the LORD and He will sustain you; He will never allow the righteous to be shaken"* (Ps. 55:22 NASB). Be patient and pray for insight for the right time to offer comfort from the Scriptures. Some believers look for Scripture comfort immediately and some need more time.

A good listener allows another person to express his feelings without interruption. A caring listener offers a response about what he has heard. Express your concerns with comments like, "That is difficult." "I sense you are upset about this." "I can see how much you are hurting." We may ask how we may help. We may phone or send a card to show support.

When we show our care and concern, we are "bearing one another's burdens" (Gal. 6:2). We share or bear with them. We must not "carry" them—regard their problem as our own. In other words, we maintain boundaries. We practice giving the person and his problems over to the Lord. When the time is right, we can point that person to our loving Father, our God of all comfort who will carry him.

Pray for Discernment

How can we show that we care for others during times of suffering without interfering? When people seek our help with problems, we aren't obligated nor dare we try to solve their personal problems. We can't rescue another and neither should we try. Furthermore, we must guard against becoming excessively involved in another person or the problem. Pray for understanding the difference between interfering and offering help or support as unto the Lord (Prov. 3:27; Luke 10:33; 2 Cor. 1:11).

Guard yourself against hindering the Holy Spirit's ministry. The Holy Spirit may use a trial or use discipline to draw someone closer to Christ, so we should stay out of His way. God alone is in the human soul rescue business. We must let go and let God the Holy Spirit intervene and perform His recovery work. Thus, we respect the boundaries of others and the work of God.

But how do we disconnect from the problems of others? The best way to detach from the troubles of another and still care is through prayer. We can give the problems to the Lord and continue to pray for our loved one. We can pray that the unsaved person would be responsive to the gospel and for an opportunity to share it with him. When praying for the carnal (out of fellowship) believer, pray that the trial would restore him to fellowship with the Lord. When a believer suffers a lifequake, we can pray that the trial leads him to depend more consistently on the Lord.

How can we befriend another believer? We can listen attentively to the problem, and then direct him to the Word of God. We may pray and read Scripture with him and share the faith-rest approach to circumstances. Allow him to search for God's will and make his own decision based on God's principles.

Key points to remember when comforting other believers:

1. God's comfort must be the common characteristic.
2. God is the God of all comfort (2 Cor. 1:3).
3. God is with us and comforts us in all trials (Rom. 8:35).
4. Comfort others with the same promises that the Lord has comforted you (2 Cor. 1:4; 1 Thess. 4:18; 5:14).
5. God comforts us, so that we may be able to comfort others (2 Cor. 1:4b).

Channels of His Comfort

Have you ever thought that God will use your trials to comfort others? What might you say to someone going through a trial similar to yours? Having similar troubles may help us identify with others and perhaps lend words of comfort. Hearing comments such as, "Oh, I went through that" may comfort us for a time. However, telling others how we survived our trial *by our strength* or *determination* isn't the "comfort" God wants us to share. Highlighting our trials in the wrong manner or at the wrong time can focus the spotlight on us instead of on the God of all comfort.

The Lord Jesus offers more comfort than sharing a self-centered, parallel experience. The suffering person benefits more by knowing that God understands his pain and can comfort him. Pointing people to the God of all comfort, His specific character, and promises is of greater benefit than talking about parallel trials and ourselves. Sharing with others how God comforted you in a trial is beneficial.

The Lord comforts us with His promises and then He helps us to comfort one another. The apostle Paul wrote of God's comfort and comforting others. *"Blessed be the God and Father of our Lord Jesus Christ, the Father of mercies and God of all comfort, who comforts us in all our affliction so that we will be able to comfort those who are in any affliction with the comfort with which we ourselves are comforted by God"* (2 Cor. 1:3-4 NASB). Some people misunderstand or misapply what God is saying about His comfort in these verses. They take the phrase "that we will be able to comfort those who are in any affliction" out of context. Some think this means that because they suffer, they can comfort others and consequently, they miss the point of the verse. By taking the phrase out of context, they shift the focus from God's comfort to themselves. Since God is the God of all comfort, greater comfort comes from emphasizing God. Our Father, the God of all comfort, must be the common characteristic, not our common problems, when we offer comfort.

We are merely the channels to express His comfort and mercy. Our experience of God's comfort needs to spill out in an overflow of His comfort into the life of another believer. For example, Joni Erickson Tada, a quadriplegic through a tragic diving accident, gradually learned to depend on the Lord. Because of God's comfort to her, Joni pours out God's comfort on others through her Christian writings. As a channel for the Lord's comfort, Joni comforts others with the same comfort of God that consoles her.

This verse promises the more we suffer, the more His comfort will be available to us. *"For just as the sufferings of Christ are ours in abundance, so also our comfort is abundant through Christ"* (2 Cor. 1:5 NASB). We will have more than just enough comfort. We will have overflowing comfort in proportion to the sufferings we share because we belong to Christ.

God, the Sovereign Lord, reigns and comforts us, and through us comforts others.

Reflection Questions

Use Scripture verses to prove your answers whenever possible.

1. Define God's grace and give two examples from your own life.

2. What must be the emphasis when comforting another?

3. How must we correctly understand 2 Cor. 1:3-5?

4. What does "God gives more grace" mean to you?

5. What have you learned to apply to your Christian life?

CHAPTER 15 PREVIEW

༄ The Riches in Your Spiritual Account

༄ Your Real Position and Identity

༄ Account Withdrawals Available 24/7

༄ Expect Triumph and Thrive

༄ Joy–A Blessing of the Victorious Life

CHAPTER 15

Are You Living Victoriously?

Millions of people live without a second thought whether they are saved because they assume they are. In the same way, most believers are unaware of the victorious Christian life or have no idea how to experience it. The following story has applications for both the unsaved and for believers.

Don't Leave It on the Desk
Author unknown

A professor of religion named Dr. Christianson taught at a small college in the western United States. For many years, Dr. Christianson taught a required religion course to freshmen.

Although Dr. Christianson tried hard to communicate the essence of the gospel, most students considered the course as nothing but drudgery. Despite his best efforts, most students refused to take Christianity seriously.

This year Dr. Christianson had an outstanding student named Steve, who intended to enter the ministry. Steve had an impressive physique, was the starting center on the school football team, and was popular with the other students.

One day Dr. Christianson asked Steve to stay after class so he could talk with him. "How many push-ups can you do?" Steve said, "I do about 200 every night." "That's pretty good, Steve," Dr. Christianson said. "Do you think you could do 300?" Steve replied, "I don't know; I've never done 300 at a time." "Do you think you could?" Dr. Christianson repeated. "Well, I can try," said Steve.

"Can you do 300 in sets of 10? I have a class project in mind and I need you to do about 300 push-ups in sets of ten for this to work. Can you do it? I need you to tell me you can do it," said the professor.

Steve replied, "Well...I think I can..."yeah, I can do it." "Good," Dr. Christianson responded. I need you to do this on Friday. Let me explain what I have in mind."

On Friday, Steve went to class early and sat in the front of the room. When class started, the professor pulled out a large box of doughnuts. These weren't the typical kinds of doughnuts; they were the extra fancy, big kind filled with cream centers and frosting swirls. Everyone was excited it was Friday—the last day of the school week. They were eager to get an early start on the weekend with a party in Dr. Christianson's class.

The professor went to the first young woman in row one and asked, "Cynthia, would you like one of these doughnuts?" Cynthia said, "Yes." Dr. Christianson then turned to Steve and asked, "Steve, would you do ten push-ups so Cynthia can have a doughnut?" "Sure!" Steve jumped down from his desk to do a quick ten and then returned to his desk. Dr. Christianson put a doughnut on Cynthia's desk.

Next, the professor went to Joe and asked, "Joe, do you want a donut?" Joe quickly said, "Yes." Dr. Christianson asked, "Steve, will you do ten push-ups so Joe can have a donut?" Steve did the push-ups so Joe could have a doughnut. The test continued, down the first aisle, Steve did ten push-ups for each student so each one could have a doughnut.

In the second aisle, Dr. Christianson came to Scott who was also on the basketball team and in good condition like Steve. Since he was popular, he never lacked for female companionship. When the professor asked, "Scott, do you want a doughnut?" Scott's reply was, "Well, can I do my own push-ups?" Dr. Christianson said, "No, Steve has to do them." Scott didn't like this and said, "Well, I don't want one then." The professor shrugged and turned to Steve and asked, "Steve, would you do ten push-ups so Scott can have a doughnut he doesn't want?" With perfect obedience, Steve started to do ten push-ups. Scott said, "HEY! I said I didn't want one!" Dr. Christianson said, "Look! This is my classroom, my class, my desks, and these are my donuts. Just leave it on the desk if you don't want it," and he put a doughnut on Scott's desk.

With perspiration flowing from his brow and fatigue setting in, Steve had begun to slow down. Steve was too tired to get up and down, so he stayed on the floor between sets.

Dr. Christianson started down the third row. Now the students were getting angry. The professor asked, "Jenny, do you want a doughnut?" Sternly, Jenny said, "No." Then Dr. Christianson asked, "Steve, would you do ten more push-ups so Jenny can have a donut that she doesn't want?" Steve did ten and Jenny got a doughnut.

By now, a growing sense of uneasiness filled the room. The students were beginning to say, "No!" and many uneaten doughnuts were setting on the desks.

Steve was exerting more effort to do push-ups for each student to have a doughnut. Beneath Steve's face was a small pool of sweat, his arms and brow were red because of the physical exercise.

Professor Christianson was having difficulty watching Steve work so hard for all those uneaten doughnuts. He asked Robert, the most vocal unbeliever in the class, to watch Steve to make sure he completed each set of ten.

As the professor started down the fourth row, other students wandered in and sat along the side steps of the room. Realizing more students, the professor did a quick count—now there were 34 students. He started to worry whether Steve would be able to do push-ups for four more students.

Dr. Christianson went to the next person, the next, and the next. By now, Steve was having a rough time doing push-ups. He was taking longer to complete each set. Steve asked the professor, "Do I have to make my nose touch on each one?" The professor thought a moment, "Well, they're your push-ups. You are in charge now. You can do them any way that you want." The professor continued to the next student.

A few moments later, Jason, a recent transfer student, came to the doorway. As he was about to enter the room, the students yelled in one voice, "No! Don't come in! Stay out!" Puzzled Jason wondered what was happening. Steve raised his head and said, "No, let him come." Dr. Christianson replied, "You realize that if Jason comes in you will have to do ten push-ups for him?" Steve said, "Yes, let him come in and give him a doughnut."

Professor Christianson said, "Okay, Steve, I'll let you get Jason's set out of the way right now. Jason, do you want a doughnut?" Jason, new to the room, not knowing what was going on, said, "Yes, give me a doughnut." Steve, will you do ten push-ups so Jason can have a doughnut?" With great effort, Steve slowly did the set. The professor gave bewildered Jason a doughnut and he sat down.

Dr. Christianson finished the fourth row, and then started on those visitors seated on the steps. Steve's arms were shaking with each push-up as he struggled against the force of gravity. Now the sweat was dropping profusely from his face and the only sound in the room was Steve's heavy panting. By now, the students were emotional and there wasn't a dry eye in the room.

The last two students in the room were two young women, both popular cheerleaders. The professor went to Linda, the second to the last and asked, "Linda, do you want a donut?" Linda sadly replied, "No, thank you." Dr. Christianson quietly asked, "Steve, will you do ten push-ups so Linda can have a doughnut she doesn't want?" Grunting from the effort, Steve did ten slow push-ups for Linda.

Professor Christianson turned to the last student and said, "Susan, do you want a doughnut?" With tears flowing down her face, Susan pleaded, "Why can't I help him?" Dr. Christianson, with tears of his own, answered, "No, Steve has to do it alone. I have given him this task. He is in charge of making sure everyone has an opportunity for a doughnut whether he wants it or not.

"When I decided to have a party this last day of class, I looked at my grade book. Steve is the only student with a perfect grade. Everyone else has failed a test, skipped class, or offered me inferior work. Steve told me that when a football player messes up in practice he must do push-ups. I told Steve that none of you could come to my party unless he paid the price by doing your push-ups. He and I made a deal for your sakes.

"Steve, would you do ten push-ups so Susan can have a doughnut?"

As Steve slowly finished his last push-up, he understood he had done what was required of him. Having done 350 push-ups, his arms buckled beneath him and he fell to the floor.

Dr. Christianson turned to the students and said, "And so it was, that our Savior, Jesus Christ on the cross called out 'It is finished.' Jesus had done everything required of Him to pay the penalty for your sins. Our Savior yielded His life to give you the gift of eternal life. And like some of those in this room, many leave His gift on the desk, uneaten." Two students helped Steve up from the floor to a seat. Though physically exhausted, he was wearing a thin smile. "Well, done, good and faithful servant," praised the professor and added, "Not all sermons are preached in words."

Turning to his class the professor gave this appeal. "My desire is that you might understand and fully comprehend all the riches of grace and mercy that have been given to you through the sacrifice of our Lord and Savior Jesus Christ. God spared not His Son, but gave Him for us all, now and forever. Whether or not you accept His gift, Christ paid the price. Wouldn't you be foolish and ungrateful to leave it lying on the desk?"

This classroom exercise demonstrated Christ's work of salvation by grace, without any work or merit on your part. The demonstration has additional application for believers who have accepted Christ but have left something on the desk. Are you one of millions of believers who accepted His gift of salvation but left part of His gift, His riches lying on the desk? Do you realize that the riches of His grace are your spiritual inheritance? When you leave part of His gift on the desk, you choose to live the Christian life in spiritual poverty instead of spiritual wealth.

Many believers fail to claim their riches in Christ and live in spiritual poverty their entire life. They fail to draw on Christ's spiritual riches daily. Because you share in His riches, you have all the "gold" you need to live a supernatural, victorious Christian life.

Drawing on the Spiritual Treasures

Beth, a Christ-centered mother of four, enjoyed spiritual stability through faith resting. However, the diagnosis of an incurable, muscle-weakening disease tested the consistency of her faith. Her first response was grief and concern for her family, but she remained confident in the Lord's perfect will. Even though she experienced times of mourning, she continued to draw on her riches in Christ. By faithfully reading, hearing, and applying God's Word, Beth continued to have the same peace and joy in Christ that she had before her illness.

A sign of spiritual steadiness is waking up in the morning with prayer and praise to the Lord. "Father, this is Your day. What do you have for me today? Thank you for this time of difficulty to mold me to be more like Christ. I know this trial is your will for me now."

> *A believer unbound to the world can enjoy Christ.*

Are You Living Like Royalty?

Every believer is a member of God's royal household in the family of Christ, the King of kings. As spiritual royalty, you have limitless spiritual riches to spend every day. Although you live on earth, your spiritual family position is in your heavenly palace. Dear believer, are you merely surviving in a state of spiritual bankruptcy? Or, are you thriving as a spiritually wealthy aristocrat who lavishly spends your riches in Christ?

The Lord wants you to live from your position of spiritual health and wealth in Christ. He desires that we, His princes and princesses, live in a manner that represents our heavenly calling in Christ (Eph. 4:1). God our Father expects us to look, think, and act like spiritual nobility. Consequently, draw on your spiritual heritage; claim your inheritance every day. Live like you own the peace that passes understanding, His joy, His love, and all the riches of God because you do! Believe that the same power that raised Christ from the dead is available to you for overcoming sin, Satan, and his world. Act as though you have all the spiritual endurance of the God of the universe in your possession because you do. Spend your spiritual legacy with daily withdrawals of the wealth of His promises and character traits. Cherish your position of privilege by claiming your spiritual riches, and then you can be victorious in daily living and during trials.

Think and behave like spiritual royalty who lives in the palace with Christ. Then you are living worthy of your calling—your spiritual status of royalty (Col. 3:12-14). How are you living worthy of your calling in Christ? Ask yourself, am I living looking up? Am I striving toward my position is Christ, which I already possess? Since you already have a wealthy spiritual position of royalty, you don't need to strive to gain it, just enjoy it. Instead of looking up from yourself to Christ, you can keep looking down on your trials and circumstances in life from your position in Christ. In other words, think about who you are—a child of the King, and where you belong—your royal position in Christ. View life from the perspective of life in the royal family of God. Have a mindset of your position in Christ with a heavenly inheritance to use to enjoy the highest quality Christian life.

> We belong to another sphere altogether. We have died, and our life is hidden with Christ in God (Col. 3:3). We are like a tree that has its roots in heaven and its branches down here. No doubt our branches are fretted and ripped by the atmosphere here, but nothing can touch the roots up there. Planted inside, they flourish. —J.B. Stoney (1814-1897)

Because of your union with Christ, you can be victorious. You have no need to ask for what you already have—all His riches including His power to be victorious. The issue isn't your weakness but His strength; not your efforts but His life expressed through you; and not your inadequacies but His sufficiency. Are you viewing spiritual victory "looking down" from your position of His strength and victory through you? Live from the position that is already yours in Christ.

I am not a spiritual peasant; I am spiritual nobility, an aristocrat.

More than Conquerors

As previously noted, the Lord provides replacements—His strength for my weakness, His thoughts for my thoughts and His security for my fear. *"But whoever listens to me will dwell safely, And will be secure, without fear of evil"* (Prov. 1:33; also, Ps. 4:8; 121:7-8). When we obey by trusting, He is dependable and strong to help us fight the good fight.

Overcoming sin, Satan, and the world is part of the superior life that God promises every believer in Jesus Christ. *"Yet in all these things we are more than conquerors through Him who loved us"* (Rom. 8:37). Trusting His promises encourages us to continue the fight of faith and then to thrive in the battle.

In his book, *The Complete Green Letters*, Miles J. Stanford encourages us regarding the victorious faith-rest life when he writes,

> If there is a great trial in your life today, do not own it as a defeat, but continue by faith to claim the victory through Him who is able to make you more than a conqueror, and a glorious triumph will soon be apparent. Let us learn that in all the hard places our Father brings us into, He is making opportunities for us to exercise such faith in Him as will bring about blessed results and greatly glorify His Name.

Dear believer, focus on Christ, and His power not your defeats or victories. If we look at our failures of faith, we will be discouraged. If we look at our victories, we may become proud. Neither perspective will help us in fighting the good fight of faith (1 Tim. 6:12). Victory is from and through the Lord. *"But thanks be to God, who gives us the victory through our Lord Jesus Christ"* (1 Cor. 15:57). When we view our spiritual victories as God's grace though faith in Christ Jesus, we give Him the glory.

Expect Triumph and Thrive

Look for victory over negative thoughts and the feelings that result from them. Expect the true, consistent peace that God intends for you through faith. Our Lord Jesus gives us His supernatural peace, which replaces depression, hopelessness, or worry. Just take the Lord at His Word: *"Peace I leave with you, My peace I give to you; not as the world gives do I give to you. Let not your heart be troubled, neither let it be afraid"* (John 14:27). With His peace, enjoy a clear mind, energy for the tasks before you, and purpose for living. Never question if you can thrive in a trial; instead, have confidence that you can triumph by claiming your spiritual riches.

Dear believer in Christ, when you live by faith you can expect victory in the form of peace (Ps. 4:8; 121:3-4; 127:2); courage in the face of trouble (Ps. 46:1-2); deliverance (Ps. 34:19); and blessings (Eph. 1:3).

Take time now to evaluate your last lifequake. Were you a smoking smudge pot or a victorious blazing torch of living faith? Did you trust the Lord:

1. when you couldn't see?
2. for His timing?
3. to do His will?
4. by faith resting?
5. to provide for you?
6. for His wisdom?
7. for victory to be a blazing torch?

Did you live from your royal position, draw on your spiritual riches, and then thrive in your trial?

Victorious Living Looks to Christ

When we respond in faith, our trials deepen our attachment to Christ. Take time now to ponder these verses: *It is good for me that I have been afflicted, That I may learn Your statutes* (Ps. 119:71). *I know, O LORD, that Your judgments are right, And that in faithfulness You have afflicted me* (Ps. 119:75). Trials are often bitter, but gaining a deeper affection for the Lord Jesus is so sweet.

God rewards the use of faith rest in our circumstances. *"But without faith it is impossible to please Him, for he who comes to God must believe that He is, and that He is a rewarder of those who diligently seek Him"* (Heb. 11:6). When you depend on the Spirit, He will work in your life. Then you will experience the spiritual riches reserved for you from eternity past.

> *The confidence of a heart clinging to God alone delights Him and He rewards such faith.*

Jesus Christ is the basis for victorious living by faith. By our own ability, we can't develop faith; we can't grow spiritually by our striving. Spiritual growth can be compared to a baby who grows from the milk he drinks, not from the determination to grow. Similarly, believers mature spiritually from consistent intake of spiritual food, the Word of God — not from intake alone, but from "digestion" (meditation, understanding, and believing). Christ plants, encourages, and develops our faith.

A believer who is occupied with the Word of God will draw closer to the Lord in dependency on Him. A believer stays focused by looking to Jesus moment by moment. Meditate on Jesus, the source of your faith, as you read the next hymn.

LOOKING OFF UNTO JESUS
"Looking unto Jesus, the author and finisher of our faith" (Heb. 12:2).

O eyes that are weary and hearts that are sore,
Look off unto Jesus and sorrow no more;
The light of His countenance shines so bright,
That on earth, as in heaven, there need be no night.

"Looking off unto Jesus," my spirit is blest;
In the world I have turmoil — in Him I have rest;
The sea of my life all about me may roar,
When I look unto Jesus I hear it no more.

> "Looking off unto Jesus," I go not astray;
> My eyes are on Him, and He shows me the way;
> The path may seem dark as He leads me along,
> But following Jesus I cannot go wrong.
>
> "Looking off unto Jesus," my heart cannot fear,
> Its trembling is still when I see Jesus near;
> I know that His power my safe-guard will be,
> For, "Why are you troubled?" He says to me.
>
> Soon, soon shall I know the full beauty and grace
> Of Jesus my Lord when I stand face to face;
> I shall know how His love went before me each day,
> And wonder that ever my eyes turned away.
>
> ~ Anne B. Warner, 1820-1915 *Hymns of Truth and Praise* ~

A Faith Adventure
Take a Deep Faith Breath!

Paul expects spiritual triumph when he draws on His spiritual account. He shares some thoughts to encourage you to use your spiritual riches. Paul writes,

> Recently I was diagnosed with invasive cancer. Its ramifications, surgeries, and chemotherapy have redefined what used to be "normal" for my family and me. Indeed, we are grieving the loss of normalcy in almost every part of our lives these days.
>
> Stethoscopes in hand, medical professionals often listen to my lungs while instructing me to take deep breaths. They try to determine whether I am taking in oxygen properly. The test is an important one, so much so they refer to this listening process as "checking my vitals." And vital it is, for without oxygen one doesn't live.
>
> Before each treatment and surgical procedure, or when I am faced with yet another nasty reality of the cancer, I take deliberate breaths of another sort—both physical and spiritual. Let me explain.

I take a series of deep physical breaths. This helps bring fresh oxygen to my bloodstream, slowing down my anxious heartbeat, calming my raw emotions and steadying my mind in preparation for the physical and emotional assault to come.

Also, I take what I call "faith breaths"—deliberate and intentional reviews of what I know to be true about God's attributes and of all I possess in Christ by His wonderful grace! Faith breaths have a way of sending divine truth cruising through my spiritual veins, like spiritual oxygen. They settle down my anxious soul at the deepest level with a peace and a comfort that really, as the Scripture says, "passes understanding." Indeed, I find this exercise is vital to my spiritual well-being.

Dear reader let me urge you to breathe deeply of all God's pure attributes. Breathe deeply of your unsearchable riches of God's grace in Christ! Such deep faith-breaths are vital to your spiritual well-being. Next time you face trials, try taking deep faith breaths.

Account Withdrawals Available 24/7

As you know, the Lord Jesus provided hundreds of promises—some for today, others for eternity. Many believers may be familiar with or know God's promises by memory. Those who live by faith cherish the depth and richness of His promises.

In addition, claiming the promises about your heavenly future provides confident assurance about our life with Christ. God has promised you a body like Christ's. "[He]*who will transform our lowly body that it may be conformed to His glorious body, according to the working by which He is able even to subdue all things to Himself*" (Phil. 3:21). When you feel sorrowful, spend His promises such as, *"And God will wipe away every tear from their eyes; there shall be no more death, nor sorrow, nor crying. There shall be no more pain, for the former things have passed away"* (Rev. 21:4). When your thoughts turn towards health concerns, uneasiness about getting older, or the possibility of national collapse, access your spiritual bank account of promises. Spend the promises about your eternal future for your confidence for tomorrow. Oh, the joy we have when we anticipate heaven's perfect environment living with the Lord Jesus.

When I consider God's command to think about heavenly matters, a promise in the book of John comes to mind. We will live in a mansion forever. *"In My Father's house are many mansions; if it were not so, I would have told you. I go to prepare a place for you. And if I go and prepare a place for you, I will come again and receive you to Myself; that where I am, there you may be also"* (John 14:2-3).

Best of all, I have eager anticipation of living with my spiritual Bridegroom. *"We are confident, yes, well pleased rather to be absent from the body and to be present with the Lord"* (2 Cor. 5:8). Our perspective improves when we think about the Lord Jesus and His promises. *"For I know that my Redeemer lives, And He shall stand at last on the earth; And after my skin is destroyed, this I know, That in my flesh I shall see God"* (Job 19:25-26). Claiming the riches of His promises reminds us that life is temporary. Thinking from His viewpoint causes us to anticipate the joy of living with Jesus Christ forever.

> *The best is yet to come—forever with the Lord!*

Keep Your Fork
Author unknown

An elderly woman with a terminal illness had just three months to live, so she was getting her things "in order." She asked her pastor to come to her house to discuss her final wishes. She told him which songs she wanted sung at the service, what Scriptures she wanted read, and in what dress she wanted to be buried.

Everything was in order. As the pastor was preparing to leave, the woman suddenly remembered something important. "There's one more thing," she said excitedly.

"What's that?" the pastor asked. "This is important," the woman continued. "I want to be buried with a fork in my right hand." The pastor stood looking at the woman, not knowing what to say. "That surprises you, doesn't it?" the woman asked. "Well, to be honest, I'm puzzled by the request," said the pastor.

The woman explained. "In all my years of attending church socials and potluck dinners, I always remember that when the dishes of the main course were being cleared, someone would inevitably lean over and say, 'Keep your fork.' It was my favorite part because I knew that something better was coming—like velvety chocolate cake or deep-dish apple pie—something wonderful and with substance! So, I just want people to see me there in that casket with a fork in my hand and I want them to wonder, 'What's with the fork?' Then I want you to tell them, 'Keep your fork...the best is yet to come.'"

The pastor's eyes welled up with tears of joy as he hugged the woman goodbye. He knew this might be the last time he would see her before her death, but he also knew the woman had a good grasp of heaven. She knew something better was coming.

At the funeral people were walking by the woman's casket. They saw the green dress she was wearing, and the fork placed in her right hand. Repeatedly, the pastor heard the question, "What's with the fork?" Repeatedly he smiled. During his message, the pastor told the people of the conversation he had had with the woman shortly before she died. He also told them about the fork and about what it symbolized to her. The pastor told the people that he couldn't stop thinking about the fork and they probably wouldn't be able to either.

So the next time you reach down for your fork, let it remind you oh so gently, that the best is yet to come. Jesus is coming soon, either to call us home through death or take us home in the Rapture. The best is yet to come—living forever with our best Friend and Savior, Jesus Christ!

A Faith Adventure
Victory in Living and in Dying

A few years ago Dave went home to be with the Lord. In his battle with cancer, Dave and his wife Kathy traveled to Mexico for nontraditional treatment. When Dave developed a medical complication during treatment, he was transported to a hospital in San Diego. The Lord had arranged a change in their plans to fulfill His purposes of drawing people to Himself.

In His grace, the Lord blessed Dave with consciousness and alertness even near the end. As Dave grew weaker, his children flew in to be with him, as did a longtime friend with whom Dave shared the gospel.

As the family prayed, read Scripture, and sang hymns, the peace of God and joy in the Lord filled the hospital room. The Lord gave Dave and his family various occasions to share the gospel with others. On one of the last days, the doctor came in to break the news that death was imminent. He was hedging yet trying so hard to say what he needed to say when Dave said to him, "Just say it." The doctor replied, "You are dying." Dave confidently yet humbly responded, "I, this body, may be dying but I have eternal life in me, do you doctor?" This comment opened the way to share the gospel of Christ.

God used the opportunity of Dave's trial to plant gospel seeds in the hospital personnel. The hospital staff commented that in all the years of seeing dying patients, they had never seen anything like this in a hospital room. The staff heard the family and friends singing hymns of praise and comfort. The staff saw peace in the dying patient and the family when they talked about their Savior. One interested nurse called the family asking for information about eternal life. Hearing about Jesus, the Savior, at a patient's deathbed was new to the staff.

Since the message at the funeral service emphasized Christ's work at Calvary and not Dave's life, it was comforting and uplifting. Highlighting the life of the deceased is a typical funeral custom but offers little comfort. Dave's pastor offered comfort by reminding believers of our confidence in Christ and our home in heaven, reminding us the best was yet to come!

Looking back, God's plan for Dave was traveling to a Mexican clinic and then a California hospital but not for his physical healing. The Lord's concern was the spiritual wellness of others. Sharing the good news of Jesus Christ was one of the "good things" that God arranged through Dave's trial (Rom. 8:28).

> *In life or on your deathbed, you can have the victory when you keep your thoughts on the Lord* (Isa. 26:3).

Joy—A Blessing of the Victorious Life

In his book, *Victorious Christian Living*, Alan Redpath explains,

> There is nothing—no circumstance, no trouble, no testing—that can ever touch me until, first of all, it has gone past God and Christ, right through to me. If it has come that far, it has come with a great purpose, which I may not understand today. But as I refuse to become panicky, as I lift up my eyes to Him and accept it as coming from the throne of God for some great purpose of blessing to my own heart, no sorrow will ever disarm me, no circumstance will cause me to fret, for I shall rest in the joy of my Lord. That is the rest of victory.

Joy is one of the fruits of the Spirit that we experience as believers in fellowship with the Lord. Joy may include an ecstatic or excited response to God's magnificent grace.

> *Because of God's grace, I have joy.*

Victorious Faith Comes from His Grace

Because of our position in Christ, we have the victory that He won for us. *"For whatever is born of God overcomes the world. And this is the victory that has overcome the world—our faith. Who is he who overcomes the world, but he who believes that Jesus is the Son of God?"* (1 John 5:4-5)

Victorious faith believes that Christ carries you during trials by His grace, that He is stronger than your inadequate attempts to hold thing together. Christ is the "cement" that holds us together amid tremors and lifequakes. Faith in our Lord Jesus gives us the victory, not somehow by chance, but triumphantly out of the riches of His grace.

Are You Living Victoriously?

The wonderful hymn, "Faith is the Victory," depicts believers as soldiers in the spiritual battle against our enemies. Through faith in our victorious Savior, we are more than conquerors. We are triumphant! The hymn concludes with a beautiful word picture of believers standing in glory with our conquering Lamb and triumphant King, Jesus Christ.

FAITH IS THE VICTORY
"And this is the victory that has overcome the world—our faith" (1 John 5:4).

Encamped along the hills of light,
You Christian solders rise,
And press the battle ere the night
Shall veil the glowing skies.
Against the foe in vales below,
Let all our strength be hurled;
Faith is the victory, we know,
That overcomes the world.

REFRAIN: Faith is the victory! Faith is the victory!
O glorious victory that overcomes the world!

His banner over us is love,
Our sword the Word of God;
We tread the road the saints above
With shouts of triumph trod.
By faith they, like a whirl-wind's breath,
Swept on o'er ev'ry field;
The faith by which they conquered death
Is still our shinning shield.

To him who overcomes the foe
White raiment shall be given;
Before the angels he shall know
His name confessed in heav'n.
Then onward from the hills of light,
Our hearts with love aflame;
We'll vanquish all the hosts of night,
In Jesus' conquering name.

~ John H. Yates, 1837-1900 ~

> *The Christian's motto: Faith is the Victory!*

Reflection Questions

Support your answers with Scripture wherever possible.

1. What does your "position in Christ" mean to you?

2. What does it mean to live from your position in Christ versus striving toward that position?

3. What guarantees do we have that our Lord keeps His promises?

4. How will you live worthy of your position in Christ?

5. What is the victorious Christian life?

6. Why should you expect triumph in trials?

7. Now that you have read *LifeQuakes: God's Rescue Plan in Hard Times*, list major points you will apply to your life.

To God Be the Glory, Great Things He Has Done!

Definition of Terms

Carnal—used of the believer who is out of fellowship with the Lord; a carnal believer is one who follows the sin nature (self or flesh) and not the Holy Spirit. (See Flesh below)

Dependency—reliance on in order to function; the state of relying on something; the state of being subordinate to something; in Christian life it is a reliance and subordination to Christ to enable the believer to live the Christian life by faith, that is, the faith-rest life.

Faith/Trust—"firm persuasion," faith, the confirmation of things not seen and a conviction based upon hearing; is used in the New Testament always of "faith in God or Christ, or things spiritual," a ground for "faith," an assurance.

Fellowship—*koinōnia* (a) "communion, friendship (we were once God's enemies), sharing in common" (from *koinos*, "common"), is translated "communion" in 1 Cor. 10:16; "fellowship," "communication;" it is most frequently translated "fellowship;" *metochē* "partnership" (akin to *metochos* under fellow), is translated "fellowship" in 2 Cor. 6:14. Fellowship with the Lord indicates a believer who is following the Spirit, not the sin nature.

Flesh—*sarkikos* from *sarx*, "flesh," signifies "having the nature of flesh," that is, sensual, controlled by animal appetites, governed by human nature (Rom. 6:19; 1 Cor.3:3), instead of by the Spirit of God. Flesh (but this is not the same thing as in the body) is "the seat of sin in man" (Rom. 7:5; 2 Peter 2:18; 1 John 2:16) and is centered on self, prone to sin, and opposed to God. The flesh is the sin nature—that inborn part of human nature that seeks its own will, desires independence of God, and lives contrary to God's will (Rom. 8:8-9).

God's Glory—His glory is the composite of His characteristics that make Him holy, that is, that make Him distinct and unique from all others; His radiance.

Grace—God's undeserved favor. All that God is free (justified) to do on man's behalf because of Christ's finished cross work. In other words, God's grace is everything that God is willing to give you in blessing, apart from human merit or works because of Jesus Christ.

Heart—In Scripture, the word heart usually refers to the inner control center of a person's being. It is the seat of emotions (1 Sam. 2:1); the mind (Prov. 23:7), and the will (Dan. 1:8). Therefore, all decisions are made in the heart.

Hope—In New Testament it means "favorable and confident expectation."

Mercy—the loyal love of God, His faithful commitment to take care of His people.

The Mind of Christ—the Word of God reveals the mind of Christ; the promises and principles of the Word of God.

The Old Man—All you were in Adam; your position in Adam.

Son of God—The Bible term son signifies that a son has the same nature as the father. In the Old Testament and other later writings, the Hebrew words for son were often used to indicate their relationship. God the Father, God the Son and God the Spirit are equal in nature and deity.

The World—That organized system headed by Satan, the enemy of God; a system with godless rulers, people, teachings, ideas and temptations which are all opposed to God.

Appendix A: His Emergency Phone Numbers

Call upon your heavenly Father anytime and anywhere.

When in sorrow, call John 14.
When men fail you, call Ps. 27.
When you have sinned, call Ps. 51.
When you worry, call Matt. 6:19-34 .
When you are in danger, call Ps. 91.
When God seems far away, call Ps. 139.
When your faith needs stirring, call Heb. 11.
When you are lonely and fearful, call Ps. 23.
When you grow bitter and critical, call 1 Cor. 13.
When you feel down and out, call Rom. 8:31.
When you want peace and rest, call Matt. 11:25-30.
When problems seem bigger than God, call Ps. 90.
When you want God's reassurance, call Rom. 8:1-30.
When you experience illness, call James 5:14-16.
When your prayers grow narrow or selfish, call Ps. 67.
When you need courage for the task, call Josh. 1.
When you experience suffering or persecution, call Matt. 5:3-12.
If you are depressed, call Ps. 27.
If you are losing confidence in people, call 1 Cor. 13.
If people seem unkind, call John 15.
If discouraged about your work, call Ps. 126.
If self pride/self importance takes hold, call Ps. 19.
If you want to be productive, call John 15.
For understanding of Christianity, call 2 Cor. 5:15-19.
For nourishment for your soul, call Isa. 55.
For getting along with others, call Rom. 12.
For Paul's secret to happiness, call Col. 3:12-17.
For confidence in the Lord, call Ps. 34:19 and Ps. 37:39.
For reliance on God, call Ps. 77; 2 Cor. 3:18; Heb. 12:1-3.

Alternative Numbers
For dealing with fear, call Ps. 34:7.
For security, call Ps. 121:3.
For assurance, call Mark 8:35.
For reassurance, call Ps. 145:18.
Seeking God's help, call Ps. 119:169-176.

PLEASE NOTE: You may dial all these emergency numbers directly. No operator assistance is necessary. All lines to heaven are open 24 hours a day, 7 days a week. Our Lord is waiting to hear from you!

Feed your faith with His Word and pray, and doubt will starve to death.

Appendix B: Supplemental Scripture Directory

Where to look in the Bible concerning:

When in affliction:
Ps. 103:10; 119:71; Isa. 49:13; Rom. 5:26; James 1:2-3

When anxious:
Matt. 13:22; Luke 12:34; Phil. 4-6; 1 Peter 5:6-7; Heb. 13:5

Regarding belief:
Mark 9:23; John 1:12; 3:16, 18, 36; 6:35, 47; 12:46; 20:29; Acts 10:43; 16:31; Rom. 9:33; 1 Peter 2:6

When bereaved:
Luke 6:21; 1 Cor. 15; 1 Thess. 4:13-18

When it seems impossible to pay bills:
2 Chron. 15:7; Ps. 37:23-24; 102:17; Prov. 30:8-9; Jer. 33:3; Hab. 3:17-18; Matt. 6:25, 33-34; Luke 6:21; Rom. 8:38-39; Phil. 4:6, 11-12

When feeling blue:
Ps. 91; Matt. 5:4, 10-12; 10:29-31; 11:28; John 14:1-3, 16, 18, 27; Rom. 8:28, 35-39

When you feel burdened:
1 Sam. 12:22; Ps. 30:5; 55:22; 138:8; Prov. 4:22; Isa. 40:31; 41:10; 49:15-16; Rom. 8:28-30; Phil. 4:6-7; 2 Tim. 1:7; Heb. 10:23; 1 Peter 4:12-13

When facing a crisis:
2 Tim. 1:7; Heb. 4:16

For comfort:
Job 5:19; 11:16; Ps. 9:9; 18:2; 22:24; 25:5; 27:14; 30:5; 37:24, 39; 42:5; 46; 55:22; 103:13; 119:50; 138:7; Lam. 3:31-33; Nah. 1:7; Matt. 11:28; John 16:33

When you desire contentment:
Luke 3:14; Phil. 4:11-13; 1 Tim. 3:8; 6:6; Heb. 13:5

For courage:
Deut. 31:6-7; Josh. 1:6, 7, 9; 10:25; 23:6; 1 Chron. 19:13; 22:13; 28:20; Ps. 27:14; 31:24; 138:3; Prov. 28:1; Isa. 40:31; 41:6; 43:2; Acts 5:27-29; Heb. 13:6

When in despair:
Ps. 45:5-6; Isa. 61:3-4; 2 Cor. 1:-9; 4:8-18

When disaster threatens:
Ps. 20:6-9; 34; 118:5-9; 121; 126

When discouraged:
Ps. 23; 37:1-17; 55:22; 90:12-17; Isa. 49:13; Phil. 4:4-7; 1 John 3:1-3

For disbelief – For freedom from doubt:
Heb. 10:19-22; 1 John 5:14; Col. 4:12; John 14:2-4

When heartbroken by divorce:
Deut. 4:29-31; 31:6; Eph. 4:32; 6:10-18; Phil. 4:6, 7, 13, 19; Heb. 13:4; 1 Peter 5:7

When you need assurance from doubt:
John 14:2-4; Col. 4:12; Heb. 10:19-22; 1 John 5:14

For freedom from emptiness:
Eccl. 1:2-3; Ps. 73: 16-17; Matt. 28:18-20; John 11:25; 14:16; Eph. 2:8-10; Rom. 12:2

When you experience personal failure or loss:
Deut. 31:6; Neh. 8:10; Ps. 30:5; 34:17-18; 46:1; 55:22; 147:3; Isa. 43:3; 50:7; 51:11; 61:3; Rom. 8:35-39; Phil. 4:6-7

When fearful:
Ex. 14:13, 20:20; Ps. 27 56:4; 118:6; Isa. 41:10; 43:5; Matt. 6:25-34, 11:28-30; John chapters 11; 17; and 20; Rom. 8; 2 Cor. 4; 5; 12:9

When friends fail:
Ps. 35; 41:9-13, 55:12-23; Luke 17: 3, 4; Rom. 12:14, 17, 19

For your relationship to God:
2 Chron. 7:14; Ps. 27:8; 42:8; 55:16-17; 105:4; 145:18; Prov. 15:8; Isa. 55:6; Matt. 6:6; Luke 18:1; Rom. 8:26; Eph. 6:18; Phil 4:6; Col. 4:2; 1 Thess. 5:17; 1 Tim. 2:8; Heb. 4:16

For your study of God's Word:
Ex. 24:3; Deut. 4:2; 6:6; 8:3; 29:29; 30:14; Josh. 1:8; Job. 22:22; 23:12; Ps. 1:2; 19:7; 37:31; 119:11; Isa. 40:8; Matt. 7:24-25; 13:31; 22:29; Rom. 10:17

For freedom from guilt:
Isa. 1:18; 53:6; John 3:16; Eph. 2:8-9; 2 Cor. 5:19-21; 1 Peter 1:18-19

When feeling loneliness:
Matt. 27:45-46; 28:20; Mark 3:31-34; John 13:34-35; Gal. 3:26; Eph. 3:14–4:3; 1 Cor. 10:16-17; 11:27-29

When overwhelmed by responsibility:
Ps. 23:2-3; 25:4-5, 21; 27:14; 37:7, 23; 130:6; Prov. 8:34-36; 17:1; Isa. 40:31; Matt. 16:26; Mark 6:31; Luke 21:34; 1 Tim. 5:8; James 1:5; 1 Peter 5:8-9

For peace:
Ps. 1:1, 2; 4-8; 85:8; 46; 107; Rom. 5:1-5; Col. 3:15; 2 Cor. 4:8-10, 16-17

When worried about what people think:
Josh. 12:42-43; 1 Sam. 15:24; Prov. 29:25

When people withdraw from you:
Ps. 3:3; 18:28; 26:12; 36:11; 37:6-7; 44:5; 73:26; 91:11-12; John 3:18-22; 1 John 4:4

For prayer:
Ps. 4, 6, 25, 42, 51; Matt. 6:5-15; Luke 18:1-14; John 17; 1 John 5:14-15

When in severe trouble:
Prayer Psalms— 4, 5, 11, 28, 41, 55, 59, 64, 70, 109, 120, 140, 141, 143.

When afflicted:
Ps. 44, 60, 74, 79, 80, 83, 89, 94, 102, 129, 137.

When sick or in pain:
Matt. 26:39; 2 Tim. 2:3; Heb. 12:1-11; James 5:11-15; 1 Peter 4:12, 13, 19

When you have thoughts of suicide:
Ps. 9:18; 31:24; 33:22; 38:15; 43:5; Isa. 12:3; Jer. 17:7; Lam. 3:24, 26; John 14:27; Rom. 4:18; 15:13; 12:2; 1 Cor. 13:13; 2 Cor. 12:10; Phil. 4:7; Heb. 11:1; 1 Peter 1:13, 21; 4:12-13

When people become unforgiving towards you:
Deut. 4:31; 31:6; 1 Sam. 12:22; Ps. 37:25: 43:5; 91:14-15; 94:14; Isa. 41:7; 43:3: 49:15-16; 63:4; Matt. 28:20; 1 Peter 5:7

For freedom from uncertainty:
Ps. 105; 119:9; John 8:31-32; 17:17; 20:31; 2 Tim. 3:15-16

When weary:
Deut. 33:27; Ps. 55:22; 73:26; Isa. 40:31; Jonah 2:7; Matt. 11:28; 2 Cor. 4:16

Resources

Many of these Bible churches have useful resources including downloadable messages, helpful literature, and other resources. Materials and messages vary from church to church.

Duluth Bible Church
201 W. St. Andrews St.
Duluth, MN 55803

Pastor Dennis Rokser
(218) 724-5914 (Office)
www.duluthbible.org

Grace Gospel Bible Church
Meeting at: Calvin Christian School
4015 Inglewood, Edina, MN

Contact information:
Pastor Dave Knutsen
10623 Drake St. NW
Coon Rapids, MN 55433
(763) 862-7292
www.gracegospelbiblechurch.org

Heritage Trail Bible Church
5266 Heritage Trail
Gilbert, MN 55741

Pastor Gus Layman
(218) 741-7418
www.heritagetrailbiblechurch.org

Itasca Bible Church
32253 Harris Town Rd.
Grand Rapids, MN 55744

Pastor Shawn Laughlin
(218) 327-0422
www.itascabible.org

North Stonington Bible Church
100 Jeremy Hill Rd.
North Stonington, CT 06359

Pastor Larry Chappell
(860) 535-2872
www.nsbiblechurch.com

Word of Grace Bible Church
2660 S. 88th St.
West Allis, WI 53227

Pastor Rick Gerhartz
(414) 321-8880 (phone & fax)
www.wogbc.org

Sacred Music You Can Trust
Majesty Music, Inc.
733 Wade Hampton Blvd.
Greenville, SC 29609
Phone: Toll Free (800) 334-1071
www.majestymusic.com

Recommended Reading

Ingram, Chip. *I Am with You Always.*
Baker Books, 2004

Keathley III, J. Hampton. *The ABCs for Christian GROWTH.*
Biblical Studies Press, 1996-2002.

Pierson, A.T. *George Mueller of Bristol: His Life of Prayer and Faith.*
Grand Rapids, Michigan: Kregel Publications, 1999.

Showers, Renald. *Those Invisible Spirits Called Angels.*
The Friends of Israel Gospel Ministry Inc., 1997.

Stanford, Miles J. *None But the Hungry Heart.*
Available at *www.mjsbooks.com*

Taylor, Dr. and Mrs. Howard. *Hudson Taylor's Spiritual Secret.*
Chicago: Moody Press, 1989.

About the Author

For more information about the author, Leah Weber Heling, you may visit: www.linkedin.com/in/leahweberheling

www.ingramcontent.com/pod-product-compliance
Lightning Source LLC
Chambersburg PA
CBHW050611300426
44112CB00012B/1460